SUPERGRASSES
AND INFORMERS

Also by James Morton

NIPPER (co-author with Leonard Read)
GANGLAND
GANGLAND Volume II
BENT COPPERS
MAD FRANK (co-author with Frankie Fraser)

SUPERGRASSES AND INFORMERS

An Informal History of Undercover Police Work

James Morton

LITTLE, BROWN AND COMPANY

A *Little, Brown* Book

First published in Great Britain in 1995
by Little, Brown and Company

Copyright © James Morton 1995

The moral right of the author has been asserted.

A CIP catalogue record for this book
is available from the British Library.

ISBN 0 316 87527 9

Typeset by Palimpsest Book Production Limited,
Polmont, Stirlingshire
Printed and bound in Great Britain by
Clays Ltd, St Ives plc

Little, Brown and Company (UK)
Brettenham House
Lancaster Place
London WC2E 7EN

For
Dock Bateson
with love

Contents

Early on one Monday morning
In his dreary prison cell
British soldiers tortured Barry
Just because he would not tell
The names of his companions
And other things they wished to know.
'Turn informer or we'll kill you.'
Kevin Barry answered, 'No!'

Prologue

'Justice was blindfolded,' said Lord Justice Winn, giving the judgment of the Court of Appeal in *Macro and others* on 9 February 1969. 'Let us hope to God it does not happen again.' Cedric Macro, Melvyn Colman and Richard Cork had all appealed against their convictions for robbery with aggravation together with a man unknown. They had all pleaded guilty; they had received four years apiece, and the court substituted a sentence which meant they could be released that day.[1]

Macro and Co. had taken part in what, on the face of it, was a typical raid on a sub-post office. Appearances were deceptive, however. Cork had driven the car to the sub-post office and the fourth man, Raymond Scrutton, entered the building.

As was now known, although not revealed to the judge, he spoke to the sub-postmaster and confirmed the sub-postmaster had already received a warning from the police that a raid would take place that afternoon, with the assurance that he would not be hurt and the police would protect him.

What Lord Justice Winn described as 'the charade' began. A

1 *The Times*, 10 February 1969.

ix

police officer was in an inner room on the premises. Scrutton called out, 'Be quiet or you'll get yourself hurt.' He tied the hands and feet of the sub-postmaster, put tissues in his mouth, and put him behind the counter. Macro and Colman took postal orders to the value of some £700. Macro was stopped by the police outside the shop; Colman managed to make it to the car but he and Cork were arrested later. Scrutton was given two rewards; one from the police and the other from the Post Office. Macro and the others made statements saying they had been talked into it by Scrutton, whom they did not name.

Lord Justice Winn laid about him: 'It is a horrible experience for any judge to find that justice had been perverted in this fashion even though the degree of blame has not yet been allocated.' An inquiry had been instituted but the whole circumstances had still to be revealed: 'Fortunately very rarely could such a situation have arisen, and it is to be hoped that very rarely indeed would it arise in the future.'

In fact it had already happened, for on 19 May 1969 Frank Alexander Birtles left the Court of Appeal in London a slightly happier man than he had entered it. On 7 February 1968, at what was then West Riding Quarter Sessions, he had pleaded guilty to burglary and carrying an imitation firearm for which he had received a total of five years' imprisonment. His arrest had been preordained.

Birtles had spent a good deal of a previous prison sentence dreaming up an elaborate plan to rob a post office on his release. Once out of prison, he was approached by an informer who in turn introduced him to one of London's 'top' criminals, in fact a police officer. Cars and an imitation firearm were provided for the hapless man, who on his appeal at least had his sentence reduced from five to three years.[2] Lord Parker, the Lord Chief Justice, added:

Before leaving this case, the court would like to say a

2 *Birtles* [1969] 2 All E.R. 1131.

word about the use which, as the cases coming before the court reveal, is being made of informers. The court, of course, recognises that, disagreeable as it may seem to some people, the police must be able in certain cases to make use of informers and further – and this is really a corollary – that within certain limits such informers should be protected. At the same time, unless the use made of informers is kept within strict limits, grave injustice may result. In the first place the court of trial should not be misled.

Secondly, it is vitally important to ensure so far as possible that the informer does not create an offence, that is to say, incite others to commit an offence which those others would not otherwise have committed.

It is one thing for the police to make use of information concerning an offence that is already laid on. In such a case the police are clearly entitled, indeed it is their duty to mitigate the consequences of the proposed offence, for example to protect the proposed victim, and to that end it may be perfectly proper for them to encourage the informer to take part in the offence or indeed for the police officer himself to do so. But it is quite another thing, and something of which this court thoroughly disapproves, to use an informer to encourage another to commit an offence or indeed an offence of a more serious character which he would not otherwise commit, still more so if the police themselves take part in carrying it out.

After Macro the Home Secretary announced that H. M. Inspectors of Constabulary had been asked to inquire into the current practice where information had been received from informers, and to review what was happening to that information. The material was duly obtained and guidance was given but never published on the ground that it related to 'an operational police matter'. It did, however, take account of the following points:

If society is to be protected from criminals, the police must be able to make use of informants in appropriate circumstances, Informants, appropriately employed, are essential to criminal investigations and, within limits, ought to be protected. The police must not embark on a course which will constrain them to withhold information from or mislead a court in order to protect an informant.

What follows is an account of what has happened in the courts in England and America, both before and after Frank Birtles and James Macro made their small piece of British legal history. Not only the role of the informer and super-informer (the grass and supergrass) will come under scrutiny, but also the inextricably linked behaviour of the police and private detectives in infiltrating criminal enterprises.

The police do not regard all people who give information to the police as informants. The other three groups are what they describe as public-spirited citizens, eccentric or nuisance individuals, and contacts. People in the first category are, of course, to be encouraged, whilst those in the second category generally fall into two sub-categories: eccentrics who are suffering from some mental aberration or delusion short of certifiable insanity; or inquisitive busybodies who imagine that offences of a certain type are being committed. Their information is regarded as being usually completely unreliable and valueless. Many confess to crimes they could not have possibly committed. Officers are enjoined to treat them with caution and tolerance and not to dismiss their claims out of hand.

The urge to confess is an interesting one. In the case of the killing of Elizabeth Short, the 'Black Dahlia', who was literally cut in half in Los Angeles in 1947, over forty people, both men and women, confessed to being her murderer. The spate of confessions was not unexpected. Dr J. Paul de River, the psychiatrist working on the case on behalf of the Los Angeles police, said that those who confessed did not do so out of a desire for publicity but rather this would spring from masochism, exhibitionism or a guilt complex engendered by some forgotten incident of childhood.[3]

The third category, of contacts, comprises individuals – such as bank managers, caretakers or DSS investigators – who whilst supplying information of value and expecting protection do so without thought of payment. It is envisaged that contacts may develop into informants, and they are divided into four categories:

(i) the informant who gives information about crime and criminal associates either for money or the kudos; (ii) the participating informant; (iii) an individual who has been registered as a police informant on the authority of an officer of the rank of Assistant Chief Constable or above, in the knowledge that he may play a part in a crime or its preparation; (iv) a resident informant who has been an active participant in serious crime and who after arrest or conviction is willing to give evidence against his former colleagues. Serious crime is defined as one which on conviction would generate a prison sentence of ten or more years.

The last category is the overlapping protected informant: someone who informs on associates who participate in crime, and who subsequently becomes known, thus placing him in danger. Generally people in this category, which includes participating informants, will not be prosecuted. It is on the stories of people in the last three categories as well as the so-called undercover agent – a police officer who adopts a false identity or cover story to enter into an existing conspiracy with individuals involved in criminals acts, and whose purpose is to facilitate the arrest of the individual as well as to recover money, stolen goods or drugs – that this book is based. It is in these roles that the definitions have become blurred.

Nowadays police surveillance and infiltration has become an industry in itself, with high-technology gadgetry employed for electronic eavesdropping and intelligence systems. I propose,

3 The unsolved case of the 'Black Dahlia' is examined in detail by Richard and Molly Whittington-Egan in *The Bedside Book of Murder*, pp. 91–118.

however, to concentrate on the men and women on the ground who are, so to speak, at the coal-face. They may now have gadgetry at their disposal if things go wrong and, to use a police expression, the wheels come off. Twenty years ago – and even less – they certainly did not. This is the history of the infiltrator and the undercover agent who operated, and still largely does, alone and with little in the way of day-to-day protection. Primarily, however, it is the story of the use of the informer by the authorities, and of the authorities by the informer.

I have endeavoured to limit the book to the role of the informer, *agent provocateur* and undercover agent in the criminal field rather than the political one. Profit, not politics, is again the key word. Of course, matters overlap and it is not entirely possible to separate them completely. At the beginning of the chapter on informers I have therefore put together a very brief history of the use made of these men in the political field. Those who wish to look at that other side of the fence more closely may care to turn to Bernard Porter's double bill of *Plots and Paranoia* and *The Origins of the Vigilant State*, as well as Philip Knightley's *The Second Oldest Profession*. I have deliberately avoided a discussion and history of the use of the supergrass in Italy. Those who are particularly interested in the work of the informer there may care to read *The Dishonoured Society* by John Follain.

Given the use of the rise and fall of the supergrass system in Ireland, I have also included an account of their troubled history there. I accept, of course, that this is almost wholly politics and not profit, but since it largely runs parallel with the use in criminal cases *per se* in England I thought it appropriate to include it.

There is a variety of colourful words and definitions, both English and American, for informants, all denoting the opprobrium of society. None can be seen as a synonym for a hero. In alphabetical order they include *Bertie Smalls*, from the first of the modern British supergrasses; *canary* (from singing); *fink* (originally a police officer); *grass, nark* and the less derogatory term *nose* (both Victorian or earlier), *peacher, snitch, squawker, squeaker, squealer, stag* and *stoolie* and *supergrass* itself.

The derivation of the usually British term *grass* is obscure. In America it usually means lettuce, the straight hair typical of Caucasians and marijuana. Here it most likely comes from the rhyming slang *grasshopper* = copper. Another version of its derivation is that grass whispers in a wind and the phrase was popular in the 1930s following Fred Fisher's song *Whispering Grass* popularised by The Inkspots. Recently I came across the phrase *in the grass* meaning to be on the run from the police or prison. Perhaps this is the real derivation of grass – the person who informs on a person on the run. It has some logic to it. A *nark*, often used as copper's nark, is Victorian and comes from the Romany *nak* meaning nose; in fact, in the eighteenth century a *nose* was a term for an informer. Copper itself comes from to cop or to catch, and dates from around 1700. In American slang, a *copper* can mean not only a police officer but also an informer. To *peach* derives from Shakespearian times, and one of the informers in John Gay's *The Beggar's Opera* was Polly Peachum. Although *snitch* dates back to the beginning of the eighteenth century, it is now more common in American slang than in British. Originally it referred to a cardsharper who, when his colleagues had refused to share their winnings with him, went to tell the victim of the crooked game how it had been worked against him. In Scottish slang, *snitchers* were also handcuffs.

Squeaker comes from the end of the seventeenth century and certainly lasted until the middle of this one, when Edgar Wallace wrote his successful novel *The Squeaker*. It has largely faded from use in the last seventy years.

The American word *squealer* probably derives from the noise made by a pig, which is said to resemble that of an informant. Another version of the origin of the term is that an old-time thief was caught when villagers heard the squeals of a pig he was abducting. Certainly, the squealer or informant had been regarded on a par with the child molester in criminal and particularly prison society.

A relatively early American criticism of the behaviour of a squealer comes from the Kansas newspaper *Kinsley Graphic* in the 1870s, when four train robbers were convicted on the testimony of the fifth, Dave Rudabaugh. With a fine command of journalese the newspaper editorialized:

> Rudabaugh testified that he was promised entire immunity from punishment if he would 'squeal', therefore he squole. Someone has said there is a kind of honour among thieves. Rudabaugh don't think so.[4]

Squawker, originally meaning a protester, first shows up as an informer in American slang in the latter half of the nineteenth century when *to play baby* was also common. A *squawker* was also a burglar alarm. A *stag* was originally an enemy, but by the middle of the eighteenth century it had come to mean an informer, and the term was used in mid-nineteenth-century America. *Stoolie* or *stool pigeon* was originally a man made use of by criminals, but by the end of the nineteenth century in America it referred to a man who had been turned by the police to betray his colleagues; the derivation is from a decoy duck. *Stool pigeon* was also an uncommon term for the moon; no doubt because it betrayed a criminal's whereabouts. More often it was used in the same way as *shill*, meaning a person in the pay of a gambling house who attracted players to a faro table.

All the words indicate a dislike and distrust of the informer and the concept behind it. Of course, no police force can function without it, however. From an early age a police officer learns that informers are useful. In a questionnaire devised by one American force, one question read:

4 Carl Sifakis, *An Encyclopedia of American Crime*, p. 680.

The best arrests are made:

(a) As a result of hard work and intelligent dedication to duty
(b) As a result of good information from an informer
(c) Coming from the 'coop' (a police resting place on duty such as a café).

Out of a total sample of 186, 44 per cent thought the correct answer was (b), a figure which rose to 52 per cent in patrolmen of 2–12 years' standing and remained at 50 per cent for patrolmen with up to 19 years' service. 47 per cent of detectives thought that (b) was the correct answer.[5]

Here is the District Attorney of New York County making a pitch for the good guy and misunderstood grass before the New York Grand Jury Association in February 1947:

. . . we appear to have developed a public morality which condemns – rather than praises – any private citizen that we – as members of a free society – have called into being.

We want the laws enforced and to this end we hire men at good salaries to secure obedience to the law, to preserve order, and to protect our persons and property. They, by declining to co-operate and, indeed, by bringing social pressure against those who would co-operate we make it difficult, if not impossible, for those men to serve us effectively. They would fight our enemies, but we refuse to point them out. We make a sort of game of it, between law enforcement officials and criminals, and sit complacently quite ready to applaud a brilliant stroke on either side.

Seven years later J. Edgar Hoover had this to say in further bolstering the low self-esteem of the informer:

5 Arthur Niederhoffer, *Behind the Shield*, p. 218.

Experience demonstrates that the cooperation of individuals who can readily furnish accurate information is essential if law enforcement is to discharge its obligations.

The objective of the investigator must be to ferret out the truth. It is fundamental that the search includes the most logical source of information – those persons with immediate access to necessary facts who are willing to cooperate in the interest of the common good. Their disservices contribute greatly to the ultimate goal of justice convicting the guilty and clearing the innocent. Necessarily unheralded in their daily efforts, they not only uncover crimes but furnish the intelligence data so vital in preventing serious violations of law and national security.

There can be no doubt that the use of informants in law enforcement is justified. The public interest and the personal safety of those helpful citizens demand the zealous protection of their confidence. Unlike the totalitarian practice, the informant in America serves of his own free will, fulfilling one of the citizenship obligations of our democratic form of government.

The criminal and subversive underworld has long sought to destroy our effective informant system.[6]

What must be remembered is that because it is essentially a secretive subject and because the lives of their officers are at risk, the police are naturally and rightly reluctant to say how much undercover work is going on at any one time. 'Very much more than you think,' says a London solicitor with a major criminal practice. Whether this is deep cover work or, more likely, short in-and-out assignments such as playing the role of a hit-man and conducting negotiations with a sulky wife or husband, is impossible to say. Even awards made to undercover officers are done privately, and no mention is made in official police papers.

6 *Law Enforcement Bulletin*, June 1955.

Prologue

Throughout the text there are numerous quotations and I have endeavoured to give an attribution to them. This does not mean in any way at all that the words quoted were actually spoken. Many of the recollections have been written years after the incident was supposedly recorded verbatim. In recent years, however, more efforts have been made to ensure that there is a good deal of accuracy in what criminals in particular have to say. Gone (or nearly gone) are the days of the sensational reportage of, say, the Jack Spot autobiography. For example, before the autobiography of the Mafia hit-man, the ferocious Donald 'Tony the Greek' Frankos, the tapes of his voice were analysed by a voice-stress analyst who thought that the confessions were 'free of mendacious stress'. Similarly other writers have begun to triangulate the stories told to them by major criminals by checking with lawyers, newspapers and court papers. Nevertheless, in the case of criminals there have been scores to settle and debts to be paid, let alone memories genuinely impaired. It is impossible to guarantee that what they say is the whole truth or in some cases even a great percentage of it.

The quotations from Robert Fleming and Hugh Miller's *Scotland Yard* are made with the permission of the Peters Fraser and Dunlop Group Ltd.

My thanks are due to Al Alschuler, Michael Bailey, J.P. Bean, Rowan Bosworth-Davies, Andrew Boyd, Dave Critchley, Oliver Cyriax, Clifford and Marie Elmer who tracked down countless books for me, Sean Enright, Jeremy Fordham, Frank Fraser, Dominique Harvie, Brian Hilliard, Gabriel Jewel, Jennifer Kavanagh, John Kaye, Joan Lock, Cal McCrystal, David Martin-Sperry, Jean Maund, Adrian Neale, Clive Norris, Bill Pizzi, Nipper Read, John Rigbey, Jack Slipper, Edda Tasiemka, Graham Tutthill, Alice Wood and many others on both sides of the fence who have asked not to be named.

As is always the case, the book could not have been written without the endless patience of, and help from, Dock Bateson.

1

There's Always an Excuse

There is a belief amongst police officers that all but the most staunch villains are capable of being turned into grasses. In *Crime Inc.* Martin Short points out how, when it suited them, the major crime figures, Lucky Luciano and Meyer Lansky, were quite capable of telling the police something which might get them off a temporary hook.[1] In England, members of one major London gang of the 1960s were reputed to be protected at Assistant Commissioner level because of the quality of information supplied by them.

An ex-detective sergeant (Flying Squad) says:

> They will all do it, from the biggest professional villain down to the kid just starting out on the back streets – it's just a question of catching them right. They do it for all sorts of reasons but money is always the big draw and if the reward is high enough, there's always someone . . .

1 Luciano admitted his convictions, for running a gambling house in 1930 and for narcotics in 1916. He claimed he had never touched dope again but Dewey (Thomas E. Dewey, the special prosecutor) proved he had been caught selling drugs in 1923 when police had found morphine and heroin at his home. Luciano told them that at 163 Mulberry Street there was a trunk full of narcotics. Thirteen years later Dewey revealed his treachery, showing that even the great Luciano would turn stool pigeon when it suited him. Martin Short, *Crime Inc.*, p. 153.

Repentance and rehabilitation, at least a sufficient amount to dollop before the court and jury, are necessary requirements of any self-respecting supergrass's confession.

> I have been in police custody since Sunday 18 May 1980 during which time I have been asked by Detective Chief Inspector Peters about jobs I have done with Tony Fiori, Christopher Wren and others. I have had time to consider all these matters and I had the opportunity of speaking to my wife. I now want to admit all these matters and to completely wipe my slate clean, because I have decided to finish my life of crime and start a new life with my family. I should like to tell you today about a burglary . . .[2]

Indeed one of the least palatable excuses of the defendant in general and the informer in particular is that he has found religion. It is as old as the hills, but two examples may be picked from more modern times. In America in the trial of Big Bill Haywood, Pettibone and Moyer in 1907, the assassin Harry Orchard, who had been put on death row for a ten-day period, was seen by the Pinkerton agent James McParland and hectored on the benefits of repentance and with tales from the Bible. Eventually sufficient seeds had been sown in the mind of the man who, quite apart from blowing up fourteen non-union miners and later the ex-Governor, had

> begun his career of crime by short-weighting the farmers who brought milk to his Canadian cheese factory; who burned down the factory to collect the insurance; who abandoned his wife and six-months-old daughter to run away with another man's wife; who married a third

2 Michael Gervaise (1 July 1980), beginning one of his many statements, this time against a man who was acquitted. Gervaise subsequently retracted this statement.

woman without bothering to divorce his first wife, spent the money she had inherited from her husband and deserted her when she had become so destitute that she had to take in washing; who had stolen from his miner roommate the possessions of his truck; who had robbed mines for their ore; who had burned down a saloon for a hundred dollars so the owner could collect his insurance; who had plotted to kidnap the child of a former partner to rob streetcar conductors, to sweat gold coins; a man who for years had roamed the West, living off the kit of burglars' tools found in his truck . . .

Now:

I am ready to make a full confession. I am asking no leniency. My lonely imprisonment will drive me crazy if I do not confess. My conscience will not permit me to keep the guilty secrets. If ever a man suffered the torments of hell, I am that man, I can only hope that God in his infinite mercy will heed my prayers. I have been a wicked man. I want to tell.[3]

In his piece about the killing of his daughter, Dominique, and the subsequent character assassination by her killer, her boyfriend John Sweeney, the novelist Dominick Dunne comments acidly on Sweeney's new-found state of grace:

It is the fashion among the criminal fraternity to find God, and Sweeney, the killer, was no exception. He arrived daily in the courtroom clutching a Bible, looking like a sacristan. The Bible was a prop; Sweeney never read it, he rested his folded hands on it. He also wept regularly. One day the court had to be recessed because he claimed the

3 Irving Stone, *Clarence Darrow for the Defense*, pp. 199–200.

3

other prisoners had been harassing him before he entered and he needed time to cry in private.[4]

On 24 May 1992 thirty-eight-year-old George Woodhatch was shot twice in the head and twice in the chest as he was using the telephone at the Royal Free Hospital, Hampstead, where he was recovering from an operation for piles. It was a contract killing and although his business partners, Paul Tubbs and Keith Bridges, were charged with his murder, initially the magistrates found there was no case to answer and they were discharged.

The prosecution's case was that Woodhatch had swindled them out of £50,000 in their roofing business. Despite a lifestyle which included a Porsche and a Japanese-style house in Hertfordshire, he was in serious financial trouble, owing £400,000 in tax and having substantial business debts. Woodhatch was also becoming increasingly irrational and at the time of his death was on bail for threatening to kill his secretary. A twenty-seven-year-old Maori woman, Ti Rangimara Ngarimu, was hired by Tubbs and Bridges for a fee of £7,000. She had met Bridges, another New Zealander, when she was working as a barmaid in London in the late 1980s. At first when Bridges put the proposition to her she thought he was joking, but almost immediately agreed.

The plan was that she would shoot Woodhatch while he was in hospital and then immediately fly out to New Zealand. On her first effort she could not find the ward and, now wearing a baseball cap, tracksuit and gloves, returned the next day. This time she shot him from a distance of three feet. Bridges, she said, had told her, 'Shoot him twice in the head and twice in the body to be sure of death.' She then caught the 4.30 flight from Gatwick, leaving the clothes and gun at Bridges' flat in Camden Town to be disposed of.

4 Sweeney was acquitted of first degree murder and sentenced to six and a half years' imprisonment for voluntary manslaughter. Dominick Dunne, *Fatal Charms*, p. 24.

It seems that, at first, it was thought that Woodhatch had died from a brain haemorrhage and it was not until five hours later, in the mortuary, that the bullet wounds were discovered. After the killing, Tubbs telephoned a friend and asked him to meet Bridges to help in getting rid of the holdall. The friend looked inside and threw the holdall in a pond, later helping the police retrieve it.

In early 1994 Ngarimu returned to England. She had been contacted by the police but at first told them, 'I couldn't kill a chicken. I am a vegetarian.' Over the years, however, she had embraced religion and after at first fighting extradition procedures she voluntarily returned to England as she wished to clear her conscience. Bridges and Tubbs were re-arrested and were convicted largely on her evidence. They had already pleaded guilty to conspiracy to pervert the course of justice by disposing of the gun and clothes she had worn. Bridges and Tubbs were sent to prison for life, with a recommendation they serve fifteen and sixteen years' imprisonment respectively. The trial judge added that he thought the Home Secretary should consider making each man serve a further third of the sentence. 'In my view it is necessary to protect the public from serious harm from each of you,' said Sir Lawrence Verney, the Recorder of London. Ngarimu was sentenced to life imprisonment.

The case has two interesting features. The first is that this appears to be the first use of a female hit-man in this country. The second is that during the trial, which began in May 1994, Bridges was shot in the chest and leg while walking in Ruislip, Middlesex. No arrest was made over that attack.

The motives of the first of the so-called Mafia informers, Joe Valachi, were described by narcotics agent James P. Flynn who eventually gained his confidence.

Revenge was a large part of it, but it was also a cold calculated move for survival. Don't think for a moment that this was a repentant sinner. He was a killer capable

5

of extreme violence. He was devious, rebellious against all constituted authority and he lived in a world of fear and suspicion. Fear especially marked him. Fear of what he was doing and at the same time fear that nobody would believe him.[5]

In general, though, in common with many supergrasses, Valachi believed that nothing was his fault at all. James Flynn's view was that:

Joe thought everybody was responsible for Joe. He only took up crime, for instance, because he never had a chance as a kid. It was the prison administration's fault that he had to kill a man he didn't even know. He doesn't consider himself a traitor to the Cosa Nostra; in his mind Vito Genovese was the real traitor.[6]

Sometimes the reasons can be personal. Former Ghost Squad officer John Gosling recalls an instance where a small-time thief informed on his daughter's boyfriend in order to break up the relationship.

Norris and Dunnighan found in their survey that one informer was a father who informed on his son and collected money, whilst another was a man who was having an affair with his neighbour's wife and found that, first, it was a good method by which to keep the husband away and, secondly, that it provided money for the relationship.[7] A senior officer recalls an early informant:

I was on the desk one Friday when a call came through giving me details of a potential drug bust. The caller wouldn't say who he was and when I checked out the address it was not known so I did nothing further. The

5 Peter Maas, *The Valachi Papers*, p. 34.
6 *Ibid.* p. 38.
7 For further details of the findings of the survey, see chapter 11: *The Police*.

same thing happened the next Friday. The man recognised my voice, asked why I'd done nothing and gave even more details. I checked out the address again. Nothing was known about it and I still waited. Third Friday the call comes again so this time I acted. It was the best bust I had that month. As I was in the front room a middle-aged man comes in and looks at me. He's the father-in-law. I thought, 'Hello, I know where those calls have been coming from.'

Others would inform on their wives, mothers, and assorted relations if it suited them. An ex-Flying Squad officer recalls one instance:

Another man who worked for me was called Pat. He lived out Woodford with his wife and several grown-up kids and was totally without scruple. He had worked for various Flying Squad and divisional officers for years and, although he was rather lazy, when he could be motivated there was no better grass in London.

Once, when he had been a bit backward in coming forward, we met him in a pub in Loughton and told him he'd better pull his socks up. He protested the usual story of there 'not being much about, Guv', but after a while and his fourth pint he perked up and said, 'Tell you what – you can have the old woman if you like.' We fell about at the double meaning but we were completely speechless when we heard what he really meant. His wife had, he said, recently purchased a television stolen from one of the TV rental firms, and Pat was suggesting we turn over his own house and charge her with receiving. There wasn't going to be much money in it, £20 if he was lucky, but as far as he was concerned that was £20 he wouldn't have had otherwise. He also complained that she did nothing but watch *Coronation Street* and he never got a chance to have a sensible conversation.

7

Oddly, when we nicked her, his wife did not have much to say at all. She pleaded guilty and was fined a fiver or something nominal. Pat sat in the back of the court and later got his £20. As far as I know she never ever sussed him.

Pat fell neatly into the category described by John Gosling.

The category of informants who give the most trouble are the ones who do it strictly for the money. These are usually the real toe-rags or slags – the dregs of the criminal fraternity – and they can cause you endless problems. If a job doesn't come off we call it a blow-out. With an informant who works for money, you can expect seven or eight blow-outs from ten pieces of information. You're doing the work, getting the warrants, setting up the searches, making yourself look an idiot if it does blow out. They're gambling on a few tips coming off, so they can scrape together £20 or £25 out of the information fund to carry them through one more day or have one more booze-up. I've always avoided that kind of informant whenever I can, but it's very easy to get trapped until you get to know the ropes.[8]

Informants could, occasionally, be used to recruit other informants.

Some time later Pat set us onto a stolen car parked up outside a block of flats in West Ham. 'The ice cream,'[9] said Pat, 'lives in the flats and he's driving the motor every day. When you nick 'im, be a bit shrewd – 'e'll be shit scared and you can get him on the firm.' We had to sit outside the flats for less than an hour: the ice cream came

8 Jack Slipper, *Slipper of the Yard*, p. 33.
9 Ice cream freezer = geezer.

out, got in the vehicle and promptly had his collar felt. Pat's assessment of his character was completely accurate. After an hour in the nick he was bending backwards to tell us anything and everything he knew. All he wanted in exchange was bail and a bit of help in court. Within three weeks we had a very good receiver in Bow from him, a conspiracy to forge fifty-pence pieces, an escapee from prison who'd been on the run for years, and we passed on a couple of nice hashish jobs to the Drugs Squad.

I don't remember if he got a discharge or a fine but he was compromised. Even if he'd wanted to walk away he couldn't and we teamed him up with Pat. Many policemen go all their service without contact with one effective working grass and to those who have never experienced it, two working together is akin to having two ferrets working a seemingly inexhaustible rabbit warren.

Some men become informers because they simply cannot handle being in a police station. This was the situation of one thief recalled by a major London player:

Golly became an informer after the Silver Bullion Raid at Mountnessing. Funnily he didn't grass everyone. Instead he named four out of the eight men, and two were just buyers.

I'd had a row with him over some dough back in the 1960s and in 1972 as I was walking along the landing at Brixton who was there but Golly. I said, 'Forget about the argument. We were in it all together.' He showed me his body and it was black and blue. He'd been caught running across the fields. He was a man who'd been at it for years. He'd been arrested for loitering and he'd done approved school but he'd never been tested. That's why he'd named names but he wouldn't go in the box to give evidence.

Years later I was in a restaurant in Romford and called

a cab to go home. Who was the driver but Golly? I didn't recognise him at first but then he said who he was and I replied, 'Do me a favour. Stop the cab. I'm getting out.' He said he hadn't really been a grass and if he'd wanted he could just about have got me life. I said, 'For old times' sake what I'm going to do if I bump into any of the others I'm going to have to tell them where you're working, so turn the job in.' In the end I never ever mentioned it but he quit the job.

Some informers turned, or at any rate said they did, because they thought that they were likely to be killed by their employers. Cecil Kirby, a Canadian former member of the Satan Choice motorcycle gang who became a hit-man for the Toronto-based Commisso gang, was convinced that they were plotting to do away with him. He had found them unreliable employers in the first place, welshing on deals and undercutting his payments for arson, beatings and murder plots on the pretext either that they hadn't been paid or that he had not completed the work satisfactorily. Now, in 1979, he was sure that his health required a change in occupation. They had, he claimed, suggested he go on a mission for them to Calabria to kill Girolamo 'Momo' Piromalli – then a powerful, if not the most powerful, Calabrian boss in Southern Italy. They would, they said, arrange for his travel there and back and pay him 10,000 Canadian dollars. He was afraid that all that would be paid was his fare to Italy, and that he would become part of a foreign field that was for ever Canada.

Kirby is also honest enough to admit that he was due to face a long sentence for a substantial breaking and entering offence: 'My choice was doing a long stretch in jail and probably being killed there by one of the Commissos' people or being done by the Commissos outside prison walls.'

He also had problems knowing to whom to turn. The previous year he had tried to work with an officer in the Ontario Provincial Police – assisting, he says, in saving his life by tipping him off that the Vagabonds, a particularly unpleasant Toronto motorcycle gang, had put out a contract on him. He had expected some tangible assistance from him with future court cases, but received none. Now out of the blue he called the Royal Canadian Mounted Police National Crime Intelligence Section and found safety if not redemption.[10]

Thank God for the telephone! Small-time thief Vito Zaccagnini was unable to pay the juice or interest on his loan. By 1963 he owed more than $22,000 to Cosa Nostra money-lenders, with total weekly repayments running at $1,500. Now he found himself in Winnebago County Jail at Rockford near Chicago. He arranged for a bondsman to obtain his release and was, he says, given a message by Pete Cappelletti, the bondsman, that there was a contract out on him. On 14 March 1964, on his way back to the wing, he saw a way out.

> I knew I couldn't pass up that telephone. If I didn't grab it then, I never would. So I called the FBI office in Chicago. I'd hardly started to talk when I froze with fear. I'd never done anything like that before. I knew what the code was. And I knew what would happen to me if I broke the code and they [the mobsters] got to me.
>
> They'd capture me to torture me, that was what I was afraid of. They kill you slow. I know what happened to Jackson [William Jackson, murdered in 1960]. They hung him on a hook and left him there. It took him a couple of days to die.[11]

One man who knew, or should have known, how the Mafia worked was Donald 'Tony the Greek' Frankos who at the end of a long career as a contract killer, during which time he had worked for both the Italians and the Westies, eventually decided discretion was the better part of valour. He was

10 Thomas C. Renner and C. Kirby, *Mafia Enforcer*, pp. 3–13.
11 Sandy Smith, 'How an informer traded mob secrets for his life', in A. Halper, *The Chicago Crime Book*, p. 455.

arrested on 15 October 1981 in Jilly's nightclub (named after
Frank Sinatra's then bodyguard) and identified as one of the
killers of Clarence Jones, a former basketball star and then
drug-dealer, who had been shot to death outside his apartment
in the Bronx, one of the few hits of the time with which Frankos
actually denies involvement. Convicted, he was sentenced to
25-years-to-life. Whilst in prison he negotiated a contract for
himself to dispose of another prisoner who was to be a witness
in a major drugs trial. He then discovered that his potential
employer had decided to extend the number of people who
were to be hit, and these included the prosecuting attorney and
the arresting officer. Frankos decided to look after himself. In
a touching passage, this killer describes his feelings:

> I hated the idea of being a rat. I know everybody says
> that, but I believe my entire life points to this truth: the
> main satisfaction I obtained as a criminal came from being
> acknowledged as a tough guy, a hitter, an individual who
> knew the consequences and accepted them . . . and if I
> went to the cops I'd become a pariah.
>
> The thought wouldn't leave my head, though I tried to
> banish it, order it to go away. It made my stomach churn,
> and I cursed myself repeatedly, calling myself every name
> in the book. I became physically sick, retching in the toilet
> bowl, but the thought wouldn't go away.

Eventually he heard a prison guard joke that 'the walls have
ears' and in his paranoid state decided that the plot had been
uncovered: 'A few days later I whispered in a guard's ear, I
want to talk to the U.S. Attorney.'

What he would not do, however, was to give evidence, and
as time went on he came to realise that unless he did the
protection he was being offered under the Witness Protection
Program extended only to being kept safe in prison. A return to
the street was not available. He testified before a grand jury and
then thought better of it. He was returned to the general prison

12

population in Attica, where he lasted only a short period before being badly beaten and shanked. Frankos agreed to return to the Witness Protection Program but apparently has consistently refused to give evidence. He is continually shifted from prison to prison for his own protection.[12]

Becoming a supergrass is not confined to the lower echelons of criminal society. The best can become one. Warwick Reid, the head of Hong Kong Legal Department's Commercial Crime Bureau went down the grassy path. He admitted accepting $1.6 million in bribes to fix fraud cases, but his original eight-year sentence was reduced in return for his testimony against his accomplices. He served four years and eight months and was released in November 1994. The Hong Kong Government hopes to recover about half the bribe money by selling Reid's home and fruit orchards in New Zealand. He said the rest of the money had been spent in an effort to flee Hong Kong justice. He had disguised himself as the adopted Caucasian son of a Chinese fishing family, and had so managed to slip into China. He then made his way to the Philippines where he was traced in Manila.

On his release he said he would not go into the Witness Protection Program and had been offered consultancy work throughout Eastern Asia. 'I have a very, very deep sense of regret about many things,' he told the press. 'I regret that I betrayed my office and took money in the first place.'

Of course, even a temporary intention to 'go straight' may be sufficient self-justification for an informer. As Jack Slipper says:

I was less impressed, though, by the reasons O'Mahoney[13] gave me for wanting to become a supergrass. He told me he was sick of crime and wanted to make a complete break from it. If he grassed on everyone, he said, no one would ever invite him into another team, and that way he

12 Donald Frankos, *Contract Killer*, Ch. 21.
13 For the career of Mr O'Mahoney, see pp. 65–73.

wouldn't be tempted back into the criminal world. But supergrasses need excuses – excuses they can make to themselves – more than they need reasons.[14]

There are some who become informers simply because they are getting old. Men who in their youth would have been the lions of – and been lionised in – the prison, in middle age no longer hold that same position. No matter how many repetitions are done in the prison gymnasium, no matter how many pounds are lifted on the Nautilus equipment, the reactions and the ability to inflict, and more importantly to receive, punishment are not the same. The once king of the prison is now relegated to a role where, instead of ruling and protecting, he is ruled and often needs to be protected.

Others do it because, having grown old, they cannot keep at their old trade. In the nineteenth century the Pinkerton agency was particularly good at recruiting old American burglars. One was the sixty-one-year-old William Forrester, who had been a prime suspect in the killing of millionaire Benjamin Nathan.

At 6 a.m. on 28 July 1870, Washington Nathan went downstairs in his home at 12 West 23rd Street, New York, to get a glass of water. Passing by his father's bedroom he looked in. On the floor lay Benjamin Nathan, said by some, almost certainly inaccurately, to be the richest man in the world. At least when his death was announced the flag over the New York Stock Exchange was flown at half-mast. He had been hit over the head a number of times with a carpenter's tool. There were signs of a struggle and a safe in the room had been opened. It appeared that the killer had washed his hands in a basin in the room but had not bothered to remove a handprint from the bedroom wall. The science of fingerprints was, however, unknown in America at the time.

Young Nathan was known to have been in financial trouble and to have quarrelled with his father over money. He had,

14 Jack Slipper, *Slipper of the Yard*, p. 114.

however, an alibi for most of the time-of-death bracket, provided in part by what the newspapers coyly described as a 'lass of the pavements'.

Nathan was not the only son of the family under suspicion. His brother Frederick was also in the house, as was William Kelly, the son of the housekeeper, a man with at least a passing acquaintanceship with the Underworld. Curiously, neither of them appears to have heard anything of what must have been a violent incident.

As is often the case in a high-profile murder, over the months and years a number of people confessed. One man, John T. Irving, was brought from California but was unable to persuade the authorities of his guilt. A prisoner in Sing Sing later implicated a burglar, William Forrester; he said he had heard that Forrester had intended merely to rob the house, but was surprised by Nathan and killed him. Forrester denied, almost certainly falsely, that he was in New York that night, but there was no hard evidence against him except that of the squealer and he was never charged. One puzzle was the question of the street door. Everyone in the house said it had been locked up for the night, but when Washington Nathan went down to get his glass of water he found it unlocked.

In 1879 Washington was shot in the neck by a former girlfriend, Fanny Barrett. The Chief of the New York Police then had the ingenious idea that whilst Nathan was recovering from the anaesthetic he would be questioned about his father's murder. Unfortunately the scheme came to nothing when the bullet worked its way out of its own accord. He remained under a cloud for the rest of his life, finally leaving America to live in Europe, where he died in 1892 at the age of forty-two. His hair was said to have turned prematurely white.

Now William Forrester, down on his luck, became a poacher turned gamekeeper. He dressed in old clothes and, staying in rooming houses in Toledo and Canton, became a mine of information. His street (or should that be hotel) credibility was, of course, first class.

Other Pinkerton informants included John C. Archer who, after a none too successful career as a pickpocket and burglar, opened a rooming house in Dayton, Ohio, along with his wife, herself a rather more successful pickpocket.

Archer, writing under the engaging name of Birdstone (it had previously been Brimstone), reported to his supervisor, Seymour Beutler, on the growing menace of the Yegg, or safebreaker:

> I don't know what connections you've got in Toledo, but if you're interested in Yegg work throughout the country that's your town. There are now about three mobs in there, one of whom came in about three months ago $10,000 strong, and they frequent only three places, Bill Downey's on Erie St., Johnnie Henry's, also Bill Herbert's place. If you've got a hot Yegg kick take Toledo for it and win.[15]

Archer kept his cover by coming out of retirement to execute raids on his own behalf. There was honour amongst thieves, and an informer could rely on at least tacit help from his employers. In December 1903 Archer was arrested in Indianapolis and put on an identification parade attended by a Pinkerton superintendent, Irle, who helpfully failed to pick him out. Seven years later, when he was charged with a bank robbery, the agency gave no effective evidence against him.

Some inducements to turn informer may not receive the hoped-for response.

In the spring of 1992 the Tokyo police offered a reha-bilitation programme for Yakuza gangsters who wished

15 Quoted in Frank Morn, *The Eye that Never Sleeps*, p. 146. The derivation of Yegg is interesting. In this context it almost certainly refers to John Yegg, said to be the first safe-blower to use nitro-glycerine. There are, however, alternative suggestions on offer. One is that the word was used for a professional killer employed by Chinese Tongs. Another is that it comes from the German *Jaeger*, meaning hunter, and yet another that it meant a beggar.

16

to retire and cross over to the paths of righteousness, that is the Tokyo police. One of the problems is the disconcerting habit of self-mutilation to be performed ritually if, in any way, a junior member has offended a senior. Off comes the top joint of the little finger (and for repeated offences other joints and other fingers). This makes the former Yakuza easily identifiable, and the police offered a package which involved reconstruction with toes substituting for the missing joints. It was not a success.

On the other hand, some do.

Later in the year the Italian police devised a package offering informers a new name, home and nose. Special telephone lines were installed so that viewers of teletext p.166 who dialled Rome 33170804 could ring in. In the first nine months of the operation some 280 *penititi* telephoned, a substantial increase on the dozen who had grassed in the previous forty years.[16]

The use of informants has long been regarded as good control policing. Commenting on corruption in the Metropolitan Police, a PC with twenty-two years' service said:

Prior to the Mark era, it was getting to such a state that particular squads just ran London. But it kept a lot of the villainy down. Now they're not keeping it down. They're not allowed out drinking so they don't get their informants in pubs.[17]

Says John Gosling:

Some did it for the excitement which, in cases where

16 O. Cyriax, *Crime*, p. 444.
17 Roger Graeff, *Talking Blues*, p. 326.

the snout had ceased to be a crook, compensated for the loss of thieving's thrill. Minor snouts worked for you for a variety of reasons: from motives of spite, envy or jealousy, or to try to evade the worst consequences of their crimes. A few did it to enjoy the thought that they were in a sense private detectives.[18]

One of the other problems for the police is how to keep their charges happy in isolation from the prison population as a whole. The technique does not seem to have changed over the last century. In the Haywood trial of 1907 it was thoroughly desirable to find someone who would back up Orchard's confession. He had implicated a Steve Adams and that man had promptly been arrested. At first he was placed in a cell with Orchard, who worked on him for five days to warn him of the dangers of non-cooperation and recount the good things which would follow if he helped out. Adams was then introduced to the Pinkerton agent McParland and signed a confession corroborating Orchard on a number of crimes against property.

> He was instantly taken out of his cell 'and placed in a sunny room in the hospital'. His wife and children were brought from Oregon and the family was set up in a bungalow outside the penitentiary walls. Three meals a day were brought in from the guards' table.
>
> Unfortunately Adams did not appreciate all the blessings which were being heaped upon him as an informer and State witness. He retracted his statement and was immediately arrested and taken three hundred miles north to Wallace where he was charged with murder.[19]

When Bertie Smalls decided to become the first real supergrass

18 John Gosling, *The Ghost Squad*, p. 39.
19 Irving Stone, *Clarence Darrow for the Defense*, p. 214. Defended by Darrow, Adams was acquitted after two jury disagreements.

in 1971, he received numerous benefits such as a suite in a Wembley hotel and then a series of safe houses. Others, such as Maurice O'Mahoney and Billy Williams, were lodged in Chiswick police station where they had colour television, games of snooker, rounds of golf and walks in the countryside and, according to O'Mahoney, drink and visits from his girl-friend who conceived a child in the cell. The cell conception was something he denied at a subsequent trial, but there is a picture of Billy Williams in a policeman's hat holding a bottle of champagne.

As Jack Slipper recalls:

Billy Williams was not a likeable sort of man. He was only too pleased to bite the hand that fed him. He was getting more extra facilities than he ever dreamed of, but he still saw fit to bite the hand that fed him and have photographs taken of him wearing a policeman's helmet.

When the *News of the World* photographs were published I expected to be called in to explain how it could have happened. I was quite pleased to find my immediate superiors accepted this could happen when you had a man like this.

Informers had to be treated with kid gloves. Once they had received their five-year sentence they could, and sometimes did, decide to have little more to do with the case.

Even with regular exercise O'Mahoney went into his shell and wouldn't talk with anyone. I spent a fair bit of time with him, not necessarily coaxing him to pull him out of his depression but to find out what interests he could safely be allowed to have put into operation.

One of the better-class North London villains, John Moriarty, also ended as a supergrass. By this time he was, however, heavily into drugs. He introduced smack to one of his partners, Tony 'Carrots' McLean, the son of Ginger Dennis from the

Spot slashing and cousin of the street fighter, Lenny 'Mean Machine' McLean. As one old face recalls, 'Carrots always said to me, "If only I could go back in time I would kill that bastard stone dead or anyone else who gets kids on drugs."'

By then the supergrass system was becoming more and more complicated. There now seemed to be competing teams of supergrasses: those who gave evidence under Scotland Yard detective Lundy's aegis and those, such as John Moriarty, who gave evidence against Lundy's friend Garner. Moriarty had twice been shot by rivals and had served periods of imprisonment. Now he decided to give evidence and to implicate Roy Garner.

'I never knew why he did it,' says former local police officer, Dave Brady. 'After all I was the officer called to The Favourite, the pub in Hornsey Rise where he'd been kneecapped. I asked what had happened and all he said was, "I fell down the fucking stairs, didn't I?"'

In the early 1970s Garner, together with a friend Kenny Ross, had purchased premises in Upper Street and then tried to evict the tenants. When this failed the premises were fired. Now, after the two shootings, Moriarty was prepared to name them in his statement as the organisers of the arson attacks.

Often the most loyal of supporters was a hidden blade of grass. One ex-CID officer recalls the double career of Charlie Clark, highly thought of by the Kray twins. It shows how easy it is for a police officer to lean on a villain.

Some time in 1967 when I was stationed at Walthamstow I got some information that a man living near Walthamstow dog track was an active receiver. With another officer I obtained a search warrant and called to see the man, who I had been told was named Charlie Clark. He lived in a bungalow off the main road and as soon as I saw him I knew that he was not the normal, run-of-the-mill denizen of East London's suburbia. Aged over fifty and a widower, he looked ill and gaunt, and I concluded that he had either 'prison pallor' or the type of complexion which results from too many late and very heavy nights on the tiles. The bungalow was clean and tidy in a bachelor sort of way and as we meticulously searched the house I became more and more aware that something was amiss, but for the life of me I could not put my finger on it. Charlie Clark was the perfect gentleman: wearing a smart cardigan and suit trousers, he showed us round and was almost too happy to co-operate fully and answer any questions we put to him. He didn't work, he said, he was 'on the panel', and did a bit of gambling.

We found no stolen property, and as Clark pressed a cup of tea on us the niggle in my mind suddenly resolved itself. Leaving him and my colleague in the small kitchen I had another look round the little bungalow, and sure enough I was right: there were two beds made up – one in a bedroom which was certainly that of Charlie Clark, and another single bed in a front room. Also in this room was a clothing rail of the type used by dress and clothing shops, and hanging from this in plastic covers were eight or nine expensive-looking men's suits. The suits weren't stolen; they were obviously in current use. I pointed this out to Clark and after some prevarication he said: 'They're Ronnie's, aren't they? He stays here on and off, when he feels like it.' 'Ronnie', it turned out, was Ronnie Kray and on being taxed further about his association with the Twins, Clark said he did a bit of driving for them, a bit of this and a bit of that – all in all a general factotum. I should point out at this stage that this was at a time after the Twins had been acquitted of the McCowan fiasco, and as far as the run of the mill CID officers were concerned no major inquiry into their activities was current.[20]

At that time, though, we knew that the Krays had

20 The Krays had been charged with blackmailing Huw McCowan, and after considerable shenanigans and a retrial had been acquitted. For a full account of the case, see L. Read, *Nipper*.

21

interests in premises in Hoe Street, Walthamstow and that a well-known Walthamstow hardman Tommy 'The Bear' Brown was believed to be a close associate, so we were not too surprised at the revelations. Clark, though, looked very sheepish and was foolish enough to say that it would not go down too well with the Krays if they knew that his house had been 'turned over' and that in addition to having incurred their wrath by having been stupid enough to draw police attention to the address, he would also lose considerable income as they would certainly ditch him.

From his point of view this, of course, was the worst thing he could have said. Within a few minutes he had been left in no doubt whatsoever that unless he was prepared to 'help' me with information, no matter what about, the Krays would certainly get to hear from one source or another that the bungalow had been visited and further that Ronnie's temporary digs had been noted. We left the bungalow with Clark's assurances that reliable information would be forthcoming ringing in our ears. We had, of course, no intention of ever 'leaking' what had taken place to anyone at all, let alone the Krays. We had played 'the game' with Clark and if he was fooled and went along with it, all well and good, but to be honest I had little hope.

Much to my amazement Clark was in touch by telephone within a few days and thereafter on a fairly regular basis. Obviously it would never have been a very good idea to call at the bungalow and as far as I can recall I never actually saw Clark in person again. His information, though, was always one hundred per cent reliable: there were several small receivers, a couple of stolen cars – all that sort of thing, but nothing about the Krays, which I suppose was very much on the cards. From time to time I would ask him what 'the Firm' were up to, where they were drinking and who they were annoying, but he never seemed to know anything apart from what was common knowledge.

Then, after a few months something very odd happened. One morning the Walthamstow Detective Inspector Frank Nichols called me into his office and told me I had been summoned to the Yard to see a Chief Superintendent named 'Fergie' Walker. Nichols said he had no idea what it was about but I had to go and that was all there was about it.

I arrived at the Yard to see Walker with no small feeling of apprehension: the man was a senior officer in C.1 department, which amongst many other things dealt with discipline and complaints against police at that time. I knew it was odd to be summoned in person but just the same I was concerned. As it turned out, my fears were misplaced and I knew there were no problems as soon as I went into Walker's office and he called me 'Sarge'. He had become aware, he told me, that I had an informant named Charlie Clark who was closely associated with the Krays. I had done very well to cultivate such a snout, he said, and he was just wondering if Clark had ever had much to say about what the Twins were up to. I told him that he had not, but assured him that if he ever did I would contact Walker or his sergeant immediately.

Driving back to Walthamstow, I thought over what had happened. No one knew that Clark was working for me – with the exception of the DC who had accompanied me on the original search of the bungalow – so how had Walker found out? There could only be one explanation: Walker had a telephone intercept on Clark and had therefore overheard all of our mutual conversations. A year or so later, after the arrest of the Twins by Nipper Read and Henry Mooney, and when I knew that Fergie Walker had started off the second major investigation into their activities, this was confirmed to me.

Over the months, he faded out and I did not pressurise

him. I had drawn his criminal record file and noted that he had a few minor convictions years before both in the name of Clark and Bateman, but apart from that there was nothing of any interest at all.

During the whole period of our association, he told me only a few small pieces of information relative to the Firm and these, I imagined, were pretty common knowledge in any event. He told me that Ronnie was intent on becoming some sort of country squire and was spending most weekends in Suffolk, and told me that the Twins had persuaded the writer, John Pearson, to do their biography. He stressed that this was to be in the manner they saw fit and, very tongue-in-cheek, he told us that they were well on the way to convincing Mr Pearson that they were some sort of Saviours and Benefactors of the East End Poor and Needy as well as the Well Known Sporting and Philanthropic Twins they encouraged the press to refer to them as, and that suggestions that they were engaged in criminal activities – let alone gangsterism – were wicked lies. Years later Nipper Read told me that after the arrest of the Krays and on their first appearance at Bow Street magistrates' court Pearson had offered to bail them. 'You just sit here for a couple of weeks, Mr Pearson, and listen to what's going to be said,' Nipper told him, 'and then come and tell me if you want to bail them.' Needless to say, the offer was not repeated!

Clark also told me of Ronnie's predilection for homosexual activities, which at that time came as something of a surprise to me, although according to Clark's informant this was well-known amongst London's criminal fraternity.

In his book *Villains We Have Known*, Reggie Kray refers to Charlie Clark as being some sort of King of the Cat Burglars – a master climber. I never saw any evidence of this and there was nothing in his criminal file to give even the slightest indication that he was any

24

sort of a villain at all. Kray also alludes to how loyal to the Firm Clark was, how fond he was of Ronnie and that he was a dependable and unswerving associate. Countless CID officers over the years have maintained that there is no such beast as a criminal who will not give information if needs must; the Krays, perhaps, should have borne this in mind![21]

The informer can expect a hard time in prison with much, if not all, his sentence served on Rule 43.[22] Some were reasonably fortunate:

There were four men, Johnny R., Billy T., Kenny Baker,[23] he's dead now, and another old-time villain from Manchester were arrested up there over a set-up by a man who was very well respected, Billy E.

During their sentence when they got a lot of bird he turns up in Ford. I'm in there as well. Billy T went over to Billy E and said something. The man went white and went over to the screw in charge. That was at midday. He was taken to the security room and by 1.30 he was

21 In the early hours of 10 March 1989 Charlie Clark, now known as Bateman, was found stabbed to death at his home in Beaufoy Terrace, Dover. He was then seventy-one and after having had a leg amputated, spent most of his time sitting looking out of the window of his home. In July 1990 nineteen-year-old Shane Keeler was sentenced to life imprisonment for his murder. Keeler, who had been in care since the age of five and was suffering from an abnormality of the mind, had pleaded guilty to manslaughter on the grounds of diminished responsibility, but the plea had not been accepted. He had broken into Clark's home and, when discovered, had stabbed him in the neck. He made off with £5, which he spent at the docks on video games and a cup of tea. Clark's neighbours challenged the prosecution's description of him as a 'likeable old man'. They referred to the court case the previous year and some said they had been obliged to move because of his behaviour.
22 Rule 43 allows the separation of certain categories of prisoners from the main congregation. These include men who are convicted of sex offences and those who are informers, as well as convicted police and prison officers. The governor of a prison may also order a disruptive man to be detained under Rule 43 for the good order of the prison.
23 On 27 November 1990 Baker was shot dead by the police when he and three members of the South-London-based Arif family were cornered after they had ambushed a Securicor van at a filling station in Reigate, Surrey.

in a van on his way out of Ford. No one knew where they took him.

Some were not so fortunate:

> So one day when this grass was at work in the bag shop one of the chaps asked the screw if he could fall out to go to the recess, having got permistion he went into the recess; had a shit in his handkerchief, holding it behind his back he went up behind the grass (who was bisily sewing away at a mailbag, and he was not expecting anything to happen to him) and emptied the contence of his handkerchief into this unsuspecting geezers bin, and then just walked away as inocent as you like, sat down in his place and carried on with his work. After a while the grass put his hand in his bin for something or other, and was horryfied at what he found, he went and showed the screw what someone had done, but the screw began to raw with laughter, at this every one began to laugh untill the whole place was in an upraw. [*sic*]24

Some had it even worse.

> In 1967 I nearly took Joe Cannon's eye out in Pentonville. I was back there for visits and now Joey was doing his seven for armed robbery and he had a name as a grass in prison.
> I got this great big, long needle which was used for sewing mailbags. When he came in and was locked up, I crept up to his cell. He said, 'Who is it?' I said, 'It's me, look through the spy-hole,' and as he did I stabbed it through. He screamed out and immediately rung his cell bell. I just drifted away. He told the authorities it was me, but there was nothing they could do because by the time

24 F. Norman, *Bang to Rights*, p. 85.

they got to me the needle was long gone and I was back in my cell. It was his word or mine, and the screws weren't going to act just on his word. He was immediately taken to the hospital and then transferred out of the prison.[25]

Many informers both in history and in more recent times have found that they could not manage to bear the burden they had brought on themselves and the damage they had done. In modern times Richard Piggott, who sold forged letters to try to implicate Parnell in the Phoenix Park murders, gassed himself in Madrid. In June 1927 a man named Johnstone – who had, it seems, been the paid spy of Scotland Yard, keeping them informed on the National Unemployed Workers' Movement – committed suicide on a beach at Southend by drinking a bottle of disinfectant. David Smith, the robber, now planning to repeat his career as a supergrass, changed his mind and hanged himself in his cell shortly after his birthday.

25 F. Fraser, *Mad Frank*, pp. 112–113.

2

Grasses – The Early Days

It is not given to everyone to leave his name in the English language. Lord Cardigan did; so did the Duke of Wellington. Leotard, who invented the art of the flying trapeze at the Cirque d'Hiver in Paris, also fashioned a body-suit. The Earl of Sandwich left his name as a type of food, and a poker-playing man named Reuben had his given to a variety of that food. Opera singers and ballet dancers have given their names to meringues, puddings and toast. The early 1970s introduced a new word – supergrass – into the English language. It also gave a new phrase to criminal slang – *to do a Bertie*, or inform to the police. Even Capone and the American gangsters of the twenties and thirties did not reach that height of acclaim, neither did Jack Spot, Billy Hill or the Krays. Now Bertie Smalls of Edmonton, North London, reached the pinnacle of fame. The phrase quickly passed into more general usage; schoolchildren in London used the phrase of others who had sneaked to their teacher. It had taken centuries for a criminal to attain that position of fashion-making.

There is no thing new under the sun, said Ecclesiastes, and informers themselves are as old as history. Although, in English law, strictly speaking he was probably an ordinary person acting under duress rather than an informer, one of

29

the first recorded uses of the confidential informant seems to be found in the Old Testament:

> *24:*And the spies saw a man come forth out of the city, and they said unto him, Shew us, we pray thee, the entrance into the city, and we will show thee mercy.
> *25:*And when he shewed them the entrance into the city, they smote the city with the edge of the sword; but they let go the man and all his family.[1]

In around 200 BC, Scipio Africanus had his soldiers dress up as slaves in order to spy on the Carthaginians. A problem arose when one of the 'slaves' was recognised as having been at the same school as a Numidian general. In about 100 BC Quintus Servius offered to spy on the Teutons who were then threatening Roman Gaul. His idea was to put on Celtic dress and acquire 'the commonest expressions of that language for such conversations as might be necessary'. His undercover mission seems to have been successful; he 'mingled with the barbarians, and after seeing or hearing what was necessary, came back'.[2]

These were rare examples, however, and quite clearly military and political. More germane, in Ancient Greece there were sycophants or fig-blabbers who informed the authorities on those who were exporting figs illegally. In the Roman Empire the fire-brigade was used for the purposes of the secret police:

> A soldier, dressed like a civilian, sits down by your side, and begins to speak ill of Caesar, and then you do too, just as though you had received from him some guarantee of good faith in the fact he began the abuse, tell likewise everything you think, and the next thing is – you are led off to prison in chains.[3]

1 Judges 1 24–25.
2 J. Haswell, *Spys and Spymasters*, p. 12.
3 Chester G. Starr, *Civilisation and the Caesars*, p. 141.

In sixteenth-century India scavengers, refuse collectors, merchants and pedlars were employed as police spies, and in Arabian countries eunuchs often headed networks of secret police. England long had a political spy system going back at least to Harold, and this reached a relatively early apotheosis in Francis Walsingham and his spy system for Elizabeth I.

Historically, in England, the individual was required in law to inform on a man whom he knew to have committed a felony – an offence which, on conviction, could lead to the forfeiture of possessions to the Crown. If he did not, then he could be prosecuted for the offence of misprison of that felony and in turn could himself be fined or imprisoned.[4] There was therefore a large body of people who were quite prepared to inform on their neighbours and friends. In Walsingham's case he was prepared to take the matter a stage further and pay for the information.

There was also the related concept of the hue and cry. A person witnessing a felony had a duty to sound a general alarm, calling, 'Out! Out!' Those hearing the call then, under pain of fines and imprisonment, had a duty to turn out with bows, arrows and knives to chase down the felon. This was the *posse comitatus*. There was also an obligation to take part in a night watch.

There is now some doubt amongst legal writers as to whether the obligation still exists. If it does, it now exists more in its breach than its observance. It has certainly persisted in the requirement that a citizen should go to the assistance of a police constable in uniform who calls for help. However, in a recent case in 1993, although a prosecution was brought against a man who had declined to assist a police officer trying to catch a burglar, it was abandoned. Possibly this was due to the fact that, the previous week, a man who had done

4 Felonies were the serious crimes such as murder, rape, robbery. In mediaeval times they carried not only the death penalty but also the forfeiture to the Crown of the felon's property. Other crimes were called misdemeanours and did not carry forfeiture. The difference between a felony and a misdemeanour was abolished by the Criminal Justice Act 1967.

just that had been shot and killed. In any event the prospect of a conviction seemed unlikely.

Given there was no such animal as a police force as we know it in England and Wales until 1829, one of the ways of controlling crime was the use of the dedicated common informer. He was described by Radzinowicz as:

> a person who brought certain transgressions to the notice of the authorities and instituted proceedings not because he, personally, had been aggrieved or wished to see justice done, but because under law he was entitled to a part of a fine which might be imposed.[5]

By the end of the seventeenth century, with the rise of the highwayman, the coiner and other serious criminals, the reward for apprehending felons was a judge's certificate which exempted the holder from any obligation to put in a spell of duty as a part-time parish constable. It soon came to be known as blood-money or a Tyburn Ticket, and could change hands at auction for up to £300 although between £10 and £50 was a more usual price. The proceeds of sale would be divided between the informer and the arresting constable. One result was that small-time criminals had a virtual licence to commit crime in the hope that they would graduate from misdemeanours to felonies and so make their arrest financially worthwhile to the informer. A second was that anyone of substance and intelligence, if not integrity, could buy a lifelong exemption from duty. As a result many of the parish constables were illiterate or foolish and very often both.

By the beginning of the nineteenth century a common informer, as now, could make a good living from receiving part of the penalty imposed. The awards for bringing to the notice of the authorities 'offences leading to corruption of morals'

5 L.Radzinowicz, *A History of the English Criminal Law*, vol ii, p. 138.

could range from 1s 8d (8p) to the much more worthwhile £200. A publican who was found to have allowed his licensed premises to be used for gaming by 'journeymen, labourers, servants or apprentices' could expect to pay the informer 10s (50p) for the first offence and £2. 10s on subsequent occasions.[6]

Common informers could not expect to be popular and indeed they were not.

> . . . popular prejudice has attached odium to the common informer not because the thing itself is wrong since the law has made it necessary but because many dissolute characters have taken up this state, seldom with a view to benefit the public . . . Informers are indispensibly necessary to the execution of the law.[7]

Certainly in London the common informer, as a legal entity, faded from view shortly after Peel's New Police marched into the streets in 1829. By the end of the next decade the magistrates had power to reduce the part of the penalty which was paid to the informer or deny him the right to any payment, and as they imposed this practice more and more often the sport became less profitable. As it took longer to establish police forces throughout England and Wales, so it took rather longer for the practice to die out in the provinces.

On the other hand the decision of the supergrass, as opposed to the common or garden informer, to assist the police has almost invariably been taken at a moment when his professional life, for one reason or another – very often because

---

6 *Ibid.* p. 142.
7 P. Colquhoon, *A Treatise on the Functions and Duties of a Constable etc.*, p. 57. Colquhoon was a metropolitan stipendiary magistrate who was obsessed with the idea of establishing a proper police force to replace the often inefficient and corrupt Bow Street Runners who operated at the time. By 1800 his *Treatise on the Metropolitan Police* had reached its sixth edition.

he has been arrested and finds that death, transportation or more recently a long term of imprisonment is looming large – has become impossible, so as to cut himself a better deal. It also happens when he finds that his life on the outside is similarly threatened by his employers or former friends.

Possibly the first of the British supergrasses was a professional housebreaker, John Smith. On 5 December 1705 he appeared at the Old Bailey on four indictments including the theft of fifty pairs of men's shoes, 900 yards of cloth, 400 lb of China silk and 128 pairs of gloves. Ironically in the case of the shoes an accomplice gave evidence against him to the effect that they had been stealing as a team for some six years. There was accomplice evidence in the second case (the cloth), which was dismissed, and he was acquitted over the matter of the silk. There was nothing much he could do about the matter of the shoes, since he was caught in the shop with the goods packed up neatly awaiting disposal. Since, at the time, conviction for any offence of theft where the value of the goods was more than five shillings carried the death penalty, he was sentenced to be hanged.[8]

Smith appeared at Tyburn on 12 December, having travelled west from Newgate prison, a journey which coined the expression 'to go West' well before either Mae West or the American newspaper proprietor, Horace Greely, put their names to the phrase. There he was hanged, or rather half-hanged because while he had been swinging on the

8 The practice was for a merciful jury to return a verdict that the prisoner had stolen goods value 4s 11d and so avert the death penalty. Even if they did not do so, there were still a number of ways in which the prisoner could escape the gallows. There was the Oath of Clergy under which if verses of the Bible could be read (or memorised) then the prisoner went free. There was also branding which, as the years went by, was often done with a cold iron.

From 1706 onwards Smith appeared on an infrequent basis in the London courts until in 1720 he was sentenced to transportation. At the age of sixty-six he had been found trying to break into a warehouse. There is a full account of the activities of John Smith in James Bland, *Crime, Strange but True*, pp. 183 *et seq*.

gibbet for between seven and fifteen minutes, his reprieve was announced. He was cut down and resuscitated.[9]

A reprieve then was not necessarily a complete escape for a prisoner. It was more in the way of a stay of execution. Many would be subsequently pardoned, and a good few not. Smith was fortunate; and it may be that fortune favours those who help themselves because on 20 February he received an unconditional pardon. By 3 March he had informed on 350 pickpockets and housebreakers who had joined the Army to avoid detection. In the November of that year he named two sergeants and six soldiers in the Second Regiment of Footguards in which he had served. The men were acquitted.

One of those who was not so fortunate in obtaining a pardon was John Poulter, otherwise known as Baxter. In one of those gallows repentance books which were so popular, and which were the ancestors of the 'true crime' books of today, Mr Poulter was condemned to hang for robbery and then in Ivelchester jail purportedly wrote an account of his life and crimes:[10] 'I have followed Gambling and Defrauding these five years passed, and lived on the Spoil of other Men's Substance.'

He had met John Brown, alias Dawson, Mary Brown and Mary Davies at Lichfield in Staffordshire on a fair day and

> after some ceremony we all agreed to go and drink a glass of wine; accordingly we went to Mr Wm Brook's at the George Inn, in the said town, and were shown up stairs; we had not been there long before Mary Brown espied a large chest, and said here is a chance, the lid being loose, and her hand but small, she pulled out of the said chest

9 Failed executions were not all that uncommon. In November 1740 the seventeen-year-old William Duell had hung for half an hour before he was cut down from Tyburn and resuscitated. He was later transported. In 1782 John Hayes was revived after his hanging and was later given a passage to America paid for by a surgeon from Gough Square, London. Douglas Hay *et al, Albion's Fatal Tree*, p. 104.
10 John Poulter, *The Discoveries of John Poulter, alias Baxter.*

one yellow silk flowered damask gown, one green silk
ditto, one brown silk ditto, and one black flowered silk
capuchin, which Mary Brown carried out of the said house
in her apron, to the place where our horses were . . .

and off they went for a rip-roaring five years spent in theft and
robbery in Britain and Ireland.[11]

It ended in tears, of course, after the robbery of a Dr
Hancock of Salisbury, and, in an effort to save himself
from the scragsman, Poulter turned informer naming some
thirty-one of his friends and accomplices to the justices at
Taunton. Perhaps because there was no great success in
apprehending these villains, who included his old friend John
Brown, no reprieve was forthcoming.

The author of the postscript to the book certainly believes
Poulter was unlucky:

This unfortunate man, after having made important discoveries of great use to the public and for much less
than which many a man has not only receiv'd pardon
for capital offences, but also rewards, had the fate by a
series of unlucky incidents & circumstances, to be brought
to suffer, after having entertained the most allured and
flattering hopes to the contrary. When he first made his
informations against his accomplices, which was soon
after he was taken up, he desired they might be kept very
secret; and particularly he gave a charge to the officer
who was sent to Bath to apprehend his accomplices, not
to divulge his errand at his arrival to any one person there

11 Mary Brown had a splendid career. In the previous 4½ years she had been
tried six times all over the country. The first was in Westmorland, where she
was acquitted and her then husband Peter executed. After that she appeared in
Ruthen, Derbyshire, with Brown, alias Dawson, and then in Staffordshire and
the Fen country mostly for pickpocketing. She was transported in 1746 but had
effected her illegal return. After the death of her husband she seems to have
teamed up with Rosey Brown, who himself was transported in 1750 but also
returned before the expiration of his sentence.

except the mayor; because there were several persons who lived in good credit in the eye of the world, that yet had intelligence with his gang.

The charge did no good to Poulter or the officer. Within an hour of the man's arrival the gossip was all over town and, it seems, the names of the wanted men and women appeared in a printed broadsheet. Unsurprisingly, the birds flew.

Dr Hancock seems to have played the market both ways. In return for the confession, the return of some of his property and the information, it seems he told Poulter he would be 'very favourable to him in the prosecution'. Not so, writes the author. 'The doctor behaved against him with the greatest inveteracy, and used all his interest to prevent the judge from granting him any respite from execution.' In return for his information and the details of how transported felons could get back into the country unapprehended . . .

. . . just before they go on board a ship, their friends or acquaintances purchase their freedom from the captain, for about 10l sterling. Then the friend of the convict gets a note from the captain that the person is free to go where they please, unmolested, when the ship arrives between the Capes of Virginia.

There is also advice to retailers how to detect and prevent thefts:

The counter being covered with goods, one of the two shall look over the goods, whilst the other shall plant a piece under the rest, not opened, altho' one or more persons be behind the counter, who shall not see them, because they will open a piece of stuff and hold it up between the owner and their partner, who sits with her petticoats half up, ready for the word napp it; she puts it between her carriers (that is her thighs), gets up & lets her cloaths drop agreeing and paying for what they like, and so go off, and can walk very well without putting her hands to hold it; then going into a yard or entry, the partner takes it from them.

Respites were given and indeed there was some feeling amongst members of the community that Poulter was worth preserving. The fairly disingenuous argument was that his accomplices, who were now believed to be abroad, would never feel able to return to England because he knew their haunts and would be able to inform on them again.

Unfortunately those members did not include the local gaoler who refused to allow Poulter a bed. A campaign was begun to ensure that the repentant man was given some comfort, but it seems this may have rebounded with the authorities. Poulter was sentenced to hang in March 1752. All his good intentions and protestations came to nothing when, after forcing a window with an iron bar from his cell, he escaped on 17 February along with a debtor who was lodged in the prison. Poulter was obliged to walk in his irons, resulting in a very badly chafed leg. The intention was to make for Wales, but when they arrived in Wookey they thought they were near Axbridge. Poulter went to bed and then it was a case of the informer informed upon. He was captured by some workmen and returned to Ivelchester where the gaoler, smarting from the escape and the bedding incident, successfully petitioned that Poulter be hanged immediately.

Poulter received the news and spent the day in prayer. However, he still had one last card to play. In his book he had named a man 'F' as being involved in the robberies and having melted plate for him. On the scaffold he denounced 'F' whom he saw in the crowd.

F denied this with bitter imprecations, Poulter affirmed that, as he was going to appear before his great judge and hoped to receive mercy from him, what he had said was true: He then desired the spectators to take warning by his sad end, and to avoid ill company, acknowledging that he deserved to die, but most of his accomplices more so.

There is no record of what, if anything, then happened to 'F'.

Between this pair and under the licence of the trading justice the celebrated criminal 'thief-taker' Jonathan Wild operated with marked success. Wild, who carried a silver-mounted staff as an emblem of his self-styled rank, was a broker for stolen goods and an informer. Provided no questions were asked and there were adequate rewards, the goods were returned to the warehouses from which he had often arranged their theft. Indeed he seems to have provided a role-model for some policemen to the present day.[12]

His career was an interesting one. Born in Wolverhampton in 1683, he was apprenticed to a buckle-maker. He married and left his wife. In 1708 he was imprisoned for debt and was discharged four years later when he set up house in Drury Lane with his mistress Mary Milliner, a prostitute whom he had met in prison. Initially he was what was called a twang, the pickpocket who would take the wallets of Milliner's clients. In those days intercourse with prostitutes was almost invariably undertaken vertically. He began his criminal apprenticeship proper with a Charles Hitchin, a City Marshal, who taught him the trade of receiver which Wild was to perfect.

From then on he set up a loose association of thieves, pick-pockets and highwaymen. He was described in the *Newgate Calendar* as The Prince of Robbers. He also set himself up as a thief-taker and opened an office near the Old Bailey where he acted as agent between thief and victim, often later

12 For a full account of Wild's life, see *The Thief Takers* by Patrick Pringle. The character MacHeath in John Gay's *The Beggar's Opera* was based on Wild.

arresting the former.[13] If anyone threatened to expose him he brought a capital charge against the man, fabricating a felony charge. At the time no convicted felon could give evidence against anyone else. It is difficult, at this distance in time, to understand why anyone at all went near him, but for twelve years he was able to maintain such a successful double life that by 1723 he petitioned to be made a freeman of the City. By 1718 he had already designated himself as 'Thief Catcher General of Great Britain and Ireland' and had issued himself with his silver staff.

It was not as though the authorities were unaware of the dangers of the receiver-cum-thief-taker. In 1691 anti-pawnshop legislation had driven the receiver underground and in 1718 Hitchin, now suffering from the predations of his protégé, had published a pamphlet, *A True Discovery of the Conduct of Receivers and Thief Takers, In and about the City of London*, denouncing Wild. A bill – later known as the Jonathan Wild Act – sponsored by Sir William Thompson, Recorder of London and Solicitor-General, was passed, making it a felony to receive rewards under the pretence of retrieving stolen goods. In the debate over the bill Wild was denounced again but, for the moment, he was adroit enough to circumvent trouble.

13 An earlier example of thief-recoverer was Mary Frith, known as Moll Cutpurse and celebrated in *The Roaring Girle*, by Middleton and Dekker. She was probably born in 1584, the daughter of a shoemaker in Barbican and 'particular care was bestowed on her education'. It did her no good. Her anonymous biographer quoted in the *Dictionary of National Biography* says of her, 'A very tomrig or rumpscutttle she was and delighted and sported only in boy's play, not minding or companying with the girls.' When she was grown to a 'lusty and servicable wench' she was put out to service but she disliked housework of any kind and 'had a natural abhorrence to the tending of children'. An accomplished pickpocket, who dressed like a man, drank heavily and smoked a pipe, she was said to be scrupulously honest in her dealings with robber and robbed alike. Accompanied by her dog, she also seems to have been a highway robber. On one occasion, the story goes, she held up General Fairfax on Hounslow Heath, shooting him (in the arm) and both his horses. Her own horse failed her at Turnham Green and she was caught. Amazingly she bought herself out of prison with a payment of the immense sum of £2,000 to the aggrieved General. If the story is correct she was sixty at the time. She died of dropsy and in her will she left £20 for the celebration of the return of the monarchy. She was buried on 10 August 1659.

In an early example of international crime, stolen goods, particularly English watches which were highly prized on the continent, were shipped to Holland and kept in a warehouse in Flushing. The proceeds of sale were translated into dutiable goods which were then smuggled back to England. In 1723 Wild was still sufficiently confident of his invulnerability that he made his petition to the Lord Mayor and Aldermen for the freedom of the City of London 'in return for his services to justice'. He had, he said, sent sixty men to the gallows. By now he had a 'branch office' in the care of a manager, had become a successful slum landlord and owned a country house tended by a butler and a footman.

That year he survived an assassination attempt by Joseph Blake, known as Blueskin, a highwayman, who cut his throat in court. He and Blake had at one time been associates, and Blake expected some help in arranging his release. When it was not forthcoming Blake attacked him. Blueskin did not survive; he was hanged, to be commemorated by Dean Swift in the elegy *Blueskin's Ballad*.

Wild's end came when he was indicted under his own Act, so to speak, for receiving ten guineas as a reward for helping a Mrs Steham to recover stolen lace, the theft of which he had arranged. Convicted, he was hanged on 24 May 1725 despite another petition to the Lord Mayor of London. He tried to commit suicide, taking an overdose of laudanum the night before his execution and, still drowsy, was pelted by the mob on the way to Tyburn.

On Monday about the usual Time, Jonathan Wild was executed at Tyburn. Never was there seen so prodigious a Concourse of People before, not even upon the most popular Occasion of that Nature. The famous Jack Sheppard had a tolerable Number to attend his Exit; but no more to be compared to the present, than a Regiment to an Army, and, which is very remarkable, in all that innumerable Crowd, there was not one Pitying Eye to

41

be seen, nor one Compassionate Word to be heard; but
on the contrary, whenever he came, there was nothing
but Hollering and Huzzas, as if it had been upon a
Triumph.[14]

His body was saved from the Tyburn surgeons but one of the
Newgate chaplains betrayed his burial place and it was dug up.
Several generations later it was donated to the Royal College of
Surgeons. He was survived by both Mary Milliner and Charles
Hitchin. Ms Milliner, whose ear had been sliced off by Wild
in a temper, had been paid a pension by him to the date of his
death. Hitchin remained a City Under-Marshal for a further
three years when he was tried for sodomy. Acquitted of the
capital offence but convicted of a kindred misdemeanour, he
was sentenced to a term in the pillory, as well as six months'
imprisonment, and fined £20.

However, not everyone was pleased with the death of this
celebrated informer:

14 *Applebee's Journal*, 29 May 1725, quoted in William Robert Irwin, *The Making
of Jonathan Wild: A Study of the Literary Method of Henry Fielding*. As for
Jack Sheppard, he was born in 1702 and apprenticed to a cane-chair maker.
He fell into the company of Bess Lyon, better known as Edgeworth Bess, who
together with Poll Maggott incited him to larceny. His first recorded offence
is the theft of silver spoons from the Rummer Tavern, Charing Cross, but his
fame lies in his brilliant and daring escapes from prison. He rescued Bess from
St Giles' Round House and she returned the compliment when in April 1724
he was betrayed by his brother-in-law and sent to the New prison, from which
he escaped on 25 May by getting rid of his irons, cutting through a double grille
of oak and iron bars and scaling a 25-foot wall with a man on his back. Wild
caught him on 23 July 1724, but Sheppard escaped again on 31 August and was
at liberty for eleven days, working as a highwayman. After his capture and now
in Newgate prison, he was chained to two iron staples from which he escaped
on 13 September. He remained at large for a fortnight, burgling throughout the
City happily, and was caught after he drank himself insensible in the Maypole
Tavern near Clare Market. He was hanged on 16 November 1724 and buried in
St Martin in the Fields' churchyard. He is described by Horace Bleakley in *The
Hangmen of England* (p. 45) as having '. . . a cheery and impudent humour that
appealed to the common folk, whose love for him grew fonder when they saw
that he was always merry when everything seemed most black. Sharp of tongue
and quick of wit, he was a typical specimen of the Cockney guttersnipe, and as
such the great city of London took him to its heart. Jack's physique was also
a help to his renown. A dapper fellow such as he, subtle as a panther and with
muscles of steel, was naturally the ideal hero of his particular feats of skill. In
popular fancy he became the will-o'-the-wisp of crime.'

Tis remarkable that since the Dissolution of Jonathan Wild, not one Felon has been convicted capitally, which by some is attributed to a Reform amongst the Rogues and by others to the Want of a proper Person to detect them.[15]

Since the Death of Jonathan Wild has been so much lamented for Want of his useful Intelligence, this is to inform the Publick, that his ghost gives constant Attendance every Night at a certain House in Bury Street; where he resolves all Sorts of Questions, As his former Business was to discover Robberies committed, he has now the Gift of Revealing Rogueries intended.[16]

Horace Bleackley is another champion of Wild.

Nature intended Jonathan Wild for a sleuth, and had he been born two centuries later it is probable that he would have won a responsible position at Scotland Yard. For ten years at least, from 1715 until he died, he was by far the most efficient thief-taker in England. Fear was unknown to him. He was as tenacious as a bull-dog. Whenever he had resolved to clasp hands on a mill-ken or a bridle-cull – as burglar and highwayman were termed in his jargon – he ran his quarry to earth at whatever hazard. Scores of times this intrepid man arrested some armed desparado single-handed or rounded up a dangerous gang with a couple of his henchmen.[17]

Thief-taking did not, however, end with Wild. Four men, Stephen McDaniel, John Berry, James Salmon and a man named Egan, were convicted at the Old Bailey in February 1756 of a conspiracy to procure two other persons to commit

15 *Daily Journal*, 5 July 1735.
16 *Daily Post*, 5 February 1726.
17 H. Bleackley, *The Hangmen of England*, p. 47.

a robbery. The four men had, according to the prosecution, been practising as thief-takers for some fifteen or sixteen years. Their tried and tested methods were an example which has lasted until today. They would induce a simpleton to join them in committing crime and then denounce him to a magistrate and collect the reward.

Their come-uppance arrived when they persuaded two young men to take part in a staged robbery in Deptford, scene of the death of the playwright and spy Christopher Marlowe. Salmon was the purported victim and McDaniel came on the scene and arrested the boys. Initially they were convicted at Kent Assizes but Salmon and his friends reckoned without the abilities of a local constable, Joseph Cox, who arrested the entire gang. The truth came out and McDaniel and the members of his gang were sentenced to seven years' imprisonment accompanied by a stand in the pillory. Cox capitalised on his efforts with his treatise *A Faithful Narrative of the Most Wicked and Inhuman Transactions of that Bloody-Minded Gang of Thief-Takers alias Thief Makers*.[18]

When McDaniel and Berry took their turn in Hatton Garden up the road from the Old Bailey, they were nearly lynched by the mob and were rescued by prison warders. Three days later Salmon and Egan went in the pillory in Smithfield and neither was so fortunate. Egan was killed in the ensuing riot and Salmon died of his injuries received after he was rescued and taken back to Newgate prison. There was a story that the men were linked to the Bow Street Court and the magistrate, 'Blind' John Fielding, inserted a notice in the *Public Advertiser* denouncing the men and dissociating himself from their behaviour.[19]

Turning informer – or in legal terminology entering a plea of approvement which translated into turning Queen's Evidence –

18 Joseph Cox, *A Faithful Narrative of the Most Wicked and Inhuman Transactions of that Bloody-Minded Gang of Thief-Takers alias Thief Makers*, pp. 154–74.
19 A. Babington, *A House in Bow Street*, pp. 128–9.

was, however, a reasonable bet to save one's neck and possibly to obtain a pardon even in murder cases.

Some seventy years after the death of John Poulter, the Irish body-snatchers William Burke and William Hare arrived in Scotland to work as navvies on the Union Canal being built between Glasgow and Edinburgh. They met whilst staying in the same lodgings at Tanner's Close, West Port, Edinburgh. These they shared with an army pensioner, 'Old Donald', who died in November 1827 owing Hare £4. Bodies to be used by anatomy students – there were over 500 to be catered for in the city alone – were hard to come by, and the temptation to recoup his losses must have been irresistible to Burke.[20] 'Old Donald' was dug up and sold for £7 10s to the fashionable surgeon Dr Robert Knox of the Anatomy School, who lived at 10 Surgeon's Square, Edinburgh.

After that the enterprise burgeoned even if it did not last a full year. They had two 'wives', Helen McDougal and Maggie Laird respectively, as accomplices to lure people to their lodgings where, having been plied with drink, they were suffocated. The bodies were placed in a tea chest and carried round to Dr Knox to be sold at prices ranging between £8 and £14. On 31 October 1828 Margaret Docherty had the dubious privilege of being the last of their victims. A husband and wife, fellow-lodgers named Grey, found Burke cleaning the room after the murder and saw the corpse. On their way to the police they were met by McDougal and Laird who took them to an inn. In the meantime Knox's assistant, a David Patterson, paid £5 for the body. Eventually the Greys, no doubt fearful for their own safety, went to the police. Hare told all and gave King's Evidence, so saving himself and Maggie Laird. Burke and Helen McDougal were tried with the murders of Margaret Docherty, James Wilson and a prostitute, Mary Patterson. Burke was found guilty, and the Scottish verdict of 'not proven' was returned against Helen

20 Before Warburton's Act of 1830 everybody was required to have a Christian burial, and this prohibited the sale of the dead.

Docherty. In all sixteen people were murdered, but despite their soubriquet of body-snatchers Burke and Hare, in fact, snatched only one man.

Burke was hanged at Liberton's Wynd on 27 January 1829. For a fee of sixpence a time he had allowed himself to be sketched in his condemned cell, ranting that he had been swindled over the price paid for the body of Margaret Docherty. Appropriately his body was dissected at a public lecture by the Professor of Surgery in Edinburgh; his skeleton remains in the Anatomical Museum at the University. Both Helen McDougal and Maggie Laird were attacked by the mob outside the court and were saved only through the intervention of the police. McDougal went to Australia, where she died in 1868. Hare went to London, where he became a beggar in Oxford Street. One story is that on his way south he found work in a lime-kiln and when his fellow workers discovered his identity they blinded him. Dr Knox, hounded from his Edinburgh practice, also travelled south, in his case to Hackney, where he became a general practitioner and died in 1862.

A century later, grassing as such is perhaps the principal method by which the police obtain information which will lead either to the prevention of a crime, or to the arrest of the villains and recovery of stolen property. Any good detective keeps a small, or sometimes large, string of informers who may be active thieves themselves or who may simply hang about on the fringes of the Underworld. In the past they were paid out of a police information fund, or sometimes out of the pocket of the officer who ran them; it was regarded as a good investment towards promotion. Sometimes in the case of a drug bust the informer was given a part of the bust itself as his reward. Sometimes an informer had a licence to commit crimes, short of violence, in a particular area. Sometimes all three applied. One singularly corrupt Flying Squad officer of the 1960s, Alec Eist, is described in admiring terms by a former colleague:

46

He was the best informed police officer in London. What he took off one criminal he gave back to another. If he got £200 from a villain for giving him bail, Eist would give £195 to cultivate an informant.[21]

And another says of the practice:

You find three pounds of heroin and put only one on the charge sheet. The villains are pleased; less they're found with means less bird, and you give the other two to the informant. The job won't pay the informant so the only way is you give it back.

The grass could also expect help from his runner if he was arrested. This might well take the form of an intercession to prevent a charge being preferred.

Nipper Read, who arrested the Krays, maintains that the first of the modern supergrasses was Leslie Payne, the *consigliere* and financial whizz, if not genius, behind the twins. Payne's was a curious story, one which certainly led to the downfall of the twins. It was also part of the interesting, and extremely rare, example of the wholesale defection by a substantial part of a criminal gang not to another enterprise but into the arms of the police.

Payne had managed the Krays' financial empire and, without doubt, had built a platform from which they could have expanded possibly into the legitimate world. He had both tired of the Krays and been edged out by them as they saw his usefulness diminish. It was Payne who, unknowingly, had contributed to the death of Jack 'The Hat' McVitie. McVitie had been paid £1,500 to shoot Payne and had taken Billy Exley along with him. The expedition was neither well planned nor a

---

21 Eist, a florid, handsome, black-haired man, was acquitted in one of the trials of police officers and solicitors in the 1970s. Later he had a dress shop: 'It did no good. He was always having fires and burglaries – it was an embarrassment.' Later he owned a public house near Newmarket. He died of a heart attack.

success. They arrived at Payne's home, were told by his wife that he was not in and went away. Unfortunately for McVitie, now into the dangerous – and in his case fatal – combination of drugs and alcohol, he boasted that he had turned over the twins for the money. Naturally, it was not something which appealed to them. McVitie was lured from the Regency Club where he was drinking and stabbed to death by Reggie Kray, urged on by his brother Ronnie.

Initially the Krays were arrested over allegations of fraud, but once they were in custody all manner of their acquaintances came out of the woodwork at the urging of Read and his men. Some, such as Billy Exley and Lennie Dunn who had minded Frank Mitchell after his escape from Dartmoor, had been fearful of reprisals against them. For example, Albert Donaghue maintains he changed sides when he believed that he was being set up to take the rap for the Mitchell murder. Unexpectedly, Charles Mitchell, horse-doper, fraudsman and thieves' ponce, was another to change sides.

> Mitchell was a small, broad-shouldered man with a fresh face and a full set of sparkling white teeth; he was also completely bald. He ran his bookmaking and money-lending business from Fulham's North End Road.[22]

He had been a long-time friend, running long-firm frauds. He went with Charles Kray and some others to Toronto to talk with Don Ceville, a Canadian mafioso, when they were all arrested and deported. Rightly, Charles Kray did not trust him, but his brothers were more accommodating.

For purely pragmatic reasons he was able to tell Read that there was a contract out for both him and Leslie Payne. He, Mitchell, was to bankroll the hiring of an American hitman.

On 25 June, the day of Mitchell's defection, they were

22 Colin Fry and Charles Kray, *Doing the Business*, p. 118.

all sitting there in their usual studiously unconcerned way when Kenneth Jones [prosecuting counsel] asked that Mitchell be allowed to stand down.

'He [Mitchell] has made a complete statement and it has been decided he should be used as a prosecution witness,' he told the Court.

Mitchell walked from the back row as though he was going to collect a prize at a Sunday school. Even then the twins could not believe what was going on. It was only later they realised the full implication of the betrayal and, by then, it was too late for them to show their displeasure in a tangible way.[23]

It is curious that in no other of the gang cases, either before (Richardsons) or afterwards (Tibbs, Dixons), was there any such defection from the ranks.

---

23 Leonard Read and James Morton, *Nipper*, pp. 184–5.
Frequent threats come out of prison, I am told, mostly aimed at the relatives of anyone whom they dislike. Lip-service seems to be paid by the 'faithful', but it is all really dead. An attempt to shoot a well-known figure who had fallen out with them, Charlie Mitchell (of horse-doping fame in the past), was attributed to them by the Press. It was not true: the shooting was the result of an alleged injury much nearer home. No damage was sustained by Mitchell and all simmered down. Since the Krays are rightly credited with many black deeds, it seems only fair to exonerate them on this one! Peta Fordham, *Inside the Underworld*, p. 139.
Mitchell went on with his double career – including an incident in the Fulham Road when a car window was wound up on his throat and he was dragged for several hundred yards – before going to Spain where he was murdered.

3

Grasses – The Super Days

The Kray case aside, grassing changed gear on to a wholly different level with the arrest in 1970 of Derek Creighton 'Bertie' Smalls. It became the era of the supergrass, the criminal who, to dig himself out of trouble, would inform not just on his colleagues on a particular job but on his associates and their efforts going back years and years. In turn he could expect to receive a minimal sentence compared with that handed out to his former friends. He could also expect, through a nominee, a share of the insurance rewards.

In the late 1960s and early 1970s Bertie Smalls led a highly successful team of armed robbers in a series of attacks on banks, mainly in North and North West London but on occasion as far afield as Lloyds Bank in Bournemouth.

Peter Kelly was a part-time member of the squad. Talking of his time as a villain in the 1960s and 1970s, he recalls:

How did we look out the banks? On a Monday Georgie and I would drive round looking for a bank with a side turning. This was in the days before bandit glass – it was us made them put it in. One of us would go and change a note to see what drawers there were and then we'd go in mob-handed with pick-axe handles. One of us would stay by the door. Sometimes Bertie Smalls used to do that

51

because he was fat and unfit and I'd jump on the counter
and cause mayhem.

Each time the operational method was almost identical. The
robbers wore balaclavas, possibly with a nylon stocking
underneath, and masks. The raids were in banking hours.
A ladder was used to get over – and a sledge-hammer was
used to smash – the security grilles put up in the 1960s, but
not yet made ceiling to counter. A shotgun would be fired into
the ceiling to concentrate the minds of staff and any customers
there might be in the bank. There would be one or two getaway
cars waiting. The haul was usually substantial.

Smalls' name was 'in the frame' so to speak. He had been
wanted for a robbery on one of the branches of Lloyds
in Bournemouth in September 1970 and his wife, Diane
(sometimes confusingly referred to as Alice), had been arrested
along with others, including a Donald Barrett who had made a
confession naming names. At the trial at Winchester Crown
Court, he pleaded guilty. The only evidence against Diane
Smalls and the other defendants was that of a Stella Robinson
who worked as an *au pair* for the Smalls' children. She missed
the trial, having spent the time in Mablethorpe where Smalls
had a caravan. The trial collapsed and the case against Diane
Smalls and the others was dismissed. For a period the police
were seriously worried that she had been killed and it was
only when Smalls produced her at a solicitor's office that
they were satisfied of her safety and abandoned a potential
murder inquiry. Barrett's reward was a sentence of twelve
years and a card posted from Spain from the others, who had
all been acquitted, reading, 'Wish you were here.' In law, his
confession was no evidence against anyone but himself unless
he chose to give evidence in the witness box. On this occasion
he did not wish to do so.

Now Smalls had also been identified from a photograph in
the 'Rogues Gallery' at Scotland Yard as being involved in
the National Westminster Bank raid at Palmers Green in May

1972. The number-plate of a Jaguar car which had been used in a trial run had been noted by an off-duty police officer, and was traced back to a garage at Tower Bridge in which Smalls was known to have an interest. That was certainly not sufficient to bring a charge. After a robbery at Barclays Bank in Wembley High Road in August 1972 which had netted over £138,000 in old notes, a special unit was formed by the police under the direction of Jim Marshall; it would eventually become the nucleus of the Robbery Squad.

It was not the first time the police had eyed Smalls as a potential informant. One Flying Squad detective recalls the early 1960s:

> Living and 'performing' in Wood Green at that time was Derek Creighton 'Bertie' Smalls who years later would make his mark on criminal history by being the first of a long line of supergrasses. No matter how my buck and I tried we could not turn Bertie. There were a couple of occasions when we were very close, though. He kept a few meets in various pubs but to his credit and our chagrin he managed to withstand the pressure we were putting on him. Eventually he drifted off the manor.

This time things were much more serious. Now Smalls was remanded in custody by Harrow Magistrates' Court for committal papers to be prepared. It was when they were served on the defence that Peter Donnelly, the solicitor's managing clerk who had acted for Smalls over the years, noticed a reference in them to 'outers'. Smalls would, so the statement of a police officer read, give names if he had 'outers'.

> I went to see him in Brixton and asked, 'Did you say it?' He's hedgy. 'I've got to have guarantees,' he said. I went to see either Marshall or Wilding and asked if it was a serious proposition. 'Yes,' was the reply, 'but we don't

believe he'll do it.' 'If he does what will you give us?' I asked, and it's then they start thinking it's possible. I went back to Smalls and said, 'Go and sit tight, keep your trap shut.' Then I got word they were interested.

I went and saw him again and told him he's got to put his cards on the table. They wanted robberies, names and so on, but not unnaturally he was reluctant to go into details at this stage. Finally we got a skeleton of the jobs from him in areas.

Then I arranged a meeting with Marshall and Wilding at Wembley. I went up there with Peter Steggles, the senior partner. They've got a clip-board with a list of names and robberies I could see upside down.

I said that everything on the board they could have plus XYZ additional robberies. That seemed to take them off guard. From then we had the advantage. They were reluctant and thought it would be difficult to have anything in writing. Nothing in writing – no deal. They said they'd take instructions. It was then going to have to go to Deputy Commissioner or Commissioner level.

We then tell them that we will draft heads of agreement as to our conditions and the main concerns were one, the immunity from prosecution, and two, the security. There was no question of a reduced sentence. Another term was that it had to be agreed upon by the DPP. We had two more meetings before they agreed to write a letter which was the final document and was basically word for word our heads of agreement.

It was then lined up that on receipt of that letter Smalls was to be produced at Harrow court. The Bench had been squared to grant him bail – that had been dealt with before we arrived – and he was bailed into police custody and we're taken down to Wembley. We sat down 12–14 hours a day whilst he reminisced.

By this time I had spread the word I was going on holiday, but the day he appeared people were asking what was happening. Where was he? Where was I? The word was out. That's why I think the rest of the team had paid their money.

Diane Smalls was never happy with the whole business. Donnelly met her on Brixton Hill one afternoon when he had been to see Bertie in prison and explained things. She stood by Smalls, but their relationship was effectively over by this time anyway. One of the reasons was the appearance of Susan Mattis, attractive and divorced with three children and who graced the newspapers for some time after the case, telling how Bertie would leap out of bed in the middle of the night and how on the day of a raid he would stiffen his resolve with a quick vodka and grapefruit juice at 6 a.m. She had been to school with Smalls' sister. Smalls seems to have had a reasonably pleasant time whilst under guard. *Private Eye* reported nude swimming with a female police officer who subsequently retired from the force.

By now Smalls had given so much detail – the statement ran to 65 pages and covered 11 other suspects and 20 crimes – the police were starting to look for corroboration and . . .

They heaved in Stella Robinson, got a statement from her as to how various robbers, including Bertie, descended on a flop and when they were playing around with one of the sawn-offs had mistakenly fired it into the floorboards. They managed to identify the address, took the carpet up and the damage was still there with the pellets. But they still needed Diane and I went to her and said if you don't do it the deal won't be accepted because we didn't know whether they'd say the evidence was sufficient. I said, 'Do it or it may not go through.'

Very reluctantly she made the statement, but she then refused to take the oath at court.

One of the final conditions was that if Smalls' statement wasn't used and he was not to be a witness and immunity given, then what amounted to a total confession would remain on police files and not be used against him at a trial. But there was such a level of corruption at that time that sooner or later it would have got out and he'd have been dead.

During those three days Smalls stayed at Wembley with an armed guard. On the third day the police had to say 'yes' or 'no'. They said 'yes' and Smalls was then produced at Harrow, granted formal bail and taken to a hotel by Wembley Stadium where he and his family were put in the suite in which David Cassidy had stayed the week before; it seemed to please him. Later he was moved out to a couple of addresses, being guarded by shifts of police officers. The only time Donnelly could see him was at an arranged point which he would be given half an hour beforehand.

I'm sure there was a contract out. Publicity had it that it was £100,000 but I heard from Smalls' friend Jackie O'Connell that it was only £50,000.[1]

The sweep took place in the early hours of 6 April when over a hundred police officers rounded up twenty-seven of Smalls' former colleagues. Then the problem to be faced was whether Smalls, who was drinking heavily, would actually go through with things when it came to it.

The committal proceedings took place in a heavily guarded gymnasium in Wembley and Smalls appeared to give evidence minutes after his formal acquittal at the Old Bailey.

---

1 Jackie O'Connell, a high class safe-breaker, was another informer. Due to turn Queen's Evidence in the Bank of America safe raid case in which he was a defendant, he was shot on the way to court. It was never exactly clear whether he had organised the hit himself in an effort to put together some mitigation, or whether he wished to have his case put back so that he was tried separately. He was wounded so badly in the leg that it had to be amputated. He committed suicide some years later.

He stood in the witness box, looking towards the magistrate, resting on his elbow. His eyes seemed dead and he almost mumbled his answers, so that a couple of times the magistrate had to ask him to speak up. I was really worried at that point that Bertie might be about to crack but, just in time, there was an incident which completely changed the picture.

One of the prisoners was Danny Allpress, a real comedian and a live wire, who had always run around with Smalls and had virtually been his assistant. Danny kept quiet at first, then suddenly he leaned across the dock and said in a loud whisper, 'Well, Bertie, who's been having Slack Alice while you're away?' The remark got a lot of laughs from the prisoners, but Danny couldn't have made a more serious mistake.

'The remark brought Bertie to life. You could see the determination come into his eyes,' recounts Jack Slipper, who had chased Train Robber Ronnie Biggs to Brazil and was now one of the senior officers in the case.[2]

Diane Smalls was not popular with the rest of the wives. Once, because of friction, she had left a holiday in Torremolinos early and had later chosen to spend her time in Tangier. But was the Slack Alice joke as crucial as Slipper believes? According to Peter Donnelly:

I don't think the Slack Alice joke enamoured them to him, but I don't think it was the end of the world. His attitude was that most of them when pulled in had tried to do exactly the same but he got in first. From that point of view he felt justified. There had also been some trouble earlier when he was on remand for possession of a firearm. He got out but he was skint and one of them was meant to have given Diane money

2 J. Slipper, *Slipper of the Yard*, p. 108.

to look after her. He hadn't, and I think that annoyed him as well.

The men in court clearly had a sense of humour. The *Daily Mirror* printed a press release smuggled from the dock.

Mr Bert Smalls, the famous and solo singer who recently broke away from the Home Counties Choral Society, is about to give up the singing side of his career. Apparently Mr Smalls feels that the singing may affect his throat. On Wednesday Mr Smalls refused to comment.[3]

In July 1974 at the Central Criminal Court, Danny Allpress received a sentence of twenty-one years' imprisonment, reduced on appeal to eighteen. Donald Barrett, who had already had twelve years for the Bournemouth job, received another seventeen, reduced to twelve years on appeal. Others had sentences of up to twenty-one years reduced by the odd couple of years on their appeals.

One of them, Philip Morris, had been involved in a raid in February 1973 on the Unigate Dairies Depot in Ewell, Surrey. Morris had the job of standing guard over a young man, Frank Kidwell, who had just been named 'Milkman of the Year'. The shotgun went off and Kidwell died. The raid netted £148,000. Morris pleaded guilty to Kidwell's manslaughter and received a seventeen-year sentence. For his part in the Wembley raid he received a concurrent sentence of twenty years, reduced by the Court of Appeal to twelve. His appeal against the seventeen-year sentence for manslaughter was dismissed.

There were rumours of contracts on Smalls' life until the *Sun* gleefully reported that, following the making of a series of bankruptcy orders against the defendants in the case in October 1974, there was now not enough money available to pay the killer:

3 *Daily Mirror*, 23 May 1974.

'No one ever made threats to me,' says Smalls. 'Of course I didn't put myself about and if I went into a pub and saw someone who was a friend of the others I just left, but no, overall I had no trouble.'

In any event, Smalls had set the tone for the 1970s. The opprobrium attached to most supergrasses never seems to have stuck to him. In a curious way he appears to have been regarded as an innovator.

Here is John McVicar talking about supergrasses in general and Smalls in particular:

Some of them are very strong people. Look at Bert. He was a good worker, although there was always something odd about him.[4]

What he did have was a sense of humour. After one bank raid in the Wood Green area a woman witness who was shopping in the High Road ran more or less slap-bang into the men escaping after the robbery. She had heard what she thought was a car backfiring, but when three men wearing stocking masks rushed past her she knew exactly what had happened. She backed up against a wall and then started to walk to the end of the alleyway when a fourth man, also wearing a mask, loped towards her. Again she backed up, but as he went past he stopped.

'What a way to earn a fucking living, eh, girl?' said a sweating Smalls as he disappeared down the alleyway.

After the trial Smalls had an armed guard for some months, but eventually this was phased out and from then the family lived more or less normally under another name.

Smalls didn't do as well as he could have from his story. A book he was planning never came to fruition – due in part, perhaps, to both his and his ghost's then enthusiasm for vodka.

4 L. Taylor, *In the Underworld*, p. 82.

Later in April 1975 a short series of articles appeared in the *Daily Express* in which he offered a few pearls as to his life and times, saying he reckoned he had squandered between £250,000 and £300,000. The general consensus was that he was correct when he said, 'I did it for my wife and kids.' Well, certainly the kids. Of the present he said:

I prune the roses and I say good morning to my neighbours. And that's it – nobody knows who I am.

And of the use of guns on the raids:

I reckoned it was really safer for everybody. If you're only carrying axe handles you have to use 'em haven't you, and people get hurt, plus they might fight back and maybe hurt some of your mob. If you pull a gun they're terrified. The bank clerks don't feel they've got to be heroes in front of the birds, do they? I mean they can always say afterwards, 'Well he was carrying a gun so I couldn't do nothing.'[5]

It was only a matter of time before the defendants went to the Court of Appeal where the presiding judge, Lord Justice Lawton, was not amused.

The spectacle of the Director of Public Prosecutions recording in writing, at the behest of a criminal like Smalls, his undertaking to give immunity from further prosecution is one which we find distasteful. Nothing of a similar kind must ever happen again. Undertakings of immunity from prosecution may have to be given in the public interest. They should never be given by the police. The Director should give them most sparingly and, in cases involving grave crimes, it would be prudent of

5 *Daily Express*, 3 April 1975.

him to consult the law officers before making any promises.

Nevertheless the appeals were dismissed and off went the defendants to the House of Lords where they fared no better, but this time Lord Justice Lawton had his wrist slapped by Lord Diplock.

> I am wondering to what extent it is right for any court to give directions to the Director as to how he should conduct his business. The Director of Public Prosecutions works under the Attorney General. He does not work under any judges at all and any directions he receives as to the way in which he does his work surely must come from the Attorney General. I would have thought it quite wrong for it to come from any judicial authority at all. He may be condemned for what he has done, but he must not be told what he has to do in the future.

Nor were the police by any means apologetic. Said Roy Yorke, who had nurtured Smalls and obtained his confidence:

> I have no regrets. We were totally justified. We performed a public service. Before the deal with Smalls there were five major armed jobs a week. After the arrests were made possible by Smalls' statement, violent armed robberies went down by sixty per cent. It was the only way to break into the most exclusive and possibly violent robbery organisation ever known in this country.[6]

As for supergrasses generally, there were two spin-offs from Smalls' defection to the angels which caused the authorities some concern. The first was the curious story of Arthur John 'Jimmy' Saunders, a man from a non-criminal and by no means

6 *Daily Mail*, 25 March 1975.

poor family who in his thirties became something of a criminal groupie and who was convicted of a bank robbery in Ilford in February 1970. The only real evidence against him was a confession to the then Superintendent Albert Wickstead. He made a series of ambiguous answers and, asked if he was on the robbery, Saunders was said to have replied, 'There's no point in saying no, is there?' Later he said, 'Whatever I was doing I didn't have a shooter.'

Saunders put up an alibi defence but his witnesses did not come up to proof. His appeal was dismissed in December 1971, but now Smalls said that Saunders had not been on the raid. This presented a problem. How could Smalls be put forward as a witness of truth in one part of the case (since his evidence would, in due course, convict his old friend from the Bournemouth robbery Bobby King), but not in another? His evidence was taken on commission by Lord Justice James and accepted by the court with some reluctance.

The Lord Chief Justice in giving judgment had this to say:

> We have, as I say, approached this question with caution, because the evidence of accomplices can be as dangerous when used for the defence as it can when used for the Crown and we are not unmindful of the fact that it sometimes occurs when criminals are together in prison that they put their heads together and arrange to make statements with a view to exculpating one of them. We do look at evidence of accomplices or alleged accomplices with considerable caution in this context, as in others.

In the end the Court of Appeal quashed the conviction, resolving the dilemma by pointing out in explanation that when Saunders made his confession he had been drinking.

> . . . the appellant had been drinking appreciably before his arrest, and, although a doctor brought in by the police to examine him described him as not in any sense incapable

by drink, the Court thinks that some of the slightly jocular answers which were included in that conversation do have something of the stamp of a man who had had some drink and whose responsibility for the precise language which he used might have been affected by that drink.

And therefore had been foolish in what he had been saying. No blame attached to the police; it was indeed Saunders' own fault.[7]

Another potential embarrassment was averted in April 1978 when John Short was jailed for twenty-one years. He had provided the hideaway in Torremolinos where Bertie and his friends had sunned themselves before and after robberies. At the time of the trial he and Bryan Turner disappeared abroad. Now he was back and, it seemed, Bertie would have to be brought out of retirement to give evidence against him in the Ilford case. What would happen if the jury acquitted Short?

Short had changed his name to McGrath and whilst in Canada along with his friend, Roy Radovan, had been engaged in some horse-trading, selling trotting horses for racing in and around Montreal. Unfortunately the horses either had a touch of the slows or more seriously did not match their pedigrees. The Montreal police received discreet inquiries from 'businessmen' complaining about the horses. No, they did not want to press charges, merely to know the whereabouts of the vendors. Short returned to London where six months later he was arrested. Radovan's body was found in the Hudson river. Short pleaded guilty to other charges and received twenty-one years. Everyone's face was saved when the Ilford robbery charge was allowed to remain on the file.

Twenty-five years later Peter Donnelly, the solicitors' clerk

---

7 *Saunders*, 58 Cr. App. R.251. The experience did not do Saunders that much good although he received substantial compensation for his time in prison. In 1986 he was back in serious trouble, convicted of an attempted armed robbery in Baker Street. He and the other members of the team were over fifty at the time. He received fifteen years.

who did the deal for Smalls, has serious doubts on the
supergrass scheme from his own and a more general point
of view:

> Was the principle of supergrasses correct in the first
> place? Because Bertie Smalls was successful they used
> it here, there and everywhere. They were adopting the
> supergrass system in Northern Ireland. Trials collapsed
> here and then over there where there was a string of
> acquittals and allowed appeals.
>
> I'm not so sure nowadays that sort of evidence would
> be encouraged by the courts. The use of supergrasses like
> Smalls has largely died out.
>
> Actually I think it is an unhealthy basis for a case. It's
> open to abuse. The incentives are too great. If you have a
> supergrass who's a pathological liar – and some of them
> have been – it's extremely dangerous.
>
> So far as I am concerned it damaged the practice and
> with a large amount of hindsight and many years later, I
> don't think we should have acted for Bertie. Before he
> gave evidence there was a good deal of pressure on me
> to stop him and certainly I had to watch my back for a
> long time afterwards.

Donald Barrett, himself to become a supergrass not once but
twice, put it succinctly. 'They should have put a bullet in the
first one's nut,' he says of Smalls. 'That would have stopped
it in its tracks.'

The next in line to repent, recant and recount all was a man
who did publish his memoirs, designating himself as 'King
Squealer', Maurice O'Mahoney. Jack Slipper, in charge of the
new supergrass, recalls him:

> O'Mahoney must be one of the cunningest, not necess-
> arily cleverest individuals I've ever met. My first impres-
> sion of whether he would be suitable to become a

supergrass was that he had a fantastic memory – and what a liar he was. So much so that after discussing things with my superior officer I suggested he would be suitable because of his memory but, as he put in his book, I spent a long time explaining how detrimental it would be to a whole trial should it be proved he was telling just one lie as the defence would use it to discredit his whole evidence.

As far as I was concerned he kept on the lines I'd insisted.

O'Mahoney's has been a curious story.

On 1 June 1974, a Securicor security van was ambushed in Phoenix Way, Heston, Middlesex. There were at least five, and probably six, attackers, all of whom were masked and carrying weapons including shotguns, a Luger, a revolver and a sledgehammer. The van was rammed, one guard was hit with the sledgehammer; a pistol was fired and a rather disappointing take of a little over £13,000 was stolen. According to O'Mahoney, who was being urged by his girlfriend to give up his life of crime – to which, he said, he had been giving serious thought – the job had been offered around the Underworld by some of his colleagues. One man, George du Burriatte, who had once been an associate, if not an intimate, of some of London's classier criminals, had turned police informer. O'Mahoney believed it was he who first informed on him. He was probably correct.

Du Burriatte named between 100 and 150 criminals and by October 1979 was said to have a contract of £100,000 on his head. His career as a supergrass had ended in the June of that year when his evidence sent Ray Deck down for six and a half years over a £1 million international car fraud. Du Burriatte had been the boss of the underbelly of London Airport when he suddenly changed sides and contacted officers at Chiswick police station. Nevertheless he continued working and, to fool any of his colleagues who might see him, when he went to contact the officers at the station he would put on a wig or false moustache or, if the need arose, have his arm twisted behind his back by an officer so it would appear that he had been arrested. He never really made it plain why he had crossed over to the other side, but he was able to give this encomium to the police:

> The Yard looked after me well while I was working for them. They'd hand me out one-ers and two-ers. And I picked up £3,000 reward money from banks and insurance firms.

And, no doubt, a few shillings from the newspapers to whom he told his tale.

As for the Securicor robbery itself, in his book, as befits a man trying to get out of crime, O'Mahoney played a sympathetic part.

> As I got in through the back doors, I found an elderly man. He was obviously another guard, though he looked too frail to be doing such dangerous work. 'Please God, don't hurt me,' he said. I told him, 'Don't worry, pop, no one's going to hurt you.' Then I began throwing out boxes of money, and mentally photographing the interior again for further use.[8]

The first of the men to be arrested on 11 June were John Thorne, Joseph Stevens and Angus Smith. O'Mahoney evaded the swoop and was arrested with his girlfriend, Susan Norville, at her flat about 4 p.m. the next day.

Despite O'Mahoney's belief that du Burriatte was the villain of the piece the whisper went around that he was going to squeal. Susan Norville had made a full statement. The prosecution would later allege that Thorne, Stevens and

8 M. O'Mahoney, *King Squealer*, pp. 123 et seq.

Smith suspected O'Mahoney of tipping off the police, and that Thorne and Stevens now threatened to gouge out his eyes if he talked. Various girlfriends threatened Susan Norville in an effort to dissuade her from giving evidence. It is also possible that a contract of £2,000 was taken out on her life. In *King Squealer* O'Mahoney says:

> The troubles just mounted up for me. One day I was attacked by several members of my team who threatened to gouge out my eyes with a toothbrush. These savages, some of them weighing 16 stone, were hardened criminals and meant every nasty word they said. I managed to get free from them that time, but I knew they would eventually get me. I certainly didn't want to lose my sight for something I had never done. Later I found out someone had even smuggled a cyanide capsule into the prison and planned to slip it in my tea.

According to Detective Chief Superintendent Jack Slipper, in whose charge O'Mahoney was, this was the turning point for him.

> But before this happened I had decided to take the most momentous decision of my life – to turn squealer.

Despite his fears for his safety from the 16-stone hardened criminals, the twenty-nine-year-old O'Mahoney was no shrinking violet. In his time he had bitten the diamond off the ring of a victim and swallowed it. He was adroit with a hammer and was a kneecap breaker. He was a contract enforcer and had been paid £1,000 (the going rate) for shooting a man in the legs. His book tells of his plots to kidnap Elton John and Elizabeth Taylor (consecutively rather than concurrently). Now he asked a Brixton prison officer to call a high-ranking Flying Squad officer.

'Something like Bertie Smalls, is it?' he asked.

'Bigger,' I said.

Clearly he had to be kept out of the way of his co-accused and the rest of the prison population, and so on 22 June he was moved to Chiswick police station where he had two cells, a colour television, a record player and was allowed domiciliary if not conjugal visits. Both his wife, Maureen, and his girlfriend, Susan, visited him frequently and the latter gave birth on 4 May 1975. He claimed the child as his, but at the trial of his co-accused denied having intercourse with her whilst he was in police custody. Over a period of time he told the police he had been involved in some thirteen robberies, sixty-six burglaries and assorted other crimes of violence. He named about 150 people as being his associates in the crimes.

On 20 September 1974 he pleaded guilty to the Phoenix Way robbery, an attempted robbery and a burglary. He asked for ninety-nine other offences to be taken into consideration. He was helped by the prosecution, who described him as the most guarded man in Britain and said that his assistance to the police had been incalculable. Kenneth Machin, now himself a judge at the Old Bailey, suggested that by his action O'Mahoney 'may have already signed his own death warrant'. The man himself, allowed to address the court, emotionally explained that: 'I know that what I have done in the past is wrong and I believe that what I am doing now is right . . . I want to hit right at the heart of the criminal underworld.'

It all stood him in good stead. He received five years' imprisonment from Sir Carl Aarvold, the Recorder of London, in thanks for the help he was continuing to give to the police and to assist him to realise his protestations about giving up a life of crime. Had he not done so, he could not have complained about a sentence of eighteen to twenty years. O'Mahoney spent a few weeks in prison before he was moved back to the comfort of Chiswick police station.

He began to give evidence in trials early in the New Year. The trials in which he appeared as the principal witness culminated in that of Thorne and the others for the Heston security van robbery, a wages snatch at Greenford and a robbery at the Allied Irish bank in Hammersmith. In the meantime, in other cases eight defendants were acquitted. No one, except Ronald Cook in the Heston trial, was convicted on the unsupported word and evidence of the 'King Squealer'.

After the Heston robbery trial he was given a form of parole and immediately his enthusiasm for giving evidence vanished in a puff of smoke. There were still ten defendants against whom O'Mahoney had made statements. No evidence was offered against them. In the week beginning 11 January 1977, he gave a series of stories to the *Sun* telling of his life and hi-jinks in the police station. Now he told of how he had intercourse with Susan in his cell, the back of his head blocking the Judas window. A police investigation followed before the appeals of the Heston defendants reached the Court of Appeal. It concluded that much was untrue and that O'Mahoney had 'told a colourful and probably, in parts, a lying story to the press for money, adding little to the villainy which was known to the jury'. What was more significant, the court found, was the tendency – as with many a subsequent supergrass – to play down his role in the case. In an earlier instance involving an armed robbery in Greenford, O'Mahoney had said he had been in the getaway car and named the men who went into the firm armed with a gun and a cosh. The Court of Appeal thought it rather more likely that O'Mahoney had been the man with the shotgun.

This incident shows that when it suited him to do so he was willing to attribute to others serious criminal acts of his own. In this case he did much the same in respect of his part in the Phoenix Way robbery. The evidence showed that he had carried and fired a pistol. He said in evidence that this is what Cook had done.

Cook's conviction was quashed. As for O'Mahoney, once he

refused to co-operate the police dropped their protection. He told the *Guardian*:

> They've dropped me flat, the canary that fell from its cage. They've told me to go out and get a decent job. The only trade I know how is to break into banks. I'm in a terrible state. I could go round the corner and cry.[9]

Happily, however, he picked himself up, put himself back on the perch and was used as a security man by musicians David Bowie and Rick Wakeman who wrote the preface to his book. Then in 1993, sporting a Flying Squad tie, now known as Peter Davies, and charged once more with robbery, he was telling a most amazing story from the witness box.

Following his successful career as a bank robber, and a subsequent equally gratifying one as a supergrass, O'Mahoney kept out of public vision until he was arrested in Reading in 1990 on a charge of shoplifting. He had been found, along with his young son, pushing a shopping trolley out of a store. His defence was that he was on his way to the electrical department to obtain some guarantees before paying. The case was stopped by magistrates at the committal proceedings.

Three years later his defence to the charge of robbery was that it was a snatch carried out on the instructions of the police to incriminate another man. In the witness box he told a strange story. After his acquittal at Reading, when curiously his custody record had disappeared, his cover was blown. He now tried to see a senior officer whose job it had been to protect supergrasses but received no substantial help. In the November he went to see a DI whom he knew at Brixton police station and asked what help he could have. Again there was a negative response, but this time O'Mahoney asked when and where the station's Christmas party would be held. He entered the raffle, which carried the first prize of a ticket to Paris.

9 D. Campbell, *The Underworld*, p. 157.

According to O'Mahoney he was later contacted by the man whom he had seen at Brixton police station, and asked to carry out a small commission for him. What the police wanted, said O'Mahoney, was for him to carry out a smash and grab at a sub-post office in Shepherd's Bush, leave behind the main money and instead take a money-bag containing £250-worth of 20p pieces. The robbery was to take place on 30 June. The idea was that when O'Mahoney handed the bag over to the police they would then plant the money on another man.

O'Mahoney went on to say that, since he had packed in the job of supergrass, or more probably it had packed him in, and he had served his five-year sentence in Chiswick police station, he was a frequent visitor to Briefs wine bar, a popular haunt of villains, barristers, solicitors and the police, not necessarily in that order, which was opposite Inner London Crown Court in Newington Causeway. Briefs had been opened by three former police officers who had subsequently left the Metropolitan Police, along with solicitor Michael Relton who later received twelve years' imprisonment for his part in laundering the money from the Brinks-Mat robbery. O'Mahoney told the court he spent much of his time in Briefs and his function in life was collecting and laundering money and generally helping Relton. The wine bar was one which, from time to time, had been placed off-limits by the Commissioners.

According to O'Mahoney's evidence, he was introduced at the Brixton party to an officer known as 'Basher' who, he said, had acquired the nickname because every time he was drunk he started to fight. It was then the proposition was put to him, and it was suggested he should recruit someone who was clean to carry out the raid with him.

O'Mahoney found a man in Bristol and duly appeared in Shepherd's Bush. A white Ford Escort car was, he said, to be near the shop and a red one for the getaway outside a local public house, the Fox and Hounds. As he looked round the area before the robbery he saw a Rover motor vehicle with three officers in it, as well as two mounted police officers near by. Something, he told the court, was wrong. He had intended to do the snatch himself, but now he sent the other man in; it was completed but the alarm went off, the man got back into O'Mahoney's car and as he did so the police started shooting.

In the car provided by the police, according to O'Mahoney, was a bag of guns – one a starting pistol, a second which had been tampered with – and cartridges which had been sprayed with oil. The effect of this would make them extremely unreliable. He maintained, and there was no evidence to contradict him, that neither he nor his friend ever shot back.

According to the Home Office expert eight shots were fired, all by the police. O'Mahoney never attempted to reach the exchange getaway car. Instead he took to his feet, was caught and taken to Shepherd's Bush police station where DS Fuller, who had looked after him when he was in custody in Chiswick in his supergrass days, arrived. The custody record showed that no one knew who O'Mahoney was and that Fuller took his prints to identify him. According to O'Mahoney, Fuller told him that everything would be sorted out.

In the witness box O'Mahoney listed the officers with whom, he said, he had had dealings both commercial and corrupt, going back as far as the early 1970s. Much of his time seems to have been spent in the company of retired or serving police officers. He had, for example, rewired the house of one of his former bodyguards as well as for Detective Chief Inspector Peter Atkins whose garden lights he had rewired, putting power to his pond. He refuted suggestions that he had turned up uninvited at the Christmas party by producing the voucher for the winning flight from Gatwick to Paris.

It was, wrote Duncan Campbell of his behaviour in the witness-box, '. . . a virtuoso performance. The prosecution dismissed his case as rubbish but the jury acquitted him.'[10]

10 *Guardian*, 16 July 1993.

As Campbell went on to write, this has left O'Mahoney in something of a dilemma and his lawyer, Adrian Neale, wrote to the Home Office and indeed went to see the Home Secretary, Kenneth Baker, asking for a guarantee of his client's safety. He has been given no promises. An inquiry by the Police Complaints Authority carried out before the trial exonerated the officers involved in the Shepherd's Bush case. Late in 1993 O'Mahoney issued a writ against the Commissioner of Police for the Metropolis, claiming damages for malicious prosecution. It is being defended with vigour.

Although the figures floated as to the price may have been exaggerated, there is no doubt that the gangland rumours of contracts out against O'Mahoney after he first gave evidence were correct. Says an East End figure:

> I knew some people who missed O'Mahoney in Bayswater. Their card was marked that he'd be in the Monmouth of Westbourne Grove but by the time they got there he'd gone.

It was whilst O'Mahoney was in Chiswick police station that he met another man on his way to becoming a supergrass – Billy Williams, whose conversion to the forces of good apparently came on the road away from a bank robbery at Barclays Bank in St John's Wood, London. PC David Clements was shot at the wheel of the Panda car in which he was chasing Williams and Jimmy and Philip Trusty. Clements survived, but Jimmy Trusty turned against his younger brother when Philip – who fired the shot, and feared a twenty-year sentence if he was found guilty – tried to persuade him to take the blame. Jimmy had virtually nothing in the way of convictions. Philip Trusty had considerably more.

Jimmy also turned informer and received a two-year-nine-month sentence. Philip, on the wrong end of his brother's evidence, received twenty.

There were repercussions from this case which rumbled on

for the next half-dozen years. On 26 September 1974 Peter Wilding was arrested when he became stuck in a traffic jam in Hounslow. He had been grassed by Billy Williams. According to Wilding, Williams visited him in his cell.

One of the problems for Williams and the others was boredom, and there is little doubt that the police and the authorities did what they could to keep their charges amused and in the right frame of mind to give evidence. Williams had had his share of troubles before he pleaded guilty to three armed robberies and asked for a further thirty-three, including more of the same, to be taken into consideration. He received five years from the judge and threats from the prison inmates. Before he was moved he had scalding water thrown over him – the standard, if extra-curricular, punishment meted out by inmates in prison to informers and sex offenders.

Whilst he was in Chiswick he was allowed out of his cell to marry his girlfriend Barbara Stanikowski at the local register office. Back in the police station there was champagne at a reception. Later they took pictures of each other with a smuggled camera, and a story appeared in the *News of the World* together with a picture of Billy Williams wearing a policeman's helmet, which he had borrowed from a peg, and drinking champagne. The report said that Jack Slipper was his best man but the truth is that, in charge of the security for Williams, rather more prosaically he was merely there as a witness.[11]

When it came to it George du Burriatte was a witness in one of the O'Mahoney trials and a number of others.

At that time (1972) he had a little firm robbing banks and post offices and security vehicles. Seven or eight others were with him. They were bringing the money back to George and he was paying them a wage and promising

11 *News of the World*, 16 May 1976.

to invest their money. He was acquitted and they never saw their money.

Third in line of value was Charlie Lowe, a then fairly well respected East End villain. For a change he was not a Met informer but belonged, if that is the right word, to No. 5 Regional Crime Squad which looked after Essex. The end of that particular period of his criminal career took about a year to stutter to its conclusion – at least that is what the Court of Appeal seemed to have thought, but in all probability it did not know the real facts.

In July 1975 Lowe and another man, both armed with ammonia, were seen by the police as they ran from a garage in Stamford Hill. The other man squirted ammonia at the police but after a chase both were arrested. Lowe was committed for trial at the Old Bailey, but failed to surrender to his bail on 15 January 1976. In the meantime, on 27 September he had been given bail after being stopped in a hire-car overdue for return. He had thrown away a driving licence in the name of Crowe and had been found to have a small amount of cannabis resin in his pocket. He was committed for trial, this time to the Inner London Sessions, but again he failed to appear.

Whilst his luck with crime in general was clearly out – although if you commit crimes on a weekly basis you must expect to be caught fairly frequently – with the courts it was spilling over. In November, now on bail twice, he was seen to put a sack in the boot of an MG parked in East London. When searched by the police it was found to contain a sawn-off shotgun. Lowe said he had been 'set up' and was only selling it on; again he was given bail. Later Lord Justice Roskill sitting in the Court of Appeal remarked wryly: 'We make no comment upon the number of times he appears to have been released on bail.'[12]

On 26 June 1976 he was arrested whilst bathing on the Isle of Sheppey. Now, with the accumulation of cases lined

12 79 Cr. App. R. 122.

up against him, he could see a middle-length prison sentence in prospect and he offered to tell all.

He was kept under wraps until the October when the *Guardian* broke the bad news to his former colleagues. One of the ruses employed to keep him hidden had been to bring him before the local magistrates under a false name. During his time in the relative comfort of Southend police station, where he was allowed female visitors and a television, he made statements admitting his own involvement in ninety-one offences including fifteen robberies, and implicating forty-five different criminals in cases involving over £300,000 cash and valuables in which he admitted he and his friends had used coshes and ammonia, and sawn-off shotguns had been carried – the stock-in-trade of the professional armed robber. £100,000 of drugs were recovered. Thirty-seven people were arrested.

Then came something which must have approached shock-horror to him. After the Court of Appeal's comments on the Smalls' deal, Lowe could not have expected to walk free. However, what he certainly did not expect, on 13 December 1976 when he appeared before Mr Justice Stocker at Chelmsford Crown Court, was a ten-year sentence plus a further eighteen months of a suspended sentence. He was not happy and went to the Court of Appeal where he was duly rewarded.

Lord Justice Roskill said that not enough credit had been given to him for the enormous help he had given to the police both before and after his conviction.

It must be in the public interest that persons who have become involved in gang activities of this kind should be encouraged to give information of this kind to the police in order that others may be brought to justice and that, where such information is given and can be acted upon and, as here, has already been in part successfully acted upon, substantial credit should be given upon pleas of guilty especially in cases where there is no other evidence against the accused than the accused's own confession, and be given substantial credit for it.

From then on he gave evidence in a number of successful prosecutions against his former colleagues until, in February 1978, the Lowe Express was derailed. The defence in the case of a hi-jacking had managed to learn something of Lowe's background over and above his life as a blagger. He was not simply an uncomplicated, decent English criminal, wielding a pick-axe handle in a post-Marxist attempt to redistribute wealth; he was, it seems, an international fraudsman as well. He had, it appeared, been a part of one particular swindle which had involved millions. His stamping ground had been Europe and the Middle East, with the Lebanon as a particularly favourite spot. Why the Lebanon? Because one should always go where there is a war. It disrupts communications and it is more difficult to check stolen credit cards. He had, he admitted, also been involved in what was then a major conspiracy to import twenty kilos of cannabis from Morocco. It seems that he had told the investigating officers of this verbally. At least that is what he told the court, but he had never written it down because no one had asked him to. When it came to it, however, in the Court of Appeal's spirit of rapprochement and the rehabilitation of Charlie Lowe, it is doubtful whether it would have made that much difference to his sentence. It was, however, a big stick for the defence to wield.

Now, said prosecuting counsel, Mr John Bloefeld, the credit card fraud had been 'fully investigated' and the Director of Public Prosecutions was not prepared to bring further charges. Judge Peter Greenwood, who had presided over a number of the Lowe cases, was not pleased. Summing up to the jury, he called him disgusting, evil and brutal. The defendants were acquitted.

On his release Lowe paid for his own plastic surgery, but he could not keep his fingers out of the criminal pie and, within a year, was back in trouble.

Now with the blessing of the Court of Appeal to guide trial judges, supergrasses could expect a sentence of around five years instead of one of twenty. With time spent on remand counting towards a release date, much of their sentence would have been worked off before they actually appeared in the dock. During this time, and whilst they were giving evidence, they would be kept in police custody and, allowing for remission and parole, released immediately or very soon after the last hearing. They could expect reasonable accommodation visits from their wives and sometimes the opportunity to go out to the local pubs with the detectives guarding them. There would be reward money and a new identity at the end of their sentence. It is hardly surprising that there was now a steady queue of men willing to testify against their former colleagues.

Despite this, some commentators see Charlie Lowe as the beginning of the end of the golden age of the supergrass.

4

The Grass Withers

One of the next up to bat was Leroy Davies. According to his version of events, he was extremely unfortunate to have been caught in the first place. He was arrested for handling money stolen from a security truck robbery at Leverstock Green near Hemel Hempstead, Hertfordshire, in December 1977. It seems that the robbery of £231,000 – carried out with John Gorman, Bruce Frazer, Roy Allen, Tony Knightley and a power-saw – was successful. It was not until his then brother-in-law, Dave Stockwin, wanted to earn some money that things turned sour for him. Davies sold him £500 for £400 and Stockwin passed this straight on to another relative, forgetting to warn him it was stolen money. On his arrest and that of his wife, Christine, Stockwin told the police the money had come from Davies.

Davies really was unfortunate. According to his story, subsequently sold to the *Daily Express*,[1] Davies had been keeping out of harm's way in the Metropolitan Police area by a system of well-placed bribes.

> After a bank robbery in the West End earlier, I was pulled in and told that the 'governor', a Chief Superintendent, wanted bodies.

1 15 July 1980.

79

In other words, names of the team on the job. In those days there was no way he would get those from me. So I was told it would have to be cash unless I wanted to be nicked. Ten big ones. I did not give it direct to the governor, one of his men, a sergeant took it.

After an attempted robbery in the Mile End Road in 1974 an inspector who knew I had done it demanded £500 for keeping quiet. I paid him after I had pulled another job to finance it.

These were part of regular payments I made to a few officers between 1971 and 1977. Detectives right down to the rank of constable were involved. Some of them were on retainers of £100 to £200 a week.

Now Davies found himself in Hertfordshire well away from the Met where he might have been able to call on a friendly officer for help.

Davies believed that he was about to be fitted up for the murder of a Hatton Garden jeweller near his home in Golders Green.[2] With his then girlfriend Elizabeth agreeing to stand by him despite the attendant risks of being the girlfriend of a grass, Davies began to tell nearly all. As he wrote in the *Daily Express* over his decision to turn supergrass: '. . . she agreed that I should start paying some of my debt to society

2 In fact the real killer was one of the oldest surviving armed robbers of recent times, John Hilton, who was jailed for life in 1991. He and Alan Roberts robbed a Hatton Garden jeweller, Leo Grunhut, outside his home in Golders Green. Hilton accidentally shot his partner in the thigh and as the jeweller tried to escape shot him in the back. The proceeds of the raid were £3,000 in cash and £277,000 in diamonds. Hilton managed to get his partner into their getaway car and drove him to a garage in South London where he bled to death. Roberts was buried on a railway embankment at Dartford, Kent. Grunhut died a month later. It was this murder to which Davies was referring.

By the time he reached the Old Bailey in September 1991, Hilton was sixty-two, frail and grey-haired, but he had killed three people during his thirty-year career which had ended in Burlington Gardens, Piccadilly, London, the previous year. In 1963 he had been given a life sentence for the murder of a man in the celebrated raid on the Co-op dairy in Mitcham, South London. He was freed on licence in February 1978 and it was a month later that he shot and killed both Grunhut and his partner. At his 1991 trial he refused to allow his counsel to put forward any mitigation.

and that she would stand by me.'

He had been born in the East End, one of a large family with an elder brother, Glanford. His father had been a professional boxer. Colleagues remember that he had 'started screwing young' and then in the 1960s had become a bank robber. One man on remand with him recalls:

I was nicked and was in Brixton with Joey Cannon and George du Burriatte. Joey and Leroy decided to escape and one Sunday night they tied up a screw in the toilets where they kept Cat 'A' men. Cannon and Leroy unlocked all the 'A' men but none of us wanted to go. They escaped over the wall but it was half-baked. I don't think they even had transport waiting. Meanwhile the prison's running amok with people smashing the control rooms up. What I really remember was George du Burriatte being mysteriously taken off the Escapers list shortly after that.

As a result of Leroy Davies' statements and those of two more supergrasses, Edward Martin and Roger Dennhardt, *Operation Kestrel* run by the Hertfordshire police netted twenty-four villains who were jailed for up to eighteen years. They included Tony Knightley, who received sixteen years for another security van robbery. In his tearful recollections to the *Daily Express*, Davies remembered how he had saved Knightley's name until last and how it had grieved him finally to offer him up.

On 24 July 1978 Davies appeared at St Albans Crown Court and pleaded guilty to seven counts of robbery, one of conspiracy to rob, seven of having a firearm with intent to commit an indictable offence, and asked for thirty-three similar offences to be taken into consideration.

The trial judge, again Mr Justice Stocker who had originally sentenced Lowe, had apparently not seen the clear signals sent down by the Court of Appeal and put Davies away for ten years. Leroy Davies appealed and was represented by the

81

celebrated silk William Howard QC. His co-defendant, John Michael Gorman, who had pleaded guilty to one robbery and one firearm offence and had received a total of nine years' imprisonment, was also represented by leading counsel.

Davies' sentence was reduced to seven years by the Lord Chief Justice, Lord Widgery. He had, after all, assisted in supplying information which had led to the arrest of what were described as dangerous and violent criminals in over a hundred cases. There was a recommendation that the police should help resettle Davies and his family in another country. This meant that Davies, for all his crimes, would serve rather less than Gorman for his two. Surely this was wrong? No, said the Lord Chief Justice:

> One must necessarily ask oneself: does that matter? It is not contended that Gorman assisted the police. It is not contended that Gorman should receive a sentence reduced on that account. Gorman has received a sentence of nine years, and the argument on behalf of Gorman is that the sentence on Davies should not be reduced for considerations such as I have mentioned in order to provide Davies with a substantial discount if the result is going to be to reduce the sentence on Davies to below that passed on Gorman.
>
> We have considered this argument and we reject it.[3]

Davies also gave statements to *Operation Countryman*, which at that time was investigating allegations of wholesale corruption in the Metropolitan Police, naming the detectives to whom he had been making regular payments. No charges were ever brought against any of them.

It would be pleasant to record that Davies was able to settle down after that with his new family, but it would not be accurate. In April 1982 he appeared at the Old Bailey

3 68 Cr. App. R.321.

charged, along with his elder brother, with a robbery at the French Revolution public house in Putney where he had worked as an under-manager. His brother, Glanford, who pleaded guilty and implicated him, received five years imprisonment.

It was alleged that Leroy Davies, now known as Leslie Newton, had escaped after firing one barrel of a sawn-off shotgun at the police. Davies had told the jury, which took only ninety minutes to acquit him, that he would never have been party to such an inefficient robbery. The trial judge was not so impressed. Mr Justice Lawson invited the jury to stay behind and listen to Glanford's confession which had been excluded from the evidence against Leroy. Davies-Newton stayed behind to hear his brother's counsel say:

> In a mad, reckless, drunken moment he was lured away from his home by the person who is much more evil than he is and who carried the gun on the robbery.

He also heard Mr Justice Lawson add: 'I have no doubt as to the true identity of that gunman.'

Davies jnr had reason to be pleased. Not only had he been acquitted, but the trial judge had made an order prohibiting the publication of any photograph of him. Thereafter he faded from the London scene; he had married into a well-known East End family who were unattracted by his behaviour.

For many supergrasses, the decision to turn squealer came when they heard that one of their former colleagues was about to inform on them. Roger Dennhardt was one. He was serving thirteen years for robbing a security van on its way from the Express Dairy in Hemel Hempstead, and was on trial for conspiracy to pervert the course of justice when he heard that a man – with whom he had taken part in a 1976 robbery at Murphy's, a building company in Islington, during which a security guard had been injured – was about to tell all. 'All' would be that Dennhardt was the man who had pulled the trigger. Dennhardt maintained that the injuries

were an accident and that he had been shooting at a lock, but he
was influenced by a friend who received life for 'accidentally'
shooting a police officer.

His *apologia pro vita sua* to the police makes pretty
nauseating reading.

> During the past three years I have wrestled with a strong
> desire to confess my crimes and to a great extent put right
> the damage I have inflicted on my fellow citizens . . .
>
> It is really the only honourable course a man such as
> myself has left to take. I have caused a major schism within
> my family. This act of informing is the most positive
> proof I can give that I have concluded my criminal career
> for ever.

His confession may also not have been completely untinged by
the potential loss of his girlfriend, Melissa, whom he described
(as she did herself) to the *Daily Mirror* as a dog. Recalling his
arrest, Dennhardt spoke movingly of her.

> I could still smell her on my body. I kept thinking, it'll
> be years now before I see her again. Years, mate, bloody
> stinking years.[4]

On 24 January 1980 Dennhardt changed his plea in the
conspiracy-to-pervert trial and made a 1,000-page handwritten
statement. This case involved two solicitors, a young girl clerk
and a licensee. One of Dennhardt's problems had been explaining how he had accumulated substantial sums of money in his
bank account, and the idea had been for the licensee to explain

---

4 *Daily Mirror*, 7 September 1981. As for the 'dog' bit, in general slang terms
'a dog' is used to describe an unattractive woman. Dennhardt used the word
in approbation and Melissa spoke of the privileges of being a robber's dog,
which were denied to the common or garden criminal's wife. These included
the screw turning a blind eye if the man and the dog wished to 'have a bit
of a grope' whilst on a visit.

that this came from business dealings. Within minutes, there was Dennhardt in the witness box alleging that the solicitor had wanted £10,000 to prepare the false defence.

His subsequent evidence cleared up 329 crimes involving £3 million of stolen property. Twenty-nine people were jailed. As a thank-you for his co-operation in *Operation Carter*, he received an eight-year sentence concurrent with his thirteen-year term and was released from prison in 1981 having obtained full remission. He was able to tell the *Daily Mirror*: 'Now there is nobody, absolutely nobody, that a robber can trust.'[5]

His criminal career had started in the 1960s when he had been a member of the so-called English Bonnie and Clyde gang. He escaped from Ashford Remand Centre and, with friends, carried out a four-month orgy of robberies on betting shops, sub-post offices and banks. Scotland Yard appealed to the youths to give themselves up to avoid what they feared was going to be a shoot-out and Dennhardt walked into a police station to give himself up. Whilst on the run he had sent his mother £2,000 to tide her over while he faced what he feared would be a long sentence. In fact he received only five years and three months.

Dennhardt, who always wore black with a black hood to work, had also given his version as to how to carry out a successful raid: 'The mask is not just to hide your features. It has got to be frightening. It has got to be black so that the imprint of blackness is horrible.'

It is something of a shame that Graham Sayer, the detective sergeant who was assigned to be Dennhardt's minder, did not read the paper that morning. Had he done so, his life might have been a happier one. Sayer, who had been involved in the kudos of *Operation Carter* and had twenty-two years' service, fourteen of them as a detective, fell under the spell of Dennhardt's charms.

5 *Daily Mirror*, 11 September 1981.

In November 1986 Sayer found himself in the dock at Nottingham Crown Court where he was acquitted of a conspiracy to rob a post office in Aldershot but convicted of a similar offence at Mansfield. Dennhardt was not with him. It was claimed he had broken through a police road-block after the Aldershot raid, and had hidden in a hole in the ground for two days before slipping out of the country by mingling with the Liverpool supporters on their way to the Heysel stadium. He returned and, using Sayer's knowedge of how deliveries were made to sub-post offices, organised the raid at Mansfield. Sayer had behaved incredibly foolishly. He had used his mother's car to rehearse a getaway route, spending so much time on this that an old lady in the neighbourhood had become suspicious and noted down the number. On 7 November Sayer received nine years. Dennhardt was safely in Spain, from where he gave an interview to a newspaper saying that he denied his involvement in the raids.

He explained that when he had broken through the road-block he believed it was a trap organised by vengeful colleagues. He was certainly the subject of a contract and it is possible that he survived an attack. In October 1984 Arthur Farr, a Berkshire haulage contractor, was shot dead. He bore some physical resemblance to the supergrass and had traded as Denhardt.

> It was like reading my own obituary. I have feared something like this for a long time. There are plenty of hardened villains who would shoot me. There are a lot of people I know who have sworn to get even with me.

Others who should have taken notice of Dennhardt's comment about the safety of bank robbers included those who worked with Donald Barrett. His trustworthiness had long been in question, if not from the time when he had named names in the Smalls bank robbery case in Bournemouth, then certainly a decade later when he became a supergrass in 1981. For this string of offences he received fourteen years, but the Court of Appeal halved the sentence. When it came to it he served three years and four months and within a year was at it again. Now in 1988 the reason for his downfall was a mixture of carelessness and ill-fortune.

In 1985 a young boy had found a home-made remote-control device in a rubbish sack outside a house in the East End. Technically minded, he had taken it home and stripped it. It was similar to one he had in a model racing car and he thought no more about it. In the rubbish sack there had also been a mask, hair and glue. Then six months later, watching *Crimewatch* on television in November, he realised it was a device similar to those being used by a team of robbers who were strapping bombs to their victims, to persuade them to hand over gold bullion and cash. He eventually convinced his mother it was worth telling the police.

The house outside which the boy had found the device belonged to David Croke, its maker and leader of the team of which Barrett was a member. On 11 December 1985, as part of a robbery at the Armaguard Security Depot in Essex, one of the security guards had been attacked in his home. His wife and daughter were handcuffed and threatened, and he agreed to have what he was told was a remote-control bomb attached to him as he drove to the security depot from which £500,000 was stolen.

Now the police kept watch on Croke's house, which he had purchased for £85,000 cash in the February of that year, and they identified Barrett as one of the visitors.

The police swooped on the motorway as the men set out with a haul of £280,000 gold bullion from South London which they had just hi-jacked. Barrett, who on his arrest recognised one of the officers and gave himself up saying, 'Hello, Phil, nice little tickle you've had here', once again turned informer implicating his former colleagues. This time he received sixteen years for his trouble – a discount of 25 per cent, said Judge Michael

Coombe when sentencing him on 6 May 1988. It was reduced
to twelve years on appeal. There was said to be a contract in the
sum of £250,000 on his head, but he survived to appear in the
Gangland series on BBC television in 1994, commenting on his
life and times. The robberies had been particularly unpleasant
with, on one occasion, a security guard being doused in petrol.
Croke received twenty-three years and Croke's wife's son,
Alan Turne, a security guard on the last robbery, went down
for seven years.

Detective Superintendent MacRae, in charge of the case,
said:

> Imagine Donald Barrett carrying on with criminals, doing
> robberies, when they know he's a supergrass. It's stag-
> gering and astounding. What is clear is that there was a
> body of opinion among criminals that having once been
> a supergrass, he could never, ever, ever, be a supergrass
> again. They felt in this sense he was safer to indulge in
> criminality with than any other criminal.[6]

But one London criminal thinks that Croke was not really at
fault: 'I mean Ronnie Darke recommended him. The man
wasn't really into the scene, so there was no way of him
knowing he was a wrong un.'[7]

Indeed it does seem that the profession as a whole is
careless with whom it associates. An East End criminal now
approaching middle age and father-figurehood finds that young
criminals simply will not listen.

> I know kids who are working with fucking well-known
> grasses. When I tell them, they won't have it. They're

6 Liz Mills, *Crimewatch*, p. 157.
7 On 21 January 1995 a gang tied a 'bomb' to a security guard and told him to
hand over £1,500,000 or be blown up. The gang escaped with the cash and
left him still attached to the bomb and fearful that they would detonate it by
remote control. It was the first time that this method had been used since the
arrest of Croke and Barratt.

making so much money out of grasses they don't want to know . . .

Tony G. has to have been a grass for fifty years. His brother was a self-confessed grass. He said so at Snaresbrook[8] yet P. [a professional and successful] still goes with him.

I could never prove H.A. was a grass but his solicitor swore black was blue that he was, yet everybody has it with him in the East End.

He covers his tracks. When I was done in 1976 I thought I was going for good. They had more evidence against him than they did me but he was never even charged or questioned. I've never had it with him since. If anyone asked me for a recommendation I'd just tell them to be careful.

Were people more careful in the good old days? Frank Fraser recalls those golden times.

In my days you never knew for sure who was a grass. Street bookmakers would be informers to ensure they were only nicked from time to time, same with the brasses in the West End, so instead of being nicked four days a week they would only be nicked once a week. In those days there was hardly any crime. The population was 10 or 12 m lower than it is now; maybe even more. People could go into the Army or Navy for a career and now those avenues are closed to them. *Then* there was an open door for them.

You would get a whisper who was a grass so who could be left out. Those who didn't take that course would be the informers or people who bought themselves out. The police didn't shop their informers. Their word was God. He could swear he'd seen you climbing up a drainpipe and had a monkey with you and you'd given the jewellery to the monkey and he would be believed. It was one in a

8 A Crown Court in East London.

million where the policeman was not believed. He was believed automatically.

In the upper echelons of crime, however, he believes the thief or robber had innate protection from the informer:

In those days it was impossible for it to happen to us. Everyone we knew. You could trace their history back. Not even that. You automatically knew it. No stranger could ever infiltrate that circle. In 1949–50 I would say if there were twenty people in London doing the type of crime we were doing that was about it. At the very most thirty and that's topping it up.

Then when three people were arrested for a bank, wages, etc. the three were always together. The only ones who went to Parkhurst were those with health problems. In cases like Lewes 1938 when they were convicted [after the racecourse fight] they were split up. In the 1948 airport robbery when they were convicted they went to local prisons. Jimmy Woods to Exeter, Teddy Hughes to Bristol. In our case, the Spot case [the slashing of a London villain] we were all split up.

The beginning of the end was the dispersal. Now you couldn't trust your cellmate. With the drugs which is the thing today, what they do with the informers is have a load of drugs through – really big – the informer sells it and customs get their cut. That's part of the deal. They may do this two or three times and then the informer is allowed to slip out. All nicked. I'm allowed out. It's part of the deal.

Police would consider it demeaning to give the grass money. He would be allowed not to get nicked. The police would take a larger slice.

Last year the police arrested an old-timer – man was in his late seventies – and put a deal where he'd get £500 a week if he fed them information. The man more or less spat in their face and promptly told everybody.

90

Not all reprisals against grasses and supergrasses were violent and illegal. In giving evidence at the trial of George Ernest Turner in March 1978 at the Chelmsford Crown Court, for a robbery committed in Southgate in January 1974, Colin Saggs had admitted his part in the affair. During the trial leading counsel for the Crown had said that Saggs was giving evidence at some personal risk because although the Director of Public Prosecutions had undertaken not to prosecute him if Saggs gave evidence, he was still not safe from a private prosecution. Two months into his seven-year prison sentence in May 1978, George Turner decided to do just that. He took out a summons in the Tottenham Magistrates' Court.

The DPP stepped in immediately to protect his little lamb and wrote to Turner's solicitors saying that in accordance with his powers under the Prosecution of Offences Acts and Regulations, he proposed to intervene in the prosecution and offer no evidence. Turner was not unnaturally upset and challenged the decision, contending that it was unlawful. The Director then applied to strike out the action as being vexatious. Turner was particularly aggrieved, as well he might have been, that he was convicted on Saggs' evidence, the truth of which had apparently been bolstered by counsel's remark on his exposure to a private prosecution. Mr Justice Mars-Jones was having nothing of the argument. Apart from the harm done to Saggs by bringing a prosecution,

> the Director of Public Prosecutions had to take into consideration the possible effects of such a private prosecution being allowed to proceed upon current and future criminal inquiries and proceedings.

Quite clearly, if witness could then be prosecuted on their own admissions when giving evidence for the Crown, the supply would soon dry up.[9]

9 79 Cr.App. R.70.

The Director was not going to allow any further mistakes and misunderstandings to occur. In the same year the Right Honourable Jeremy Thorpe, the former leader of the Liberal Party, was charged with conspiracy and incitement to murder Norman Scott who had claimed to have had a homosexual relationship with Thorpe. Proceedings were also brought against David Holmes, John Le Mesurier, a carpet dealer, and George Deakin who was alleged to have recruited a former airline pilot, Andrew Gino Newton, to carry out the £10,000 contract. It was alleged that Newton had driven Norman Scott and his Great Dane, Rinka, to a hilltop near Porlock on the Devon moors in October 1975, when the dog had been shot. Now the Director wished to have as one of his principal witnesses a Peter Bessell, then living in California. The undertaking was clear that there would be no prosecution against him by the police or anyone else, and 'in the event of the private prosecution of Mr Bessell in respect of any such matter, the Director will assume responsibility for the conduct of those proceedings and offer no evidence against Mr Bessell.' In the event Thorpe, Le Mesurier and Holmes did not give evidence and Deakin said that it was a conspiracy to frighten and not to kill. Bessell stood to gain £50,000 from the *Sunday Telegraph* if there was a conviction, and only half that if there was an acquittal of Thorpe. There was an acquittal of Thorpe and all the other defendants.[10]

But whatever successes Marshall and Slipper had had with Smalls and O'Mahoney, it was nothing to the success which would come to a rising star in the Met, Tony Lundy. In May 1977 Detective Chief Inspector Tony Lundy rejoined the Flying Squad, soon to be reorganised in part as the Robbery Squad with its headquarters at Finchley. It was Lundy who developed the supergrass into a whole business of its own.

10 According to an article in the *New Statesman*, at least one juror apparently thought this half-price deal destroyed Bessell's credibility. This interview with a juror led to the unsuccessful prosecution of the *New Statesman* and the subsequent passing of the Contempt of Court Act 1981 in which s.8 prevents any research into, or publication of, a jury's findings.

Within six months he had his first major success with David Smith, arrested for an attack in September 1977 on two elderly men who collected their company's wages near The Thatched Barn, a restaurant at Borehamwood in Hertfordshire. The money was snatched but then one of the team, Alf Berkley, tore off the glasses of one of the men and squirted ammonia in his eyes. The man was almost completely blinded.

Smith turned supergrass, confessing to over sixty armed robberies. He was kept at Finchley police station for over fifteen months, at the end of which, as a result of his efforts, sixty-nine people were charged, of whom 90 per cent pleaded guilty. Two of the other robbers in the Thatched Barn team were also allowed to become supergrasses. One of them, George Williams, who had been offered the supergrass deal before Smith had rolled over but had initially held out, also received five years for a total of eighty robberies.

His evidence was necessary because there was a small problem with Smith. He had actually killed a man, and the DPP's policy was to require a plea of guilty to a murder – which carried a mandatory life sentence – and so he could not be considered a credible witness. Smith had coshed Kurt Hess, an elderly factory owner, during a robbery in Shoreditch. Hess had died three weeks later. However, Smith's luck was in. A statement was obtained from a pathologist which showed that Hess' poor health had contributed to his death. A charge of manslaughter was sufficient and so Smith could be reinstated as a prosecution witness.[11] Later the rules were relaxed and supergrasses who had pleaded guilty to murder were allowed to give evidence for the Crown, in one case with fairly disastrous results.

In fact George Williams' hands were none too clean either. In 1967 he and Smith had kidnapped the manager of a North London supermarket, Walter Price, to get the keys from his

11 Smith was also reputed to have killed a bookmaker, Harry Barham, found shot in the back of the head in his car in Hackney. £40,000 had been stolen from him. There was no hard evidence against Smith and he was never charged. In fairness, many a name was put up for the Barham killing including that of the ubiquitous West Ham hardman, Teddy Machin.

safe. The 16-stone Williams, known as 'Fat George', coshed Price, who died eight weeks later from heart failure. Price had staggered home with a lump on his head described by his widow as 'as big as an egg'. Judge Michael Argyle, his hands tied by public policy, commented that he considered Smith and Williams as 'two of the most dangerous criminals in British history', adding that whilst he accepted they were telling the truth: '. . . it was nauseating to hear these hypocrites and that as a matter of policy they have only been sentenced to five years each.'

But Smith did not last long on the outside. Throughout his adult life he had been an unsuccessful career criminal and he spent only short periods out of prison. On 29 September 1986 he was caught in a raid on a Securicor vehicle in Golders Green along with another former supergrass, Ron Simpson. Smith again turned supergrass, but this time he did not live long enough to testify. In a cell which had been hung with balloons for his birthday five days earlier, Smith cut his throat with a razor-blade on Monday 13 October. Simpson was gaoled for twenty-one years.

Recruit followed recruit through the Lundy supergrass factory, some thirty of them defended by Roland Pelly, a Bishops Stortford solicitor who had been the DPP's agent in Hertfordshire in the early 1970s when the DPP used to send cases to local firms of solicitors.

One of Lundy's least successful supergrasses was Londoner Billy Amies. Given the sobriquet 'The Snake', Amies served only two years in prison, but although he had named fifty-eight criminals it seems he was responsible for the conviction of only five.

But, so far as the police were concerned, the most serious incident had involved the Flying Squad's Detective Sergeant Bernard Craven who suffered brain damage in an attack on him whilst guarding Billy Amies in Liverpool. Versions of what exactly happened and how vary.

Amies was one of the more unpleasant of armed robbers. Amongst his other roles, while dressed as a policeman he had threatened his victim in a robbery with castration, and had the man's daughter stripped to her underwear asking, 'How would you like to see your daughter raped?' He had also been at work on Merseyside. In the first of his three cases there, a middle-aged woman had been repeatedly punched in the face; in the second another middle-aged woman, her Down's Syndrome daughter and her son had all been tied up; the latter had also been threatened with castration. In the third incident a garage owner and his family had been tied up and the owner had had his testicles bitten to persuade him to open his safe.

Lundy described him as follows:

In some ways Billy was a nutter. He was also known as Billy the Queer because he's a raving homosexual. A big hard man, over six foot, a real animal, a compulsive armed robber who was really feared, but clever too.

Amies was in serious difficulties. He was caught out of his territory and had been arrested with one of Liverpool's real hardmen, John Tremarco. Lundy was told by another supergrass, David Smith, that Amies wanted help because he feared a corrupt Liverpool police officer, John Keating, was trying to lighten Tremarco's load by placing it on Amies' shoulders. It appears that Amies was being pressured into pleading guilty. Lundy went incognito to Walton jail and saw Amies who, once he had read Smith's statements involving him, decided that the path to safety was for him to turn supergrass. Much to the fury of the Merseyside police, Amies was transferred to Brixton on Rule 43 (see Ch.1, fn. 22) and then to Acton police station. There he told his version of his life of crime, implicating Tremarco and also Keating.

In October 1977, he went back to Liverpool to plead guilty. His statement was then shown to the solicitors for the other defendants who, as soon as Amies walked into the witness box, in turn were forced to put their hands up. The public gallery howled revenge, and the case was adjourned until the Monday for the sentencing of everyone including Amies.

The new and reformed supergrass was, unsurprisingly, unhappy about staying in the North West for the weekend; he wanted to do the round trip to the safety of London. It was agreed he should be returned on the Sunday night, to be lodged overnight in a Liverpool police station. So far so good, except that on the Sunday night the London sergeants who had custody of Amies could not find him a home; nor could they manage to contact the local Serious Crimes Officers. They therefore turned up with Amies in tow at the hotel in Liverpool where Lundy was staying. Further efforts to find Amies a bed in a cell failed, and so he was booked into the hotel along with his guarding officers Craven and O'Rourke. On a toss of the coin it was decided that Craven should sleep in the room with Amies, and O'Rourke outside.

Unfortunately, Amies thought it would be a good idea to go out for a last drink. This was by no means an uncommon situation with supergrasses, and the officer agreed. Off he and Craven went to a pub in the docks called the Crow's Nest. Even more unfortunately, it was the haunt of Tremarco's friends. Lundy seems to have been full of admiration for his protégé:

> Typical of the fearless animal he is, off goes Amies with Craven into the lions' den. But as soon as they walk in, they're set upon! Amies, big strong beast, fights his way out and escapes, but Bernie Craven gets an almighty kicking. He's almost kicked to death but he manages to stagger out of the pub, he's found in the front garden of a nearby house and he's rushed to hospital.[12]

12 The quotations are from M. Short's *Lundy*, pp. 51–2. There is a full account of Amies' career in Chapter 4 of the book. An alternative view is expressed in A. Jennings and others, *Scotland Yard's Cocaine Connection*. They point out that apart from the two men in Liverpool, Amies' evidence served to convict only three more people.

Amies was badly cut and had a broken arm by the time he returned to the safety of the hotel. Craven was not so fortunate, suffering severe concussion, a broken nose and a fractured cheekbone. He never really recovered, and retired from the force on health grounds. The next morning Lundy managed to have Amies' case remitted to London, where he could be sentenced for all his offences. Tremarco received fifteen years; back in London Amies served only two. Two years later, Keating was convicted of attempting to extort half the money an insurance company had paid to a police informer. He received two and a half years.

The story in the Underworld was that Amies had been punished in the pub by a Liverpool hardman, Billy Grimwood, assisted by two London brothers from a well-known and influential family. The mystery remains as to why Amies chose the Crow's Nest, of all Liverpool pubs, in which to drink.

Amies, an only child, had grown up in the East End with his father George and mother Rosie. They lived at Carr Street, Stepney. He grew up a thief and graduated into robbery. In 1964 he was arrested for tying up a woman in a robbery along with Thomas 'Golly' Sillett – who was later arrested for the Mountnessing Silver Bullion Robbery in which he named a number of names but would not give evidence against them at the trial – and Joe Flynn. Amies was convicted – the others were acquitted – and was sentenced to four years' imprisonment. Whilst in Maidstone prison he developed a relationship with another prisoner and, when that man was upset by another inmate, Amies attacked the third person, as a result of which he received a further eighteen months. On his release he resumed his occupation. He was well respected amongst the heavy London set and was attacked by Albert Donoghue, who thought he was being kidnapped when he got in a car with him after the Kray trial. In 1970 Amies was arrested and sentenced to seven years for a robbery in Portsmouth.

As has been said, the interesting thing about supergrasses is not the people whom they name but the ones they do not. In one instance Amies named a George Almond but then proceeded to give evidence in mitigation for him saying how he, Amies, had led Almond astray and onto the particular job.

Another East End figure recalls his dealings with Amies:

He could have put me away four or five times but he didn't. I don't know why. Joey was questioned about a robbery put up by Amies and he was never on it. I fucking know because I was. I think it was because Joey had had a row with Amies over one of his boyfriends. He never ever worked with Amies but he was put up on this robbery.

He was a very dangerous man. They may have called him Billy the Queen but I would never have underestimated him. Even when he was in the police station he was blagging people. 'If you don't pull up 10 or 20 grand you'll go down for a robbery.' Someone would be put in a cell with him and he'd get everything out of the bloke and give it back to the police.

The only thing I can think of why he didn't put me in was something that happened in about 1968 or 1969 and it happened with Golly S.[13] Golly, me and Amies were looking at a robbery and then we decided to leave it alone for a month. One day I went round to the lock-up and looked in and there was nothing there – no cars, no nothing. I went round to see Golly S and he said he hadn't done nothing and we should see Amies.

It was winter and when Amies opened the door to his flat he was wearing a check dressing gown and had his hand in his pocket. I could see the shape of the gun. 'What do you fucking want?' he asked. Golly said he'd been round and the stuff was gone. 'Of course, it's fucking gone. You've had it.' He said this to Golly. He never muddled me up.

I said, 'Why did you let that pouf cunt talk to you like

13 Golly S obtained his nickname because of his shock of hair.

that?' and he said he'd had a gun. I said he'd never have used it. I saw Billy Amies about a month later and he said, 'You do know that he was on it.' I said, 'I don't know, but you was out of order coming out of your house with a gun.' He said, 'That was for him.' I said, 'You should have sat down and talked it over.' Amies then told me the names of all the people on the robbery, and they included Golly S.

I gave him £500 and, although I never worked with him again, a bit later, after the Donoghue business when he was arrested on the Embankment with guns and a mask in his car, I did all the business for him and he got out on bail. I think that was his way of saying thank you.

Mind you, I wasn't the only one. I can name a dozen people Billy Amies could have put away and didn't. There again he put Ritchie Smith, a cousin of the Twins, away. He got fifteen years and he was innocent.

Amies served his sentence and, according to an East Ender, died outside London some two or three years ago 'of natural causes'.

But in many ways, the seemingly prize catch was nothing to do with Lundy. It was Maxwell Thomas Piggott who was to turn what the police thought would be the major supergrass of the decade, and would give evidence against Ronnie Knight who was thought, perhaps with some justification, to be one of the top figures in London's Underworld.

Bradshaw, as Piggott became known, had a long and interesting criminal career. His father had a slot-machine business in cafés and clubs from the Oval to Brixton, and was well respected by people such as 'Whippo' Brindle of the powerful South London family. Bradshaw junior was educated at the same school as Commander David Powis of the Metropolitan Police. In September 1965 he was charged with housebreaking, and in November of the same year with throwing acid at the police, for which he was sentenced to seven years' imprisonment. He escaped from Wormwood Scrubs in

1968 and went to live in Putney. He set up an antiques business, but this went into decline and following a wages snatch to restore the family fortunes, he moved to the South Coast and the next year he popped up in Brighton running a long-firm fraud[14] for which he received six years at Lewes Assizes. He then lived a chequered life running a fish restaurant with Micky Hennessy of the well-known South London family and Alfie Gerard, the notorious hit-man, as well as the more lucrative business of being an armed robber, arsonist and armourer. In 1977 he was arrested for robbery and was offered the chance to become a supergrass. Initially he declined, but it was whilst he was serving the ten-year sentence he received that he decided to turn. He had already managed to have a substantial slice shaved off what should have been a much longer sentence by disclosing to the police part of his cache of guns. Now a year or so into his sentence, and still in contact with his arresting officer, he put up the deal under which he would bring down Ronnie Knight, former owner of the A & R Club, then husband of actress Barbara Windsor and a celebrated London family figure. Initially Bradshaw tried to bargain – protection for his family, which was obviously granted; immunity from prosecution which, following the Smalls' decision, wasn't; and being taken into protective police custody.

After serving only twenty months of his sentence, he was moved from Wormwood Scrubs to Twickenham police station to begin his detailed account of his association with the top brass of London's Underworld.

On 17 January 1980 he pleaded guilty before Mr Justice Comyn to his part in the Zomparelli murder, arson of the Directors Club in Drummond Street, a shooting in Woolwich

14 A long-firm fraud in its simplest form involves buying goods in ever increasing quantities on credit, and when a substantial line of goodwill has been established, buying the maximum possible amount. The goods are then sold to the public at a knock-down price and the managers of the business decamp. In its more sophisticated form the long-firm involves numerous linked companies with references being given between them and the international market being tapped.

and two armed robberies. As was the practice, he was praised for his courage in naming 105 criminals in a long confession. He was then gaoled for life but without the recommendation of a minimum term. This was his, as with other murderers, *quid pro quo*. If he played his cards correctly he could expect to be released in about five years, during which time he would be kept under wraps.

The authorities thought this was to be the start of another major breakthrough in the war against professional crime. In true supergrass fashion it was not Bradshaw who had fired the fatal shot which killed Zomparelli as he played 'Wild Life' on the pin-table in the Golden Goose in Old Compton Street, but Nicky Gerard, Alf's son. The contract had, he said, been set up by Ronnie Knight as a result of a quarrel which had involved his brother David, who had been stabbed to death by Zomparelli in the Underworld hang-out Tolaini's Latin Quarter. However, when both Gerard junior and Ronnie Knight were acquitted of the Zomparelli murder, plans to use Bradshaw in other trials were quickly shelved and he was returned to prison, going to the Rule 43 unit in Wakefield prison. He eventually served ten years for the murder before his release.[15]

Perhaps 1979 was the high-watermark for the use of supergrasses. At least twenty leading villains had queued up for their day or, more likely, weeks, in the witness box. Scotland Yard believed that serious crime had tumbled from its 1977 all-time high when it had netted £166 million. Part of the success of the crack-down on crime was the sheer ineptitude of many criminals. A new recruit to the ranks of baby supergrass was James George Gallant, who had been

15 Bradshaw had alleged that Ronnie Knight had paid him to kill Zomparelli after the man received what was seen to be the extremely lenient sentence of four years for stabbing David Knight, Ronnie's brother. This in turn stemmed from a fight in North London. The police, however, claimed that the death of David Knight had resulted from a protection racket. In January 1995 Ronnie Knight, who had returned from his home on the Costa del Sol to stand trial for dishonestly handling proceeds from the Security Express robbery at Easter 1983, received seven years' imprisonment. The Crown accepted his plea of not guilty to the robbery itself. See J. Morton, *Gangland*.

found with his share of a £4,600 robbery in his packet of cornflakes. He informed on twenty-one criminals and there was a further 'break-through' when former seaman Norman Jones, together with Raymond Fowles and Peter Rose, put their hands up to a string of burglaries and robberies. All were said by Mr Brian Leary, QC for Jones, to have the shadow of death or serious injury over the rest of their lives. It was, said Assistant Commissioner David Powis, a year when 'London's criminal fraternity is experiencing its lowest ebb ever.'[16] Statistics can mean different things to different people. In 1972 armed robberies in England and Wales had totalled 539. In 1977 they had risen to 1,234. It is true that over that period bank robberies in London had fallen from 65 to 41, but this must be viewed against the more stringent security measures adopted by the banks.

On 24 March 1980 a robbery went off which surpassed the Great Train Robbers' caper. It was also one which would have the greatest repercussions on the credibility of Scotland Yard and, in particular, Tony Lundy. Three hundred and twenty-one silver ingots of bullion, worth £3.4 million, were stolen from a lorry on its way from London to Tilbury Docks when a gang of bogus traffic officials, together with a man wearing a police uniform, flagged down the lorry into a lay-by and held up the crew at gunpoint.

The instigator of the enterprise was Michael Gervaise, six-foot tall, a fluent linguist and a skilled burglar-alarm engineer, described as a 'balding figure with the mild air of a retail tobacconist', another man who would become a supergrass. He had received eighteen months for his part in the 1975 Bank of America robbery, but otherwise had no record worth speaking of. Together with an old friend, Micky Sewell, who had been given bail on a charge of armed robbery so that he too could act as an informant, Gervaise put together a team which included Lennie Gibson, Rudolpho Aguda, and Aguda's

16 *Daily Telegraph*, 29 November 1979.

nephew, Renaldo 'Ron' Aguda. Ron's specialities included the ability to uncouple trailers from their tractor units at speed.

If not actually working on the pavement, Gervaise had on his team a number of bent police officers who were paid to overlook his activities. One, Terence Donovan, who later served a prison sentence, was employed as a 'security adviser' after his retirement from the force. His job was to advise Gervaise of suitable places to burgle. Another bribed by Gervaise was the notorious Alec Eist.

The lorry was stopped by Gervaise, flagging it down wearing his policeman's uniform – supplied by a sergeant in the Met to Billy Young, who had passed it and some others to Lennie Gibson – and directing it into a lay-by for a bogus traffic census. The guards were threatened that their kneecaps would be blown off if they did not co-operate, and off went Gervaise and Co with the silver to store it in a 'slaughter', a rented lock-up garage, near Oakwood tube station at the northern end of the Piccadilly line. Gibson and Aguda senior were the only ones to hold keys to it and they had these on them when arrested.

Sewell was on bail at the time for a £200,000 wages snatch, and was being used as a snout by the then DCI Bill Peters of the Flying Squad. His mission for Peters was to infiltrate another robbery team headed by Ronnie Johnson, and his information led to the arrest of that team hours after they had shot a guard in a robbery at a bank in East Finchley. One of the men soon accepted Lundy's offer to turn supergrass and he named Tony Fiori, an Islington thief, who graduated from grass to supergrass with some facility. In turn, he named Gervaise.

It was only a matter of time before Gervaise joined the supergrass circuit – and it was only a matter of time before someone claimed the £300,000 reward being put up by the insurers. The claimant would be Lundy's protégé Roy Garner, part-owner of a thoroughly disreputable nightclub, Eltons, which more or less backed on to Tottenham police station. He had turned down an approach to do the silver bullion job.

The important thing was the recovery of the silver. Gibson,

when arrested, held out for some time as to its whereabouts until he had spoken with Aguda senior. Quite clearly there was much to be discussed because then Gibson had a two-hour private meeting with Lundy.

On the night of 4 June 1980, the police went to the lock-up at Oakwood, kicked in the door and recovered the silver – all but twelve bars worth £120,000. No one has ever been able to establish where they went to, but there again no one has ever seemed to worry too much about it. Nor has anyone ever satisfactorily explained why it was necessary to kick the door down; after all, Aguda and Gibson had been arrested with their keys to the 'slaughter' on them. Gibson and the Agudas received ten years each on pleas of guilty, rather more than the seven they had been half promised. Micky Sewell had long disappeared – tipped off by a police officer – and Gervaise had his five years. 'Dave Granger' – a pseudonym for Roy Garner – received the £300,000 reward. Garner also submitted claims through Lundy for payment for information from a Brinks-Mat security van hold-up in Hampstead in December 1979 and a fraudulent insurance claim based on a faked armed robbery, the reward for which was £75,000. After much haggling Garner received £178,000. Over the years he is believed to have accumulated more than £500,000 through rewards recommended by Lundy.

By then the supergrass system was becoming more and more complicated. There now seemed to be competing teams of supergrasses: those who gave evidence under Lundy's aegis and those, such as John Moriarty, who gave evidence against Lundy's friend Garner. Moriarty had twice been shot by rivals and had served periods of imprisonment. Now he decided to give evidence and to implicate Roy Garner.

'I never knew why he did it,' says former police officer, Dave Brady. 'After all, I was the officer called to The Favourite, the pub in Hornsey Rise where he'd been kneecapped. I asked what had happened and all he said was, "I fell down the fucking stairs, didn't I?"'

Presumably he did it because he was tired of being beaten up and shot at.

In the early 1970s Garner, together with a friend, Kenny Ross, had purchased premises in Upper Street, Islington, and then tried to evict the tenants. When this failed the premises were fired. Now Moriarty was prepared to name them in his statement as the organisers of the arson attacks.

Yet another series of supergrasses was being run from Reading by No. 5 Regional Crime Squad under the name *Operation Carter*. In 1977 a security van at Hemel Hempstead in Hertfordshire had been taken for £34,000, and three years later a North London robber, Freddie Sinfield, was arrested. The name he put in the frame was Billy Young, Gervaise's police uniform supplier.

By now there was no great problem in allowing murderers to become the main prosecution witness. On 27 June 1979, John Henry 'Bruce' Childs was arrested in Hertfordshire following the hijacking of a Security Express armoured van seven days earlier. In his turn he had been grassed by one of the others involved. Now he admitted his involvement with Henry MacKenny in six murders and, instead of his usual role of getaway driver, became the chief prosecution witness in a bizarre trial. They had put together a small version of Murder Incorporated – hiring themselves out as killers, on one occasion, said Childs, on hire-purchase terms.

He was arrested through his own carelessness in what had otherwise been a well-planned and executed robbery. The robbers had cleared £500,000 by impersonating Security Express employees. After the robbery they changed out of their uniforms in a public lavatory, leaving the clothing behind, but in the pocket of one of the overalls were the keys to a BMW and it was not difficult for the police to trace the vehicle to its owner, an East End greengrocer. In a deal for a light sentence, he returned the money which had been left in his care and then implicated both John Childs and MacKenny as part of the robbery team.

The case was initially investigated by Tony Lundy, then a Detective Inspector. He rightly supposed that this was not the first raid the team had carried out and interviewed each member with a view to getting confessions of other jobs. One of the team was even more forthcoming and named Childs and MacKenny as being involved in the killings of Ronnie Andrews, Terence Eve and the Bretts.[17]

Lundy's initial inclination was to laugh at him, but as he recalls the conversation went on:

'There's going to be another murder shortly – and you know the victim.'

'What are you talking about?'

'Do you know a police officer called Treen?'

I said 'Yeh' because John Treen had been one of my inspectors on the Flying Squad in 1977, so I knew him well. Treen had arrested MacKenny and Terry Pinfold in December 1976, but then the Director of Public Prosecutions dropped the case against MacKenny.

He said, 'MacKenny is going to murder Treen and Butcher,' who was the sergeant on the same case.

Lundy recalled that MacKenny had been arrested in December 1976 over two bank robberies at Romford and Woodford. He was then placed on a total of eight identification parades but was not picked out. Nevertheless, he was detained on the basis of witnesses' remarks of a big man – he stood 6 foot 6 inches. He was an associate of Terence Pinfold and, so the detectives investigating the case said, he had made verbal admissions. MacKenny denied these verbals and wrote out a statement giving a detailed notice of alibi.

---

17 George Brett, a haulage contractor, and his ten-year-old son Terence had disappeared in January 1975. Robert 'White Angel' Brown – a part-time professional wrestler who worked with MacKenny – and Ronnie Andrews, a close friend, had also disappeared. For a full account of their disappearances and the subsequent trial, see James Morton, *Gangland*, pp. 281–7.

The case against him had been dropped in the July of the next year, whilst Pinfold was gaoled for ten years. When the allegations were dismissed he shouted threats at Treen, the officer in charge of the case. Later MacKenny had endeavoured to interest the media in a number of cases in which he said miscarriages of justice had occurred.

In turn Lundy had difficulties in getting senior officers to accept that the stories told by his informant were credible, and it took him some time to persuade Commander Arthur Howard that the matter should be investigated further.

In December 1979 Childs became the first serial murderer in modern times to confess and give evidence against his accomplices. He had a hard time in the witness box, saying that he was drinking a bottle of whisky a day to try to obliterate the memory of killing Terence Brett. He did admit that he had thought about writing a book on the killing but denied the potential title 'East End Butcher'.

The juries' verdicts were curious. As to the murder of their partner Terence Eve, Pinfold was convicted and MacKenny acquitted. Both were acquitted of the murder of Robert Brown. MacKenny was charged with the murder of Brett and his son, along with Leonard Thompson. MacKenny was convicted and Thompson acquitted to leave court without a stain on his character, as did Paul Morton-Thurtle who was acquitted in the case of Sherwood, the nursing-home owner. MacKenny was convicted in that case, as he was over the killing of Ronnie Andrews. All received life sentences, in MacKenny's case with a recommendation that he serve not less than twenty-five years.

He was not happy, shouting that he had never killed anybody but that through his life-saving jacket he had saved plenty. 'Straight people need protection from you,' he told Mr Justice May, 'and from mongols and mugs like you,' he added to the jury before the court was cleared.

But where did all the bodies go? Although there had been considerable forensic evidence of bloodstains and traces of hair which went to corroborate Childs' story, there was no trace of any of the six who had disappeared. Again, according to Childs, initially the idea had been to cut up the bodies using a butcher's mincing machine. This had proved too blunt to deal with Eve and the idea was abandoned.

The next suggested method was simplicity in itself and extremely efficient. The bodies were cut up and then burned in a standard-size fireplace with an anthracite fire augmented by a gas burner. Bones which did not dissolve could be pounded on the hearth. The ashes were then emptied on waste ground. The disposal of a complete body took about 24 hours.

Professor James Cameron, the pathologist, was asked whether it would be possible to cremate a body in this way and tests were carried out. The carcass of an 11-stone male pig, calculated as being the equivalent of a fully developed average-sized man, was taken to Childs' home. Cameron, using brute force, sawed up the carcass, taking just over five minutes. He described it as, 'Perfectly simple, requiring no anatomical knowledge.'

The police and the pathologist then sat down to burn the body. Later Cameron told Philip Paul:

The temperature in the fire reached over 1,000 degrees but the room never went above 75. It was all properly measured, logged and photographed. But when we put the intestines on the fire it almost went out. Because, as soon as it burnt through, the fluid ran. Later on we were told that MacKenny had washed out and dried the intestines before they were burnt.

The total burning of the pig took thirteen hours. We ended up with remains of ash, bone and whatnot which filled two large plastic bags. We then went over it twice with a hammer, as we were told MacKenny had done, and eventually finished up with a small plastic bag of ash with not a remnant of teeth or bone visible to the naked eye.

Repeated checks had been made outside the building during

the burning, but no smell of roasting pork or other odour had been detected.

Childs' reward was that he received no minimum sentence in his term of life imprisonment.

In the meantime, Roy Garner's life as a double agent continued happily. He was informing on his colleagues to the police, unaware that the customs had him in their sights.

On 19 June 1987, one of the potentially greatest of supergrasses, the forty-four-year-old German-born Nikolaus Chrastny, was arrested in a spectacular raid by armed officers as he left his flat in Baker Street. Two days later cocaine valued at £14 million was found cached in a flat in nearby Harley Street. Here was a man who could not only blow the whistle on major drug importers, but could also do the same for corrupt London police officers.

Chrastny was caught through a complicated deal which had been struck in the United States with a jewel thief, Jimmy Tullevere, and one of Chrastny's colleagues Roy Whitehorne. Now Tullevere was allowed out of prison and used as an infiltrator. He went to Whitehorne's jewellery store in Fort Lauderdale and over a period of time recorded 125 hours of tapes. In October 1986 Whitehorne was arrested and pleaded guilty to conspiracy to distribute drugs. He turned informer, in return for which he was not imprisoned but instead received ten years' probation. Now he worked with the Department of Law Enforcement. He was given total immunity from the British customs officers to whom the Bertie Smalls no immunity rule did not apply.

To keep things nicely symmetrical, it was appropriate that Chrastny named his partner as none other than Roy Garner. Garner was arrested on 23 June 1987.

Chrastny, who also went under the name of Charles Flynn, was short, fat and bald, an expert marksman, fluent in five languages and with a former policewoman for a wife. At the time of his arrest he was wanted in Munich for an armed robbery which had netted him 1 million deutschmarks' worth of jewellery; in fact he had been wanted for that escapade since 1973. His capture was a triumph for the police and the customs.

Chrastny did a deal: his admissions and help in nailing others would let his wife out of the net. He was remanded into the custody of customs officers who wanted him to sing well away from London in case the melody came to the ears of Scotland Yard officers. He was handed over to the South Yorkshire police and taken to Rotherham. Chrastny was not only a robber and drug-dealer, he was a man of considerable charm and, within days, had exerted that charm on his keepers. He was moved from the protection of the South Yorkshire force to that of West Yorkshire and into Dewsbury.

The instructions given to the force were that customs officers who wished to question him must be given access on a twenty-four-hour basis, but that apart from them his whereabouts were to be secret. His life was thought to be in danger. He was placed in a cell normally reserved for women prisoners, which had a barred gate on the outside of the door that opened on to a corridor.

As befits a high-quality supergrass, Chrastny was supplied with all sorts of goodies: cigars, chutney, books, paints and model-making equipment. He was also given a television set but, because there was no power in his cell, he was allowed to keep his door open – the gate was in place – and a power-lead extension was run through from the doctor's room across the hall. He also acquired two files – alleged to have been smuggled in by his wife in the spine of a copy of *The Hound of the Baskervilles*.

He put his files and model-making equipment to good use. Without anyone being any the wiser, by working late at night and with his television full on to conceal the noise, he filed through the three-quarter-inch bars of the cell gate which opened on to the cell block. The day he was due to be taken down to London for a remand hearing he completed his task, went through a window in the doctor's room and was, so it

110

is thought, driven off in a waiting car. He left a note behind which read:

Gentlemen, I have not taken this step lightly. I have been planning it for several weeks. The tools have been in my wash-kit for several years in preparation for such an occasion. Greetings, Nick.

After the escape, as might be expected, everybody blamed everybody else. Mrs Chrastny was charged with assisting in the escape of her husband and defended by Timothy Cassells QC. Suggestions as to various other organisers were bandied about at her trial:

Cassells: Chrastny had also given evidence about corruption in the police: who was involved?
Customs officer: Lundy and Garner.
Cassells: A number of people would have an interest in Chrastny's escape?
C.O: Yes.
Cassels: New Scotland Yard, for instance?
C.O.: I cannot comment on that.

Mrs Chrastny was acquitted but, sadly for her, with her husband out of the way such immunity as she had vanished with him; she received seven years' imprisonment for the cocaine conspiracy. The inquiry into Chrastny's escape was not all that revealing. No collusion between him and either the customs or the police was proved. Two senior officers were given formal warnings, one received counselling, there were harsh words about the muddle as to who was actually in charge of guarding the prisoner, and finally it was decided that Dewsbury police station was unsuitable for housing a man who required a high level of security. This last was unsurprising; shortly before Chrastny took up residence, three men had escaped from the station.

And what of the potential supergrass? J. P. Bean records that he has been seen in Costa Rica, but there are other reports that he is dead.[18]

One of the great problems for the police in high-profile cases has been the power the grass has to get the officer who is running him to protect him. Nipper Read found this to his cost shortly before the arrest of the Krays. He decided to charge Alan Bruce Cooper who, he believed, had instructed a Paul Elvery to collect dynamite from Scotland to be used in an assassination attempt on the Maltese Club owner George Caruana. Elvery had been arrested and implicated Cooper in, amongst other things, another attempt to kill a man in the lobby at the Old Bailey by using a suitcase with a concealed hypodermic syringe and, when that failed, a crossbow.

. . . Cooper was brought to me at Tintagel House and the interview did not begin well. He was stuttering in his fright and told me he knew nothing about either the dynamite or Elvery.

'Fine,' I said. 'Then I'm going to charge you with conspiracy to murder and that's all there is to it.'

He then protested and asked to see John du Rose [a superior officer]. I told him I was running the show and asked him why. What he said came as a tremendous shock.

'If you contact John du Rose,' he said in his stuttering American drawl, 'he will tell you I am his informant.' He had, he said, been John du Rose's informant and spy for up to two years.

I simply didn't believe it and asked du Rose to come and see me. He did so almost immediately and I asked him if Cooper was telling the truth and that he, du Rose, was running him.

He accepted that they had been in contact for some

18 J. P. Bean, *Over the Wall*, pp. 273–7.

time, but he was, he said, not really running him as an informant as such, and had really received no information worth passing on: 'If there had been, I'd have let you know, Nipper.' At the time I was furious and du Rose knew it.[19]

Meanwhile Tony Lundy was endeavouring to protect – as far as possible – his informant, Roy Garner.

Lundy has been the subject of much speculation and gossip. His great defender, Martin Short, has suggested that it 'is worse than perverse to blame Scotland Yard' for Chrastny's escape, pointing out that his whereabouts were a closely guarded secret and that if officers had been involved Mrs Chrastny would have used them as a bargaining point to get a reduction on her seven-year sentence. On the other hand, J. P. Bean regards the sentence as by no means out of the way for an involvement with £2.6 million of drugs. Short believes that Scotland Yard could not have found out the supergrass's whereabouts and that Lundy's telephone was being tapped. Bean points out that it is not difficult to find the resting place of a prisoner. When, in 1991 amidst great secrecy, Roy Garner was transferred to Attercliffe police station in Sheffield when he was making allegations against Lundy, it was not long before the local paper had the news on its front page.

The allegations came to nothing. Lundy had been suspended from duty for four years before Garner began to speak to police officers. He retired in 1988 on an ill-health pension, suffering from stress. Finally his problems came to an end in October 1994, when it was announced that the Crown Prosecution Service had found no evidence to justify a prosecution against Lundy. He told the *Police Review*:

> During the eight years this investigation has lasted, not a single officer has tried to interview me, although they've interviewed dozens of people who have never met me.

19 L. Read, *Nipper*, p. 162.

Throughout the earlier investigations, I co-operated 100 per cent with the officers making the inquiries, making my bank accounts, and my family's bank accounts, available for inspection.[20]

In 1993 the *Police Review* estimated that the investigations into his conduct would cost £5 million.

There was a brief postscript to the Chrastny affair. In May 1992 the Home Office issued guidelines to all forces regarding the supervision and handling of what were coyly referred to as 'resident informers'. Supergrasses must now be held in a special suite away from other cells and be protected by three uniformed officers, who should not be connected with the case, on a twenty-four-hour basis. They could have fifteen-minute visits from friends and family, but no conjugal visits and no alcohol. O'Mahoney and Williams would have hated the regime.

In recent times supergrasses have not had it all their own way.

Supergrass trials have fallen into disrepute and supergrasses aren't used quite as much. But what they did was present to your stock gangland criminal a real threat. Gangs haven't stayed together because of that risk. The risk of being supergrassed got very high about seven or eight years ago. Then jurors started to acquit because supergrasses were being offered immunity or extremely low sentences, money was being offered or facilities in custody, so they died off.[21]

Even so, many made substantial profits from it. A former East London friend of the family recalls the story of one successful grass:

20 *Police Review*, 28 October 1994.
21 Michael Mansfield QC in D. Campbell, *That was Business, This is Personal*, p. 135.

There was a North London family called Smith*. There was George, Phillip and Frankie who died of a heart attack in the reception wing at Brixton. Phillip and Tony Fiske were done for two lorryloads of goods at Herbert's smallholding. The law charged his mother and father and the deal was that they'd drop the charges if Fiske and him will put their hands up to the handling. Smith said no. His mother and father got three years each, Tony Fiske got a five and Herbert got an eight. He got something off on appeal but when he comes out he becomes a police informer. He went into partnership with another grass from South London, George F. He started then to frequent South London. I had my card marked by a copper and I gave both Phillip and George Smith a bashing in the Log Cabin Club which was owned by George Walker and Tommy McCarthy in Soho.

In 1971 Herbert and George F were convicted of receiving a lorryload of goods and got two and a half years apiece. By now Herbert was a well-known informer and he'd got very friendly with a Dave Bailey from Islington. This was about the time when the Sewell shooting took place. Dave's brother-in-law was a Greek who got done for hiding Sewell. The only person apart from Bailey and the brother-in-law to know where Sewell was being hid was Phillip Smith. After Sewell was caught, Smith went back to the Court of Appeal and was given a suspended sentence.

After that he changed his name. A friend of mine comes into a pub and says he's just met him. I told him not to trust him and my friend went and marked Billy Tobin's card but he wouldn't have it. Tobin and Cook and some others were caught with a mechanical digger doing a security van in Dulwich. They were all nicked and Herbert got £80,000 reward money. There was a rumpus about that. He said it

* a pseudonym.

wasn't enough. It was pretty amazing; the solicitor who defended Tobin acted for Herbert in getting the reward money. He took up with Harry's wife and went off to Australia. She died of cancer over there. I don't think he ever came back.

As for F he was involved in the drugs case in which Eddie Watkins shot and killed the customs officer. F was acquitted after a re-trial. A bit after that he was shot in the shoulder in his pub in Kent. It was a motorcycle job and F turned his head at the crucial moment.[22]

It does not appear that, as is so often the case, the Underworld had learned either of F's treachery or had learned their lesson. The same source continues the story:

In about 1984 he went to Freddy Brazil and sets up a meeting in Ronnie Scott's to discuss a load of Old Masters, etchings and other antiques. Freddy agreed to place the stuff and another meet is arranged at the Heston Service Station when Freddy takes along some people with him. When they got there it was a set-up with the police. They fought the case and it came out then that F had been an informer for years. Freddy got four years.

Quite apart from the well-known supergrasses such as Smalls

22 On 23 August 1971 Frederick Sewell shot and killed Superintendent Gerald Richardson, head of the Blackpool Borough Police, in an armed robbery at The Strand in Blackpool. Sewell and four other Londoners undertook what was considered to be a simple snatch which would net them £100,000. Instead one of the staff set off an alarm and a police officer arriving on the scene saw the men escaping. Richardson gave chase and when he caught up with Sewell he was shot twice at point-blank range. The *Daily Mirror* offered a reward of £10,000 for Sewell's capture.

On 20 October 1979 Peter Bennett became the first customs officer to be killed on duty for nearly two hundred years during surveillance of an importation of £2.5 million-worth of cannabis. He was shot in the stomach by Lennie Watkins, who later killed himself in Long Lartin prison whilst serving a life sentence.

For a full account of the Sewell case see C. Borrell and B. Cashinella, *Crime in Britain Today*. For an account of the Watkins case, see J. Morton, *Gangland*, p. 302 *et seq.*

and O'Mahoney, there has been a whole second division whispering away around the countryside. In 1987 a whole lawn was in Bedford prison. Members included Clifford Barnes, who received ten years for theft but informed on robbers and swindlers in the Midlands, and David Medin, who was said to have a £1-million Mafia contract on his head. Medin had been a high-class drugs-dealer and computer genius who had been sent from Detroit to Britain to establish a cocaine distribution centre which, had it been successful, would have flooded the market. When Drugs Squad detectives arrested him he gave the police a 100-page statement which included details of the East London gang recruited by him to distribute the drugs. In Wales John Davies, who received twelve years for armed robbery, informed on at least seventy of his former colleagues. He was said to be the 'biggest leek' in Welsh history. Steven Henry, serving nine years, was another who would disprove the theory that blood was thicker than prison. Henry, who received nine years for his part in some thirty-six armed robberies on sub-post offices, informed on his brother-in-law as well as another five of the gang. From Manchester came Fred Scott who, serving ten years for armed robberies, had named twenty-five of his friends and detailed their involvement in crime.

In more recent times, even though the killing of British supergrasses is still rare, life has become more dangerous for them than in the days of Bertie Smalls.

In February 1989 informer Alan 'Chalky' White disappeared. He was last seen walking to the off-licence in Minchington, Gloucestershire to get some lager. Three months later his body, wrapped in a blue tarpaulin, was spotted by a family at the Cotswold Water Park near Cirencester. Forensic tests showed that he had been stabbed in the heart.

White, who had several minor convictions, was due to give evidence against a Danny Gardiner with whom, so White said, he had robbed a petrol station in Stroud netting £4,800 in 1986. White, who had a drug problem, had declined the police offer of a new identity and instead was given a 'panic button' to use if he felt threatened. Most nights, however, he could be found in the local Crown public house. With the death of White, the case against Danny Gardiner collapsed and he went abroad.

With the help of Interpol the police conducted inquiries in Egypt – where Mr Gardiner was wrongly reported to have died in Cairo – France, Spain, Morocco and Israel. On 4 January 1991 Mr Gardiner flew back voluntarily from Tel Aviv. He had been found there working in a tourist hotel, having apparently entered the country under a false name. He was later convicted of White's murder.

In 1990 yet another informer was killed. He had previously told the police of a planned contract killing resulting in the arrest of the hit-man. Before the trial, the judge accepted the argument of the defence that it needed access to police information. This would have meant a disclosure of the identity of the informant and the trial was abandoned by the prosecution. At the time of his death the man had been resettled in Germany – the cost of relocating an informer, names, passports and driving licences for him and his family, is around £100,000 – and he was murdered shortly afterwards.

A second killing occurred in Amsterdam and involved a man who had given police information about a gang of drug traffickers. The third, early in 1993, was in Ireland, where it seems the link to the identification of the informant had come about through the withdrawal of the case by the prosecution.

In May 1993 the trial began of four men whom the prosecution alleged had brought over hired killers from Northern Ireland to dispose of supergrass David Norris, shot dead in July 1992 by a motorcycle-riding killer in the driveway of his home at Belvedere, Kent. Norris' death had been just another in the series where the prosecution had inadvertently blown their man's cover by dropping a case. Worse than simply being a grass:

He used to set people up on jobs that he had done himself.
He would carry out a warehouse job, tell somebody there

was still stuff to be taken and then tip the police off.

The police won't say he's a grass because being bumped off is not a terrific advert for a career in grassing. He was on Rule 43 inside which tells its own story.[23]

After nearly six weeks the trial, which had cost almost £1 million, was halted when the Recorder of London, Judge Lawrence Verney, ruled that the evidence of the two main prosecution witnesses, Renwick Dennison and Stuart Warne, was unsafe for the jury to rely on. Patrick Doherty, George McMahon – both from South London – Terence McCrory from Belfast and John Green from Falkirk were all acquitted.

The prosecution had outlined a curious but ultimately unconvincing story of hitmen hired through Northern Ireland drug-dealers who were promised cheap cannabis in return for the completion of the contracts. Two men who were never arrested were said by the prosecution to have helped organise the murder squad. One of these men, so the prosecution said, had come to London from Belfast after he had been shot for supplying Catholics with drugs.[24]

At an earlier trial Warne, the link between the English drug-dealers and the Irish, and Dennison, one of the hit-men, had been sentenced to life imprisonment after admitting conspiracy to murder. Warne had told the jury that he had been met in a South London public house by a man who had whistled up £20,000 in half an hour by using his mobile phone. This was, he said, the price for the unsuccessful attempted killing

23 D. Campbell, 'Gangland Britain', in *Weekend Guardian*, 14–15 December 1991. Rule 43 is protected accommodation away from the mainstream of the prison and is used to house sex offenders and informers along with convicted police officers.

24 This man seems to have had a chequered and eventful life. According to evidence given in the case he had been active in the Belfast Loyalist underworld since the middle 1970s as both a drug-dealer and the recruiter of Protestant hit-men. At one time he was on the run and thought to be in Spain after he had been shot in a car outside a social club in the Shankhill Road area. The IRA had indicated that he was under sentence of death. He had been lucky to survive for so long for he was thought to have had contacts with the IRA and INLA. A relative was killed by the UDA in 1992.

of a second man, John Dale, 'the object of dislike and hatred apparently because he was in the habit of ripping people off in drug deals', said Timothy Langdale QC for the prosecution. Dennison took over the contract and shot him in the back outside his London home in April 1991, and then missed at point-blank range when he shot at his head. So far as Norris was concerned, the forty-five-year-old informer was shot as he begged for mercy with his wife watching helpless.

Perhaps fortunately, America is still several steps ahead in certain aspects of criminal behaviour. The recent tale of Washington's First Street Crew gang makes for unhappy reading.

In the autumn of 1992 the uncle of Arvell 'Pork Chop' Williams was murdered. Williams, a former associate of the First Street Crew, believed gang members had information on the killing which they would not share with him and, more prosaically, that he was himself about to be prosecuted for trading in narcotics. He went to the vice unit of the 3rd Police District. On 6 October he was sitting in a car on Second Street when two gunmen shot him eighteen times. A witness identified Crew members Antone White and Ronald Hughes as the killers.

According to police officers, the intimidation of witnesses began before Williams' body was taken from the white sedan. White stood watching the proceedings eating a bag of potato crisps, noting who was in the area.

On 26 October 'Chinese' Gregg Ingram was shot dead near the White House shortly after a police officer interviewed him about the Williams killing. A week later three Crew members were shot dead; the police had been hoping to question them and two had told their lawyers they were thinking about co-operating. White, Hughes and two others were arrested two weeks later. For a time the killings stopped.

Then on 19 October 1993 a homicide detective Joseph Schwartz gave evidence in the trial, careful to identify witnesses only as W-1 etc. He gave no age, no sex or address. The aim was to ensure that Crew members in the public gallery could not make any identification. His efforts were not successful. Two days later Janellen Jones was shot in the mouth, a symbol – the police say – to warn off potential witnesses. A fifty-three-year-old man who was with her at the time was also shot. In all nine people were shot, and the police believed that seven were killed because the Crew members thought they had turned informer. White and Hughes were convicted of racketeering and were sentenced to life in prison without parole. The jury could not reach a verdict on the murder charge.[25]

Revenge is, after all, a dish best eaten cold. Retribution could come many years later and was often delivered at the most timely opportunity. Edward J. O'Hare, who had been Al Capone's silent partner in greyhound racing, must have known that something was wrong shortly before his death. He had informed Frank Williams that the jury in Capone's 1931 income tax case had been tampered with and a re-trial had been ordered. By so doing he had, in effect, ordered his own death sentence.

It was long stayed. Just before Capone was released from prison O'Hare took to carrying a pistol for protection. It did him little good. On November 8 1942, a bare week before Capone left prison, O'Hare was shot dead in his car whilst driving along Ogden Avenue, Chicago. He was the only government witness in the tax case who was killed but he had, after all, played a conspicuous part in sabotaging Capone's chances of an acquittal.

Nor, if they survive, do informers always get what they see as their proper rewards. Anna Sage was one of these. Her real name was Ana Cumpanas and she was a brothel-keeper in Chicago. A Romanian by birth, she had operated brothels in Gary, Indiana, and East Chicago, acquiring convictions for

25 *Washington Post*, 31 July 1994.

running a disorderly house in both locations. In 1934 she was convicted a third time and steps were being taken to deport her as an undesirable alien. Now at the age of forty-two she was sharing rooms with a twenty-six-year-old waitress Polly Hamilton, whose boyfriend was Jimmy Lawrence, rather better known as John Dillinger.[26] It seems possible that Hamilton did not know Dillinger's real identity and also that Sage – who, from listening to his stories and tales, did – would have not gone to her contacts in the East Chicago police had only the FBI reward of $10,000 been on offer. Sage was able to negotiate a rather better deal: the deportation proceedings against her would be dropped. An arrangement was approved by Melvin Purvis, then the star of Hoover's Bureau.

On 22 July 1934, Dillinger and the women were to go to the cinema. Sage called in to the police to say that she was not sure which film of two they would attend and both houses were staked out. To help identification, she would wear a red dress. As they left the Biograph Theater where Dillinger and the women had been watching Clark Gable in *Manhattan*

26 John Herbert Dillinger was born in Pennsylvania in 1903 and became the superstar of the gangster world as well as achieving top spot on Hoover's Public Enemy list. His bank robberies were carried out with precision. Like many another, both in the United States and England, he had learned from Baron Lamm. Dillinger was the object of a number of daring prison rescues, the last being from the so-called escape-proof jail in Crown Point, Indiana. As with so many folk heroes, many members of the public refused to accept that it was Dillinger who had been shot and believed that, in fact, a substitute fall-guy had been provided. The crime writer J. Robert Nash developed this theory in *Dillinger: Dead or Alive?*, in which he argues that the Agency was duped and had to have a cover-up to avoid the appalling embarrassment. If this is true, then it must be asked what did happen to Dillinger for the rest of his life? Or had he actually died earlier?

There is also a theory that Dillinger was shot by a policeman acting as a hit-man for the local branch of the Mafia (G. Russell Giradin with William J. Helmer, *Dillinger: the Untold Story*).

As for Dillinger's mentor, Herman K. Lamm (?1890–1930), a German officer cashiered for cheating at cards, has been described as America's most brilliant bank robber. From the end of World War 1 until the 1930s Herman K. 'Baron' Lamm's men were the most efficient in the business. Lamm's career came to an end when a tyre blew on the getaway car. They seized another which by mischance had a governor fitted by a well-meaning son to prevent his elderly father from driving too fast. They were overtaken and Lamm died in the ensuing shoot-out.

Melodrama, Purvis saw Sage and according to some versions of the story called on Dillinger to halt. The girls had either vanished or simply gone on ahead by the time he reached for a gun. Two women passers-by were shot as the FBI agents opened fire on Dillinger. One bullet passed through his left side, another went into his back and, again according to some reports, he was shot in the eye.

As for Sage, she and Polly Hamilton were taken to Detroit by federal agents to ensure their silence. Two weeks later Sage went to California where she was paid $5,000 for her part in the killing of Dillinger. On 29 April 1936, despite her complaints and protestations, she was deported.

Nevertheless some still think it is worthwhile to exchange twenty-two years inside for a lifetime of looking over their shoulders. Lawrence Cain, known as 'The Snake', and said, a trifle optimistically given the going rate, to have a £250,000 contract on him, was one of them when, in 1991, he received just seven years for armed robbery. He had given 'valuable help' to the police after admitting taking part in twenty-seven raids in South East London over an eight-year period. The money had gone on foreign travel and a £300-a-day heroin habit. Amongst those who went down as a result of his evidence were his former partner Alan Condon, who drew twenty-one years, Cain's best man when he married a Thai girl who collected sixteen, and William Harding, who netted a year less. Cain's counsel told the court that he had turned informer for the highly praiseworthy reason of divorcing himself from the criminal community. 'No one will come near me unless it is to kill me,' said Cain whilst giving evidence.

Other people discovered that being around grasses is none too safe either. Paul Olson, in the American Government Witness Protection Program, had met with federal prosecutors in Chicago in early September 1994 and was due to testify in a cocaine-trafficking case when the plane on which he was travelling nose-dived when approaching Pittsburgh International Airport. All 132 people aboard were killed. Olson had been a

Chicago bank president who, after his conviction in a financial scam, entered the Witness Protection Program in 1989.

In 1994 another threat came to the grass – exposure by television. The case involved not only an informer but also a police undercover operation. The informer and the police had combined to bring down a man who had, the police believed, been a thorn in their flesh for some time. Richard Green told the court that he had borrowed £20,000 from the man, to be repaid with interest at £500 a week. He had managed to repay the 'nut' but not the 'vig'. He claimed that the man would remit the interest if he would sell on some heroin at £28,000 a kilo. Green, a long-term informer, once more went to the police, who infiltrated the moneylender's offices with Lucy, a secretary, in reality an undercover policewoman. In December 1992 the man was convicted and received fourteen years. In December 1994 his conviction was quashed and a retrial ordered.

Meanwhile in the summer of 1994 the BBC programme *Panorama* threatened to reveal Green's new identity and show photographs. He said:

> I am angry and scared, not only about my own security but for the safety of my family, not all of whom had a new identity provided. This programme would endanger my life and make a mockery of the witness protection system.

One of the problems the police in Great Britain have faced over the last two decades has been the steady growth of ethnic minority crime. In particular the Triad operations from Hong Kong have been particularly secretive. In 1992 they must have thought their Sundays had come at once when Triad hit-man, George Wai Hen Cheung became the first Triad supergrass. 'Who better to tell you what happened than the man trusted by the Triads to pull the trigger?' said Martin Heslop for the Crown. Cheung had been ordered to shoot Lam Ying-kit in the spine, Lam's crime having been to come from Hong Kong to wrest control of British Triad crime from the Wo On Lok. The prize of control was the revenue from prostitution, gambling, extortion and loan-sharking. Lam had been shot four times and was crippled as a result of the attack.

In September 1991, after several abortive attempts at assassination, Cheung had stepped behind his target in a crowded Soho restaurant and shot him. Lam, showing considerable courage, had wrestled with Cheung, grabbed the .22 gun and forced him to drop the weapon. Cheung had fled to a waiting car. He was rounded up along with other Triad leaders within a matter of hours of the shooting. As the evidence against Cheung became clearer, he changed sides and decided to help the police.

Cheung did not seem to fit the accepted pattern of hit-man, however. Born in Leicester, where his parents owned a take-away Chinese restaurant, he resented his brother and sisters and his parents had disowned him. Only 5 foot 4 inches in height, with thick spectacles for which he was known as 'Specky', he spoke better English than Cantonese. In a letter from prison he wrote:

All my life I have been stuck in between the English and the Chinese. The Chinese treated me as English. The English treated me as Chinese. I haven't much chance of recognition in England, getting an English job and getting on.

In court it also emerged that because of his acne and generally scruffy appearance he had failed to attract women and had resorted to prostitutes as well as smoking cannabis and taking LSD. His only companion appears to have been his dog, Rambo, which befriended him whilst homeless. 'All I want in life is some love and respect,' said Cheung.

He said he had been the bodyguard of a prominent Triad, and so had enjoyed status and respect. The unsocial activities in which he had engaged included extortion and drug-trafficking as well as violence. On one occasion he had slashed a man with a double-bladed knife. Now he was at the Old Bailey giving evidence against men whom he said were former colleagues from the Sui Fong, also known in Britain as the Wo On Lok group involved in the attempted murder of Lam. Meanwhile he had been held in a special security unit. A £100,000 contract was said to be on his head.

The defence was clear that Cheung was protecting the real villains and blaming his enemies whilst currying favour with the police. One, actor Tang Wai-ming who had been the leading stuntman for film star Jackie Chan, claimed that Cheung had framed him because he was jealous of Tang's success with a Hong Kong girl. Five of the defendants were acquitted. The jury could not agree in the case of Tang Wai-ming and the court ordered the count to be left on the file. All other charges including supplying drugs, blackmail, and arson against the men – and which relied on the evidence of Cheung – were also left on the court file. The police are still some way from a successful infiltration into the workings of the Triads in the United Kingdom.[27]

27 *South China Morning Post*, 6 December 1992.

5

The Supergrass in America

From the point of view of justice and social order in the 1930s perhaps the most important of informers was Abe Reles, referred to after his death as 'the canary who could not fly', whose testimony led to the destruction, by Detective Lieutenant Jack Osnato, of the so-called Murder Inc., the professional hit squad, a gang of professional killers from Brooklyn who were made available by the conglomerate (formed during Prohibition) of Charles 'Lucky' Luciano, Meyer Lansky and the Irish interests of O'Bannion and others. The executions were only carried out for business reasons and, because of the bad publicity which would have ensued, never against politicians and journalists.

The leaders of Murder Inc. were Albert Anastasia and Louis Lepke although it seems that the 400 plus contract killings had to be approved by a council which would include Luciano, Lansky, Joe Adonis and Frank Costello. Concurrence was required or, at the very least, no committed opposition.[1] Next in the hierarchical structure came Louis Capone, no relation of the more famous Al, who ran Chicago rather than New York, Emmanuel 'Mendy'

---

[1] The attitude is not dissimilar in England. In 1993, professional criminal James Moody, who had escaped from Brixton some twelve years earlier and was thought to be a contract killer, was himself shot dead. The shooting possibly followed a row he had had with a David Brindle and that man's subsequent death in the Bell Public House, Walworth.

'Much as I knew Jim well, I can understand the feelings about David's death and that it was one that had to be done. I suppose if someone who knew it was going off had really pleaded for him it might have made some difference but I doubt it.' Frank Fraser in *Mad Frank*, p. 221.

Weiss and Abe 'Kid Twist' Reles. They provided a buffer between the killers themselves who included Vito 'Chicken Head' Gurino – so-called not from his shape but because of his use of chickens in gun practice – Frank Abbandando, and 'Pittsburgh' Phil Strauss. The killers frequented Midnight Rose's, an all-night café in Brooklyn, awaiting a telephone call to dispatch them country-wide.

One of the most famous victims of Murder Inc. was Arthur Flegenheimer, rather better known as Dutch Schultz, himself a member of the ruling committee. Schultz, under considerable pressure from Thomas E. Dewey, who had been appointed a special prosecutor to investigate organised crime, asked that a contract be taken out against the lawyer. This was not regarded as sensible Mob policy, and when it was refused Schultz indicated that he would have the matter dealt with himself. On 23 October 1935 just after 10 p.m., Schultz was shot in the men's lavatory of the Palace Chop House and Tavern in Newark, New Jersey. Though, true to his metier, he did not name his killers before he died two days later, they were in fact Charles 'The Big' Workman, and Mendy Weiss. They had also shot three men – including Schultz's mathematical genius, Otto 'Abbadabba' Berman – who were sitting at a table waiting for their master to return.[2] In the ensuing panic Weiss and another man abandoned Workman, leaving him to find his own way back to Manhattan.[3]

It was not until five years later that Osnato, through a series

2 Berman's greatest contribution to life in general and Schultz in particular was when he worked out a way to fix the numbers game, a lottery which paid out on the numbers of winning horses at a race meeting, so beloved of both the public and organised crime. He was said to earn $10,000 a week from Schultz.

3 Workman was eventually arraigned for the murder of Schultz. He had not been picked out on an identification parade by eye-witnesses at the Palace Chop House but his alibi was a thin one involving working at a funeral parlour at the time of the killing. Under cross-examination his 'employer' admitted perjury and Workman entered a plea of *non vult* which saved him from the electric chair. He was sentenced to twenty-three years imprisonment and after a life as a model prisoner was released on 10 March 1964. He is said to have been not displeased that Mendy Weiss who had abandoned him was in fact sentenced to death and executed for the killing of Schultz.

of informers, reached the high level of Abe 'Kid Twist' Reles who in turn began to inform on his colleagues and superiors. Although Reles had been arrested some forty-two times over the previous sixteen years, he had served only short prison sentences and his position in society was unknown to the police. Now he was charged with robbery, the possession of narcotics and six further charges linked to murder. He feared, probably correctly, that some of those arrested with him, including Frank Abbandando, might endeavour to arrange a deal by informing on him and, so to speak, he had the first drop on them. The police were able to clear up some forty-nine killings in Brooklyn alone. He named Abbandando and Workman in the killing of Dutch Schultz, and his evidence was in a large part responsible for the conviction of Reles' superior, Louis Lepke Buchalter, and Mendy Weiss for the murder of Joseph Rosen.

For a year Reles – like so many subsequent informers – was held in protective custody. His safe home was the sixth floor of the Half Moon Hotel on Coney Island, New York, where he was kept under constant surveillance by six uniformed police officers. It was from there that he travelled to the New York courts to give his evidence. On 12 November 1941 he fell from the window of his room, landing on the pavement, and was killed. There have been a number of disparate suggestions as to how he came to be 'the canary who could not fly'. One of the more ingenious is that he was playing a practical joke climbing out of the window on knotted bedsheets and then running back upstairs to frighten the guards outside his room. Another is that he committed suicide. To do this he must have lowered himself to the third floor and then jumped; as his body was found twenty feet out into the street, this seems unlikely.

The much more plausible account is that it was a gangland hit. At the time, Reles was due to testify against Albert Anastasia who was on trial for the killing of waterfront labour leader, Peter Panto. After Reles' death the case against Anastasia was dropped, and although it was re-opened in 1951 no progress was made. He was also due to give evidence against 'Bugsy'

Siegel. Charles 'Lucky' Luciano was later to say that the killing had been done by police officers who had thrown Reles from his room and that the contract price had been $50,000. Later, Meyer Lansky said the fee paid had been $100,000. Even so, it was money well spent. There is also some evidence that Reles' confessions were being used not simply to obtain convictions against organised crime figures but to blackmail them.[4]

The first and one of the most successful of great post-war Mafia informers was Joe Valachi. Described in 1964 by the then Attorney General, Robert F.Kennedy, as the 'biggest single intelligence breakthrough yet in combating organised crime and racketeering in the United States', Valachi turned informer not because he feared prison – he was already serving a sentence – but because he feared being killed whilst in prison.

On 22 June 1962 at the US Penitentiary, Atlanta, Georgia, Joseph Michael Valachi, fifty-eight years old, 5 foot 6 tall and weighing 184 lbs and serving concurrent terms of fifteen and twenty years for drug-trafficking, had taken a 2-foot-long piece of piping and, running up behind another prisoner, Joe Saupp, had beaten him to death. Unfortunately he killed the wrong man. He had mistaken Saupp for a Joe Beck or DiPalermo whom he believed, probably correctly, that Vito Genovese – head of the Luciano crime family, who was himself in the same prison serving a sentence for drug-trafficking – had ordered to kill him.

Valachi now had considerable problems. Quite apart from the additional sentence he would face for the murder of Saupp, he

4 On 25 October 1957 Anastasia was shot to death whilst he sat in a barber's chair in the Park Sheraton hotel in New York. No one was charged, but the contract was believed to have been carried out on behalf of Don Vito Genovese. Charles Luciano was deported to Italy on 10 February 1946, from where he continued to exert considerable authority over crime in America. He died of a heart attack at Capodichino airport in Naples on 26 January 1962, having gone there to meet a film producer with a view to making a bio-pic of his life.

On 20 June 1947 Ben Siegel was shot dead in Beverly Hills at the home of his girlfriend and Mob bag-lady, Virginia Hill. One account, and probably the most likely, of his death is that it was authorised by Luciano and Lansky because Siegel had been stealing from Mob funds. On 15 January 1983, Lansky died following a heart attack at the age of eighty-three.

knew he was targeted by Genovese who had, falsely, been told
that Valachi was an informer. Valachi had survived attempts to
murder him before.

In American prisons there are basically three inmate methods
of killing a prisoner – poisoned food, an attack in the showers,
and being provoked into a fight in the prison yard in the
confusion of which he would be stabbed. All three had been tried
and failed. Valachi had known he was a marked man following
a conversation with Genovese, with whom he shared a cell.

One night in our cell Vito starts saying to me, 'You know,
we take a barrel of apples, and in this barrel of apples
there might be a bad apple. Well, this apple has to be
removed, and if it ain't removed, it would hurt the rest
of the apples.'

I tried to interrupt him when he was saying this, but he
waved at me to keep quiet. Finally I couldn't stand it no
more. 'If I done anything wrong,' I said, 'show it to me
and bring me the pills – meaning poison – and I will take
them in front of you.'

He said, 'Who said you done anything wrong?'

There wasn't anything I could say.

Then he said to me that we had known each other for a
long time, and he wanted to give me a kiss for old times'
sake. Okay, I said to myself, two can play this game. So I
grabbed Vito and kissed him back.

I went to my bed and Ralph, who was in the next bed,
mumbled, 'The kiss of death.' I pretended I didn't hear
him and just laid on my bed. But who could sleep?'[5]

Even before he killed Saupp, Valachi had applied to be put in
the hole or solitary confinement.[6] It was a request he could

5 Peter Maas, *The Valachi Papers*, p. 26. The phrase 'kiss of death' – which
comes from the betraying kiss given to Christ by Judas Iscariot – seems only to
have become really popular after the 1950s, possibly following the publication
of an American thriller of that name.
6 The English equivalent is known as Rule 43.

make but on which he could not insist. He stopped bathing and did not go for his meals. He made attempts to contact George Gaffney, then Deputy Director of the Bureau of Narcotics, but his messages were never sent. He also tried to get Thomas 'Three Fingers' Lucchese to intervene on his behalf; again his begging letter was never sent but was, apparently, returned to Valachi for re-writing so that the new draft might reveal why he had applied to be put in solitary confinement. Valachi refused to speak and so was returned to the general prison population. It was then that he attacked the unfortunate Saupp, who had no organised crime convictions and was merely serving a sentence for robbery and forgery.

Now he faced the death penalty from the State as well as a death penalty from his former associates. Valachi managed to get a message to Robert Morganthau saying that he wished to co-operate with the Federal Government. On 17 July he pleaded guilty to the non-capital offence of murder in the second degree and left the court with narcotics agent Frank Selvagi to go to Westchester County jail near New York where he was lodged as Joseph DeMarco. He was not immediately co-operative and grateful. He maintained he had been framed on his twenty-year sentence, and that this was the one which had led to his being wrongly identified as a snitch. Nevertheless he had to co-operate to some degree if he did not wish to be returned once more to the prison population where retribution would have been immediate. It must have been clear that by being allowed to make a plea to the lesser offence he was trying to strike – even if he had not actually yet struck – a deal. Such a man was far too dangerous to be allowed to survive.

It is probable, although with the gift of hindsight difficult to believe, that in the pre-Valachi days the American public knew little of the workings of organised crime. Indeed, those who doubt Valachi's testimony use as a stick with which to beat him the scarcely credible (to us) notion that before Valachi no one had heard the phrase *La Cosa Nostra*. Valachi said the term was used in house, so to speak, in preference to the Mafia. Robert Kennedy insisted that Valachi give public testimony for two reasons. The first was to obtain additional legislation – the authority to provide immunity to witnesses in racketeering investigations; and also the reform and revision of the wire-tapping law. The second, and just as important, was the need to drum up public support against organised crime.

> We have yet to exploit properly our most powerful asset in the battle against the rackets: an aroused, informed, and insistent public.[7]

Initially, however, there was public resistance to these measures and civil libertarians' opposition was not overcome until 1968.

Valachi gave lengthy testimony on the structure of organised crime in *La Cosa Nostra* with its family units which then controlled cities including Boston, Buffalo, Chicago, Cleveland, Detroit, Kansas City, Los Angeles, Newark, New Orleans, New York City, Philadelphia, Pittsburgh and San Francisco. He said that 'open cities' were Miami and Las Vegas and pre-Castro Havana. He went on to detail the structure of the Family with its *capo* or boss, the *sub-capo, caporegime* and soldiers, something with which we are now completely familiar since *The Godfather* was released twenty-five years ago. What he also revealed was the so-called Castellammarese War, a power struggle between Italian-American gangs during the early 1930s, ending with the purge by Lucky Luciano of the old brigade of Mustachio Petes. This is another stick with which Valachi has been beaten. He claimed that up to sixty killings had taken place during that nationwide war, but was able to name only a few.[8]

It may be that, in common with many informers, Valachi simply awarded himself a rather higher status in the criminal hierarchy than he actually deserved. After all, there were few

7 US Senate: 1963: 9.
8 Writers who tend to doubt Valachi's version of events include Jay Albanese, *Organised Crime in America*, Alan A. Block, *East Side – West Side: Organising Crime in New York 1930–1950*, and Humbert S. Nelli, *The Business of Crime: Italians and Syndicate Crime*.

at the time who could contradict him over minor details. *La Cosa Nostra* did not exist or, if by some mischance it did, then the persons he named had no part of it. As the years went by, however, and other Mafia supergrasses grew out of the weeds of Brooklyn, they were quick to play down Valachi's position in polite society. 'I'm only a two dollar bum, and Valachi is dirt under *my* feet,' said Jimmy Blue Eyes.[9]

Despite the apparent inconsistencies and lack of corroboration, the Sub-committee accepted Valachi's version of matters.

The Sub-committee wanted to hear what Valachi told them, and once he had satisfied their desire there was little need to be skeptical or press for additional, independent information. It was a case of the story being true because it sounded like what ought to be heard.[10]

In his autobiography, Joseph Bonanno wrote:

Valachi gave an interpretation to My Tradition that made it look cheap and totally criminal in operation. Because he never rose very high himself, Valachi mainly came in contact with the dregs of our society, our lowlife . . . Often he described historical events in which he never participated, but nonetheless inserted himself to make himself seem important to his gullible audience.[11]

Once he had completed his testimony before the Sub-committee, Valachi was allowed to write his memoirs with the author Peter Maas. He was eventually moved to La Tuna

9 Hank Messick, 'Gold Coaster filled shoes of Frank Costello' in *Miami Herald*, 20 December 1966. For once, a gangster was being modest. Vincent Alo, known as Jimmy Blue Eyes, was a long-standing high-ranking member of the hierarchy. At one time he was Meyer Lansky's partner in the Riviera Hotel, Havana. Supergrasses did like to boast with varying degree of licence. 'I was the next big-time Judas of the Underworld,' said O'Mahoney, *King Squealer*, p. 132.
10 Dwight C. Smith, *The Mafia Mystique*, p. 234.
11 Joseph Bonanno, *A Man of Honor*, p. 164.

Federal Correctional Institution at El Paso, Texas where he died on 3 April 1971. Those who believe in conspiracy theories will be heartened to know that it was widely believed that his death was a cover-up and, like that of Mark Twain, was 'greatly exaggerated' so that he could be released and hidden on the outside. If there was a cover-up then another informer, Vincent Teresa, was in on it. In his book he gives an account of the death of the old man, now riddled with cancer and troubled by the cold although in La Tuna the summer temperature could reach 110 degrees. According to Teresa, Valachi's body was claimed by a woman to whom he had been writing and was buried in a cemetery in Niagara Falls. There was no headstone in case it was desecrated by the Mob.[12]

Regarded as rather more important by criminologists is the testimony of Jimmy 'The Weasel' Fratianno, who turned informer at the age of forty-seven. He was born in Italy but his family went to Cleveland when he was four. He was credited with at least eleven gangland killings, rising to become head of the Los Angeles Mafia as a result not of his talent for murder but because he was a good businessman. After a second prison sentence imposed in 1970, he became an FBI informer and sang happily about the skimming of Las Vegas casinos and the Teamsters Pension Fund. By 1987 he had been instrumental in the conviction of six bosses and twenty-three lesser-ranked mobsters. He had a price of $250,000 on his head and was none too pleased when he was released back into general circulation. One compensation was the money he received as royalties from not one but two autobiographies, of which *The Last Mafioso* was the more successful.

Next to the plate was Vincent 'Fat Vinnie' Teresa. He was described by his co-author, in what some might see 'as a rubbish the opposition' passage, as

. . . no ordinary hoodlum. He is no Joseph Valachi, a

12 Vincent Teresa with Thomas C. Renner, *My Life in the Mafia*, p. 272.

low-level soldier in the Mob. He is not a petulant Salvatore
Bonanno, son of a crime boss, telling a disingenuous tale
of service to crime for his father's sake. Teresa was a top
Mafia thief, a mobster and at times a brutal enforcer, and
he dealt at the highest levels of organised crime. Had he
not been caught, had he not been double-crossed by those
he worked with and trusted, he would still be a powerful
and successful criminal.

Teresa, in three short years, has become the most single
effective and important informer the U.S. Government
has ever obtained. His testimony has convinced juries
from Florida to Massachusetts. He is responsible for the
indictment or conviction of more than fifty organised
crime figures including the Mob's biggest money-maker,
Meyer Lansky.[13]

Note the clever use of Lansky's name. Certainly, he was
indicted for tax evasion on Teresa's testimony but he was
acquitted.

By the time of his testimony against Lansky, Teresa was
wearing a false beard and moustache to conceal his series of
double chins. Again he was likely to overplay his hand for the
purpose of his readers. One of his remarks was of London's
Colony Club in the mid-60s that, 'You'd see royalty there every
night.' In fact it was a club under Kray protection, and in those
days at least royalty did not go to such places *every* night.
Amongst Teresa's other grandiose suggestions was that he kept
a bowl of piranha fish into which he would threaten to push
the hands of his debtors. His crucial evidence was that Lansky
had met him to receive cash on or about 17 May 1968 in the
Dupont Plaza Hotel. David Rosen, Lansky's counsel, who later
declined to write his biography, was able to show that Lansky
had been booked into a double room at the Sheraton Plaza,
Boston, from 7 May to 28 May with his wife, Teddy. There

13 *Ibid.* p. ix.

was a gap from 8 May to 19 May when Lansky was not there, and Mrs Lansky had renegotiated the room rate downwards to reflect his absence. The crucial witness, however, was a Harvard medical professor, Dr Seymour J. Gray, who had been in the theatre in the Peter Bent Brigham Hospital when there was an operation on Lansky on 10 May. He had also seen him a fortnight later when Lansky was weak and scarcely able to walk. It is always interesting to know how a jury votes, and apparently it was split 6–6 on the first ballot but soon swung round in Lansky's favour.

Just how important Teresa was, both as a Mafia figure and as an informer, is difficult to assess. According to his memoirs he was No. 3 in the New England Mafia. Through his evidence some fifty convictions were obtained and the price of $500,000 put on his head was very much more than the paltry $100,000 on that of Valachi. He turned state's witness because, he said, whilst in prison his one-time friends stole his money, failed to support his wife and threatened one of his children.

He was certainly discredited at the Lansky trial, after which he went into the Witness Protection Program under the name of Charles Cantino. Safely installed, he was able to continue with his life of crime, smuggling endangered birds into America and dealing in cocaine. In 1982 under that name he was jailed for five years in Seattle, and about the same time was sentenced to another ten years for mail fraud. He is reported to have died in February 1990.[14]

Since those early days the use of informers and witnesses has grown to that of a well-organised business. In 1970 it was estimated that between twenty-five and fifty witnesses would be inducted each year into the Program. They would be provided with a new birth certificate and social security number, and relocated far from the area in which they had testified. A subsistence allowance would be paid until the

14 *Seattle Times*, 9 August 1981, 23 September 1981 and 12 February 1982. *New York Times*, 25 February 1990. See also Robert Lacey, *Little Man*, pp. 376–8, 382–3.

witness could once more become self-supporting, preferably without returning or resorting to crime. The annual cost in 1970 was estimated to be $1 million.

This did not work out quite so economically as had been hoped. By 1983 more than 4,400 witnesses and double that number of family members had entered the Program. The game did, however, show satisfactory results. Analysing a sample of 220 cases in the period 1979–1980 in which witnesses who had entered the Program testified, 75 per cent of the defendants were found guilty. It is open to discussion whether there was the same success in subsequently keeping the witnesses out of the court as defendants. On average they had made 7.2 court appearances before they became witnesses, over half of which were for violent crimes, and after their stint their arrest record fell to an average of 1.8 with fewer than one-third of these offences being violent.

The problem with this particular statistic is that the witnesses' pre-Program criminal career averaged ten years, whilst only three and a half years in the programme was available for research purposes. There was still plenty of time for them to rack up more convictions. Recidivism was 21.4 per cent and the annual cost had risen to $25 million.

Far cheaper was running an informer or having an undercover police officer, but even this could damage the long term budget:

Jack is a well-dressed, middle-aged man, who although short on education is well-spoken. He has a way of drawing people into his engaging narratives and would make a perfect companion on a long train ride; he is warm, and in his own unpolished style, gentle. Jack is also a crook . . . Some years ago Jack got into a jam and, as he put it, 'made the decision to go with the Bureau'. In FBI parlance he is an informant, but he prefers to think of himself as a source. Whatever the title for the relationship, it has been a mutually beneficial one: he has helped the Bureau solve some sticky criminal cases, has made some money, and has stayed out of jail.[15]

One of the more interesting undercover agents used by the CIA and the FBI was Herb Itkin, who was known to the CIA under the code-name 'Poron' and as 'Mr Jerry' to the FBI. He was described by a member of the staff of United States Attorney Robert Morgenthau:

[Itkin is] the most valuable informer the FBI has ever had outside the espionage field. He never lies to us. His information has always been accurate.

The FBI said of him: 'He is probably the most important informer ever to come to the surface. He knew the younger up-and-coming characters in the *Cosa Nostra*.'

It is probably also correct that he left a trail of disaster behind him. Born in 1926, the son of working-class Jewish parents, Herbert Itkin was brought up in the Borough Park section of Brooklyn in what was then the middle-class area of 48th Street. His father had a series of small shops and, by accounts, was mild-mannered and ineffectual whilst his mother was the dominant personality. In 1944 he enlisted in the Army and was sent after VJ day to Japan with a field hospital unit. On his return with $2,000 savings he bought a luncheonette in Bush terminal, Brooklyn, and put it about that he had been a paratrooper attached to Army Intelligence. The luncheonette, where his parents worked, was not a success. According to one account, his father tripped and knocked his head on the gas-tap, turning it on. Itkin told a friend that, when his father did not come home from a Saturday late shift, he went to find him and revived the unconscious man just as the police arrived. In another, more heroic, version protection money was demanded by a Mafia enterprise. His father had resisted their blandishments and his

15 Sanford J. Unger, *FBI*, p. 450.

head was held in the gas-oven. Itkin had set out in revenge and confronted the leader, who told his henchmen to leave the boy alone because 'He has spunk.' Whichever version is correct, Itkin senior did not work in the luncheonette again; he spent some time in hospital and was then divorced.

Meanwhile Itkin junior went to law school, working during the day for a local firm Delson, Levin & Gordon, where his mother now had a position as a bookkeeper. He married Diana Kane, one of the firm's secretaries. He qualified in 1953, by which time he had moved to Hicksville, Long Island. He appears to have been worried that his Jewish name would hold him back in his career. Diana Kane recalled:

> Herbie wanted very badly not to marry a Jewish girl. He wanted a shiksa like me. Once he was going to change his name to something less Jewish and I told him, 'Herbie, you can make it wherever you want to go with your real name. Besides, your mother would have a heart attack. You have enough ambition and talent to overcome it.'

It was now that the web of deceit was spun. In 1957, Itkin left Delsons under something of a cloud because of complaints made to the Bar Association over client poaching. He had, he said, begun his CIA career with a retainer in 1954, the year after his marriage. His version of his recruitment is that it was conducted at the highest level, that of CIA Director, Allen Dulles, who had been impressed with information supplied by Itkin to Senator Joe McCarthy in the early 1950s.

This is not a version which was accepted by Federal officials, who place the date as 1962 as a result of a CIA man meeting Itkin by chance in the Madison Avenue offices he rented with other lawyers. Itkin, the official version goes, was recruited on a part-time unpaid basis because of his contacts in the Caribbean and Asia. The lawyer who had made the introduction became his control. There seems little doubt that his life as a spy was at least a two-way traffic, with Itkin trying to use his CIA connections to further his business interests. The Itkins moved out of Hickville and into the more fashionable resort of Oyster Bay. By now he was exhibiting signs of mild paranoia; he would only eat from tins opened by himself, and if hot meals were prepared for him they had to be tasted first. He began to borrow from friends and relations. There is a story that his father-in-law telephoned the CIA to ask if Itkin did work for them. 'If he does, don't believe anything he says,' he added and hung up. By 1969 Itkin was in debt to the tune of $600,000. On the plus side, however, he clearly did have knowledge of the Mafia and the Teamsters Union system of fund operating. He was turned over to the FBI in 1964.

On 18 January 1967 Itkin flew into London with Tony 'Ducks' Corallo and Tommy Mancuso, with a view to the latter buying into British gambling casinos which were starting to take off in a big way. The visit was also in relation to gaming machines which Corallo was placing in Britain with Dick Kaminitsky, known as Dick Duke. Corallo was refused entry to the United Kingdom and the mission aborted.[16]

What he was also doing was getting out of control and making money for himself without accounting to his handler. Worse, from everyone's point of view, he was boasting about his activities. Diana Kane said that: 'Herbie told just about everybody about the CIA and the FBI. He told some fellows he commuted on the train with.'

By the end of his career, Itkin, who had been involved with countless women and had now fallen in love with a divorcée, Scotty Hersch, was a liability. He was pulled off the street and into protective custody along with his first and second wives – Diana Kane had long been replaced – and their families. He was kept at a military post in New York where, said a Government official, he was allowed the use of the recreational facilities and

---

16 Kaminitsky was later killed. During his life, he had amassed three convictions for murder. It was alleged that the financing of Corallo's machines came from a company which was convicted in 1972 of having assisted Detroit crime figures to gain control of a casino in Las Vegas.

post exchange but was not allowed to buy liquor. In December 1967 he appeared in the first of the trials in which he was to give evidence. This led to the conviction of Tony Corallo, who received four and a half years, and Carmine De Sapio as well as James L. Marcus, the former city commissioner and confidant of Mayor Lindsay. Marcus received fifteen months.[17]

Although a major figure in dozens of pending cases and described by the FBI as 'risking his neck almost every day' and being praised for his 'reckless patriotism', Itkin was not without his critics. Manhattan District Attorney Frank S. Hogan was out for his blood. In the trial of De Sapio, which resulted in a conviction for conspiracy to bribe Marcus and to extort contracts from Consolidated Edison, the court heard that Itkin had kept large sums of money from swindles, bribes and kickbacks. Now Hogan wished to prosecute him. 'They would love to get me on a perjury conviction to destroy me and all my work,' said Itkin.

A representative of Hogan's office asked:

How could the Federal officials allow an informer to take that kind of money which was admittedly made from criminal deals and keep it? What do they think informers are? Some sort of bounty hunters?

Well, yes, really is the answer to that.

17 Tony 'Ducks' Corallo was a member of the Lucchese family and had a record of grand larceny and robbery dating back to 1929. In the McClellan Committee report into the Teamsters Union, he is said to have embezzled $69,000 by recording false names on the payroll. On 13 January 1987 he was sentenced to 100 years' imprisonment coupled with a fine for participating in co-ordinating coast-to-coast criminal activities.

6

Ireland

Both the history and the literature of Ireland and the Troubles have been studded with the use by the English of informers. The dishonourable tradition goes back to 1641 when Owen O'Connally informed on the Irish rebels, Lord Maguire and Colonel McMahon, who were taken to London and hanged on Tyburn Hill. O'Connally's reward was cash and an annuity, but he does not seem to have lived long enough to gain much benefit and was killed two years later. He was but the first in a long line of informers. The next crop grew up at the time of the Irish Rebellion of 1798 – Captain Armstrong (who over a period of sixty years as an informer was paid some £30,000 by the government), Frederick Dutton, Leonard McNally (who wrote *Sweet Lass of Richmond Hill* and was said to be the meanest and most mercenary of the tribe), Thomas Reynolds (who was said to be totally despicable and to have robbed his own mother) and Samuel Turner are the better-known ones, but there were others including Dr Conlan of Dundalk, James Hughes in Belfast and Edward Newell of Downpatrick. As a result of their efforts:

> The prisons were crowded with persons denounced by those infamous informers, Armstrong and Reynolds, Dutton and Newell, with a list of subordinate villains acting under the direction of police agents, themselves

steeped deeper in iniquity than the perjured wretches they suborned . . . Numbers, innocent in most cases, through the instrumentality of those bad men, were brought hourly to the scaffold.[1]

It is often assumed that the most damage to the cause was done by Leonard McNally, but in *Secret Service under Pitt*, W. J. Fitzpatrick suggests that a lawyer from Newry, Samuel Turner, was the most dangerous and treacherous. Financed by Pitt, he kept the British government well informed on the activities of the Republican leaders. It is thought that he was responsible for the execution of Father Quigley, arrested at Maidstone on his way to France. The priest was said to be carrying incriminating documents and was offered the opportunity to save himself by turning informer, but he declined the privilege and was hanged at Peneden Heath on 7 June 1798.

Turner seems to have managed to live his double life unsuspected by the United Irishmen. He was killed in a duel in the Isle of Man in 1821 after living in his house, Turner's Glen, quite happily for the period following the rebellion. Edward Newell was apparently responsible for the arrest of nearly 230 men, and for another 300 being obliged to flee from their homes.

The stories of the early use of informers in Ireland follow the pattern of many in England and the United States. A person with an unpleasant, even trifling, secret is caught and is leaned on sufficiently heavily to persuade him to turn against his colleagues. One such was John Joseph Corydon, who was born in Liverpool's dockland and became 'the most fatal and dangerous enemy of the Fenians'. It seems he had been caught with a prostitute and allowed to go free provided he turned informer.

Sometimes the efforts to buy witnesses and informers failed;

1 W. H. Maxwell, *History of the Irish Rebellion of 1798*.

bluffs were called and exposed. Richard Piggott, a journalist, sold (for the sum of £500) forged letters to *The Times* purporting to link Charles Parnell, the Irish statesman, to the Phoenix Park murders. It was part of a plot to defeat the growing campaign for Home Rule. *The Times* sent agents to the United States offering Fenians money to come to London to testify against Parnell. An allegation that one agent offered a Patrick Sheridan £20,000 to return to England, and that Sheridan agreed to do so only to expose the plot when he arrived, was the subject of a libel action by the officer and was settled out of court. The Parnell Commission inquiry into the allegations by *The Times* followed.

The murders of Lord Frederick Cavendish and the Under-Secretary Thomas Burke took place in Phoenix Park, Dublin, on 6 May 1882. Whilst out for an evening stroll at about 6 p.m. they were attacked by four men, led by Joseph Brady, wielding long knives. The attack was witnessed by a number of people, but few were forthcoming to give evidence. Their tongues were loosened by the Severe Crimes Act 1882, which enabled magistrates to hold secret inquiries, and it transpired that the assassination had been carried out by a recently formed group, the Invincibles. It appears there was an overall commander and a council of four including James Carey, a member of the Dublin City Corporation.

Informers also abounded in the case. The police had been helped by a man called Lamie who had led them to a taxi-driver, Kavanagh, who in turn became an informer and told how he had driven Joseph Brady, Timothy Kelly and Patrick Delaney to Phoenix Park, where Carey was waiting and gave the signal for the attack by waving a white handkerchief. The men were then driven back to Dublin.

At the preliminary proceedings on 15 February 1883 Carey, who would appear to have been the ringleader, turned Queen's Evidence to save himself. He was held in custody in Kilmainham Jail, Dublin, until after the trial in April, and then in the July was sent to South Africa to join his family.

He did not survive the journey and was shot by a passenger, O'Donnell, as the ship was nearing Capetown. It is not clear whether he had followed Carey from Ireland or had simply heard that the informer was on board; it may be that he was shot in a personal quarrel. O'Donnell was returned to England and was hanged later that year.

The conspirators were hanged at various times during May and June 1883 at Kilmainham Jail by William Marwood who travelled to Dublin to execute them.[2]

Long-term undercover agents seem to have abounded. Apart from the lawyer Samuel Turner there was also Major Henri le Caron (also known as Thomas Beach), a French doctor with apparently Republican sympathies. A witness to *The Times* inquiry, he was the doctor to a number of Fenians who used him to carry messages to London, Paris and Dublin. These reached their destination, but copies also reached London. It was the good doctor who was able to give both the British and Canadian governments details of the plot to invade Canada. It does not seem to have been a particularly well-thought-out plot, since at the time the Fenians had only one field gun which the doctor was himself able to spike. For his efforts he received £50 from the British Government and the rather more substantial tribute of £500 from the Canadian one.

On Tuesday morning the 5th February 1889, the curtain was rung up, and throwing aside the mask for ever, I

---

2 When Marwood died suddenly on 4 September 1883 it was rumoured, but never substantiated, that he had been poisoned as retribution for his work as the executioner of the Invincibles and other Irishmen.

On 8 July 1882 Allan Pinkerton, head of the American detective agency, wrote to Gladstone after the Phoenix Park murders recommending him to do away with informers and to eschew rewards 'as I consider them as incentives to crime'. [HO 144/1537/4.] It was an attitude shared by the detectives of the day. 'I have to confess,' wrote John Littlechild in his memoirs (p. 96), 'that the "nark" is very apt to drift into an agent provocateur in his anxiety to secure a conviction, and therefore he requires to be carefully watched.' With a deal of chauvinism George Greenham in his memoirs (p. 61) was also aware of the problem, writing how easy it was for a detective to be deceived by a 'voluntary informer', especially foreigners with shady surroundings.

stepped into the witness box and came out in my true colours, as an Englishman, proud of his country, and in no sense ashamed of his record in her service.[3]

He was given a house and an annuity by *The Times* and is an early example of the witness protection scheme. After his revelations he was guarded day and night and moved about the country until he died on 1 April 1894. He was then fifty-two, and had apparently been living in terror of being poisoned for the past five years. As with so many deaths of this type, there were rumours that he had simply been spirited away by the authorities to go to live abroad. The date of his death may have had something to do with the story. On the other hand, *Reynold's Newspaper* on 8 April 1894 suggested 'the famous spy is now on his way to one of the most distant colonies'. The next year the same paper reported on 23 June that he had been seen 'in the halfpenny omnibus that plies between the Strand and Waterloo'.

The rise of the modern informer in Irish political and criminal history can be dated fairly accurately. It began with the escalation in sectarian street violence in the late 1960s, and escalated throughout the next few years until in August 1971 internment was added by Stormont to the list of penalties and sanctions open to courts and police. Six months later, with the British Government attempting to take direct control of the situation, Lord Diplock was invited to chair an inquiry into 'whether changes should be made in the administration of justice in order to deal more effectively with terrorism without using internment'. Two years later his recommendations were the substance of the Northern Ireland (Emergency Provisions) Act 1973. The Act withdrew the right of jury trial, establishing in its place single judge courts, extended the rights of the police and the army over stop and search and placed emphasis on accepting confession evidence. By 1975 internment had been

3 'Henri le Caron', *Twenty-five years in the Secret Service: The Recollections of a Spy.*

phased out and in its place came pressure on the police to obtain confessions of crime from suspects. The result was not unexpected; a steady stream of complaints about the physical abuse of detainees followed. Eventually the practices were exposed by Amnesty International and, four years later, the Bennett Inquiry indicated that there should be rights of access to a solicitor and a closed-circuit television system to monitor interviews as well as notice of his rights given to a suspect.

At this time there was a series of appalling sectarian murders in the Shankhill Road area, where a gang known as the Shankhill Butchers operated and where at least twenty-four people, almost all Roman Catholics, were hacked to death in north and west Belfast.

As the police in purely criminal matters have found since the implementation of the Police and Criminal Evidence Act 1984, with a monitoring of the interview and access to a solicitor the suspect tends to confess rather less frequently. By the early 1980s a supergrass system was in place. Not only would informers – 'converted terrorists' as they were described by Sir John Hermon, the Chief Constable of the RUC – be used as intelligence gatherers, they would also be used to give evidence in high profile trials, particularly against Republicans. In the two years from November 1981 seven (and possibly more) Loyalist and eighteen Republican supergrasses were used in the arrest of nearly 600 suspects in Northern Ireland.

> It is arguable that this was a direct result of the difficulty which the police encountered in obtaining confessions after the introduction of the Bennett reforms in interrogation procedures. This has resulted in large numbers of IRA and INLA suspects being held on remand, many as a result of the short-circuiting of the normal committal procedures by reliance on the *ex parte* procedure for initiating an indictment.[4]

4 Tom Hadden, a lecturer in law at Queen's University, Belfast, in *Submission to the Review of Northern Ireland (Emergency Provisions) Act 1978.*

Essentially the rules under which the supergrass had to play were twofold. Immunity would only apply to offences to which the supergrass had admitted, but would not be granted to the actual killer.

The statistics of what happened next make for interesting reading. Fifteen of the supergrasses sooner or later retracted their evidence and in the case of a UDA informer, James Williamson, charges were withdrawn against all but two who had been unfortunate enough to make confessions. In the ten trials which did take place, 120 out of 217 defendants (55 per cent) pleaded guilty or were convicted. In five cases appeals were lodged and in them, 67 out of 74 convictions were quashed. The overall conviction rate, confirmed on appeal, stands at 44 per cent.

At first, as with the English courts in purely criminal cases, there was a high conviction rate. Whether this was bolstered by the absence of a jury is difficult to tell; after all, it was juries who convicted in the English cases. Up until November 1983 supergrasses were in the ascendant and, with Joseph Bennett, Christopher Black and Kevin McGrady on the stand on behalf of the Crown, 88 per cent of the accused were convicted – 61 per cent on the uncorroborated evidence of the grass. Things went downhill for the authorities after that, however. The Jackie Grimley case was perhaps the turning point and in the trials which featured him, John Moran, Robert Quigley, Raymond Gilmour, James Crockard, William 'Budgie' Allen and Harry Kirkpatrick, only in the Quigley and Kirkpatrick cases were there convictions on the uncorroborated word of the supergrass.

It would appear at first that the judges who heard the supergrass cases were prepared to accept the word of the sinner who had repented. In the Christopher Black case Mr Justice Kelly returned a verdict of guilty when Black had admitted perjury in a case previously before Kelly.

In December 1982 the trial began of thirty-eight defendants, including five women of whom one was a seventy-one-year-old widow. The 184 counts in the indictment included allegations of murder, attempted murder, possession of firearms and membership of the Provisional IRA. It ran until the following August, occupying 117 days of court time. Some 550 witnesses were called, amongst them – indeed the principal one – Christopher Black.

Black was himself a member of the Provisional IRA which he had joined in 1975. That year he was caught in a robbery, and the following March sentenced to ten years' imprisonment. On his release at the end of 1980 he rejoined the Ardoyne-Oldpark division. He did not last long on the outside, being caught as a member of a road-block set up by the IRA as a publicity stunt the following November.

As with so many informers, Black was terrified by the thought of another long stretch in prison. Now he had a young family and he was vulnerable. When he approached the RUC to offer his services, they were quite happy. If he gave evidence, he was to have immunity from prosecution for crimes to which he had confessed, a new identity and a safe home for himself and family in an English-speaking country of his choice.

He was an impressive witness, standing up to rigorous cross-examination. Judge Kelly was impressed, saying Black was one of the most convincing witnesses he had heard. Thirty-five of the thirty-eight were found guilty. Black was reported to have been given £127,000 and re-settled abroad, where the IRA was said to be conducting an active search for him.

As with non-political supergrasses, a dose of Christianity helps the political ones as well. Kevin McGrady became a born-again Christian and decided his conscience required him to assist the RUC. His background was slightly different from that of his fellow informers. For a start, before he joined the IRA and while working as an apprentice butcher, he had no criminal record. His brothers, Sean and Michael, had been interned without trial and this, said McGrady, was a principal reason for joining the IRA. When he gave evidence at the trial of John Gibney and nine others in September 1983, he stated that he had been the driver when George Rodger Duff was shot in the legs in July 1975. He had been arrested over the murder of Ernest Dowds two months later, but there was no evidence against him and he only received three months for assaulting a police officer. After his release he had worked for eighteen months as a butcher in London and had then drifted to Amsterdam, where he became involved in two fundamental Christian organisations, Youth with a Mission and Salvation for the People. It was now that he became a born-again Christian. He had, he said, been told by his spiritual adviser, Floyd McClung, that he could only clear his conscience by returning to Northern Ireland and making a clean breast of things. This he did in January 1982. His spiritual redemption earned him a life sentence for the murders in which he had taken part and, from his cell in the informers' annexe of the Crumlin Road prison, he became a Crown witness. Despite the fact that McGrady's evidence was described by the trial judge, Lord Lowry, as being 'contradictory, bizarre and in some respects incredible', not all the charges against Gibney were dismissed. Seventeen were but he was, however, found guilty of wounding and being a member of the IRA. He was sentenced to twelve years in prison.

One of the other reasons McGrady gave for his return to Northern Ireland was his desire to clear the name of his brother, Sean, whom had he said been wrongly convicted of the murder of Ernest Dowds. The Court of Appeal, however, was having none of it. The appeal was dismissed on 6 April 1984, with Kevin McGrady's evidence being described as 'quite unpersuasive and incredible'.

Meanwhile, in January 1982, the Provisional IRA had offered an amnesty to all informers who, within two weeks, were prepared to reveal what arrangements they had had with the RUC. They also had to undertake to sever their contacts. A pamphlet put out by Sinn Fein claimed that the RUC was now offering informers 'protective custody, huge sums of money and immunity from prosecution'.

It was about that time that Thomas Charles McCormick,

a detective-sergeant in the Special Branch of the RUC, fell foul of Anthony O'Doherty, an informer whom he had been handling for several years. They drank and ate together, travelled over County Antrim in unmarked police cars, and O'Doherty was provided with money and clothes. This was, believed McCormick, part of the handler's job. It must have been repulsive to him to have to spend so much time in the close company of a man who at the age of seventeen had been convicted of housebreaking, and by the time he appeared in court on 29 October 1981 pleaded guilty to forty-seven charges, including three attempts to murder policemen, and a number of attempts to blackmail bank managers, one of whom under a death threat had travelled to Cushendall to hand over £8,000. He now informed on his handler.

McCormick had met O'Doherty in August 1969 when he was selling the Republican newspaper the *United Irishman* and McCormick was there to pick up information. O'Doherty was arrested in an internment round-up and by then, if not before, he had become an RUC agent. For the next two years he was in weekly contact with the RUC, who appear to have provided him with survival training and, according to his evidence, with a Sten gun, a .303 rifle and a pistol.

The Crown's case was twofold. First, the robberies on banks and post offices about which O'Doherty had grassed and implicated McCormick were carried out because they were short of funds. Second, attacks on the security forces were a blind to deceive the IRA. Sergeant P. J. Campbell, who was killed in February 1977, had been murdered because he knew or suspected McCormick and O'Doherty were responsible for a series of robberies. McCormick's defence was that O'Doherty's evidence was a pack of lies, and that it was being said to discredit the RUC. It was accepted that he was short of money.

Desmond Boal QC, who appeared for McCormick and who described O'Doherty as 'a killer, a liar, a hypocrite, a play-actor, a devious and plausible villain, a maker of bargains with the police and a person of considerable intellectual dexterity which he frequently used to attribute to other people crimes which he himself had committed or in which he had been involved', argued that the man had been schooled in his evidence after dozens of visits by the police during the time he was in custody. The judge accepted that such police action was open to criticism but pronounced himself 'wholly satisfied that no injustice of any kind had resulted from it'. He dismissed all but three of the charges on the basis that he was not satisfied beyond reasonable doubt, and then on the remaining three sentenced McCormick to twenty years on a charge of armed robbery, with lesser sentences for hi-jacking motor cars and possessing a rifle.

The Court of Appeal looked at things in a different way. True, McCormick was tight for cash at the time, but that was not proof that he had helped O'Doherty rob a bank. The fact that a hand grenade had been given by him to O'Doherty did not prove he intended it should be used in bank robberies. Meeting O'Doherty in Portaglenone shortly before the hi-jacking of the motor cars did not prove O'Doherty's allegation that he had been involved. It was thought that the corroborative evidence, without which the trial judge would have acquitted, did not add up to anything. On 12 January 1984 Thomas Charles McCormick had his conviction quashed.

On 22 August 1984 James Prior, then Secretary of State for Northern Ireland, announced that he had recommended the Royal prerogative to remit eight years from the eighteen-year sentence imposed on O'Doherty. This meant that he would be released in 1985. The *Sunday World* suggested that this act of clemency was 'a publicity move aimed at stopping further loss of morale' among informers and ensuring that they knew the government would live up to its side of the bargain.

The virtual collapse of the supergrass system in Northern Ireland came with what was meant to be the evidence of forty-year-old John 'Jackie' Grimley, who was an RUC agent inside the INLA. He seems to have been a minor member of Sinn Fein, from which organisation he was expelled for 'irrational behaviour'. His political activities appear in the main to have been shouting slogans, carrying flags, and the like. His expulsion came after calling a crowd in a Sinn Fein social club in Craigavon 'fucking cunts'. He had also appeared hooded in the Tullygally Tavern in Craigavon and read out a spurious proclamation about theft and sexual violence in the area. After his expulsion he joined the INLA, where his role seems to have been slightly more important. He was deputed to perform robberies, hi-jacking a bus – including shooting the driver in the face when he tried to resist – knee-cappings and to murder a sergeant in the UDR or his brother, a politician. In the event no opportunity presented itself. He informed on twenty-one men and one girl who appeared in the Belfast Crown Court on 9 November 1983. The charges were possessing firearms, murder, and being members of the INLA. A diary of the trial reads:

Thursday 10 November: An application by Grimley to have his identity concealed and to be referred to as Witness A. The defence lawyers continued to call him Grimley. Grimley said he was a truthful person and had committed no other crimes except those with which he had been charged.

Friday 11 November: Desmond Boal QC leading for the defence forced him to admit to crimes which he had not mentioned the day before and to being an exhibitionist, a perjurer, a habitual drinker, given to acts of violence, having spent six months in a psychiatric hospital and manipulating people. The trial was adjourned.

Monday 14 November: Grimley admitted that he had the facility to make people (those in authority over him) believe his lies when he had to get out of an unacceptable situation. For example, he faked suicide twice to get out of the army and succeeded both times. Grimley also told the judge, 'I'm telling some lies, I admit' and admitted that, had he been brought to court for INLA membership before, he would have perjured himself to avoid jail. 'How is the court to know whether you are again perjuring yourself in return for immunity from prosecution?' asked Boal.

Tuesday 15 November: The trial was adjourned because Grimley said he was 'very tired, physically and mentally tired'.

Tuesday 22 November: The trial resumed. Grimley said that the RUC had given him a 'free hand' to carry out crimes and he acknowledged that they had put names to him, including those of a number of people in the dock on his uncorroborated evidence, who they believed were active in the INLA and wanted to implicate in terrorist activities.

Wednesday 23 November: Judge Gibson threw out all the charges against those who were on trial on Grimley's uncorroborated evidence.[5]

Grimley had also admitted being paid £25 for each nugget of information he supplied to the RUC. When such information was scarce, he had invented it. He had a record of more than forty criminal offences including fraud, perjury and theft. He said that Special Branch men were blackmailing him over a sexual offence he had committed in the bushes near the Tullygally tavern.

From 1983 to 1987 only two new supergrasses surfaced, and they did not last long. Eamonn Collins withdrew his evidence in March 1985, and the Director of Public Prosecutions dropped the charges of those implicated by Angela Whorisky. This did not mean there was no accomplice evidence, but in the years 1983–1985 it was used in only 12 per cent of the Diplock court cases.

The system had its critics. Father Denis Faul and Father Raymond Murray, two Catholic priests who have monitored

5 Sean Delaney, 'Ups and Downs for RUC's Perjurer Strategy' in *Iris*, p. 15. I am indebted to Dominque Harvie for her permission to quote extensively from her unpublished MA thesis, *The Use of Supergrasses in Northern Ireland*.

political trials in Northern Ireland, added their weight to the criticism directed against supergrass evidence.

> [informers] . . . have a unique opportunity to pay off old scores . . . they can name persons they have fought with . . . persons whose businesses they covet or wish to ruin . . . with whose wife they have had an affair or wish to have an affair . . . they are held incommunicado from relatives and friends and can be carefully rehearsed for many months to make their evidence more credible.[6]

In *The Informers*, his analysis of the supergrass trials in Northern Ireland, Andrew Boyd looks at the methods of their recruitment by the RUC. Quoting sources of a number of priests, such as Father Pat Buckley of Kileel, he says that there was a good deal of harassment of young people in that area, while Father Denis Faul told the *Irish Times* that the police trawled the prisons for likely informers, picking on men who appeared to be weak and vulnerable. There were also allegations that, apart from pressure, regular payments were made for young people to act as spies for the RUC.

The life of a supergrass in Northern Ireland was, however, much more dangerous that that of his English counterpart. Proof was not necessarily required for a suspected informer to be killed. When Thomas McGeary was blown up in his Mercedes on 29 April 1984, an organisation called the Irish Freedom Fighters said he had been killed because he was collaborating with the RUC. No further proof was deemed necessary, nor was it forthcoming. Brian McNally died some two months later, his body being found on the road near the border of the Republic and South Armagh. He was said to have become an informer for the RUC after being detained in Gough Barracks, Armagh. It seems he had benefited from the amnesty offered. He was de-briefed and all was forgiven if not forgotten

6 A. Boyd, *The Informers*, p. 31.

but, it was said, he had informed once more which had led to an arrest and the capture of an arms dump. He had received £25 a week and the offer of a free holiday in Spain before he was killed.

The life of a supergrass seems to have been much the same as it was in England: hotels, a home provided and a good allowance for expenses. Captive supergrasses were provided with saunas, squash-courts, alcohol, and facilities for sex sessions with visiting girlfriends.[7]

From around 1983, apart from the lack of new supergrasses there was a marked reluctance for informers to go through with giving evidence based on their confessions. By 1984 the judges – who had been accepting the evidence of supergrasses as something approaching gospel, even if they were caught out – began to have serious doubts.[8] In August 1984 Lord Lowry dismissed the evidence of supergrass Raymond Gilmour as 'entirely unworthy of belief' and stopped the trial against the accused, saying it would be an 'abuse of the criminal process'. On 24 December 1984 the appeals were allowed of all those convicted on Joseph Bennett's evidence.

But even if there had been a considerable running-down in the use of the supergrass since the great days of the early 1980s, perhaps he still had a useful role to perform for the authorities. On 22 December 1994 five Ulster Loyalists were jailed for life for the sectarian murder of a Catholic mother of two who had her throat slashed open to the spine. Thought to be an informer, she had been lured from a local football supporters' club to the bedroom of Samuel Cooke's home in East Belfast. Three of the five men were recommended to serve at least twenty-five years and as they were sentenced shouted to the judge that he had convicted innocent men on the word of a supergrass.[9]

7 *Sunday World*, 16 October 1983.
8 One example of a witness caught out was Robert Quigley, who substituted the name Terence Kelly instead of Michael Doherty as the man who had accompanied him on his unlawful expeditions. (Northern Irish barrister Philip McGee, speaking at the Forum Hotel in a meeting with the clergy, 3 April 1994.) It made no difference – the men were convicted.
9 *Scottish Daily Record*, 23 December 1994.

With what it is to be hoped is the end of the conflict in Northern Ireland, it is unlikely that the supergrass system will flourish there in political trials in the foreseeable future. There is, however, a new scenario. It is reported that former Provos and IRA soldiers are now turning to organised crime *per se*. No doubt if the trend is confirmed we may see the rise of the purely criminal supergrass in Northern Ireland. It may be, however, that some lessons over their use have been learned.

7

A Cautionary Tale

The story of Paul Fisher, a medium- to high-grade northern criminal, is a good example of how the supergrass system in England has worked in theory but not necessarily in practice and of the wheeling and dealing which took place, hindered from time to time by the judicial system.

In December 1982 a burglary was reported to the South Yorkshire police. It was one in which over £1.2 million of ferro alloys were stolen from a specialist steel manufacturing firm at Stocksbridge. The report developed into a huge and complicated inquiry into a massive fraud on Napier Steel, an Oughtibridge subsidiary of Sheffield Twist Drill, which lost over £1.7 million. As a result of the investigation over fifty people, including senior management personnel of both Yorkshire-based and international companies, were arrested and eighteen charged with a variety of offences ranging from conspiracy, corruption, arson and burglary to fraud. Two people were also shot.

The first shooting, which actually occurred in November 1981 before the burglary, was in the Derbyshire police force area, when a man named Elkington was attacked. He was a company official who had been bringing – or at least, trying to bring – some pressure to bear over the alloy frauds which preceded the burglary. The second shooting was of Arthur

Davies, the brother-in-law of a South Yorkshire scrap-metal dealer, which occurred on 9 January 1983, by which time the police were making progress in their metal inquiries. Almost certainly the reason behind the shooting of Mr Davies was either to silence him or as a warning to his friends and associates.

Davies left a public house in the east end of Sheffield and, driving a pick-up truck towards Rotherham, was followed by Fisher and a colleague Barrie Walker. As they drew alongside him Fisher fired a 12-bore shotgun into the cab, missing Davies' head but badly injuring his right hand. So far as the police were concerned it was a question of a round-up of the usual suspects, and Fisher and Walker were pulled in. Both admitted the shooting but neither would say who had contracted them. Now the wheeling and dealing with Fisher began.

On 4 May 1983, whilst he was on remand in Armley prison, Leeds, he was visited by senior officers who were convinced that the shooting of Davies was linked not only to the alloy frauds but also to the attack on Elkington. There was no thought in their minds that he had been involved in the Elkington shooting, but rather that he might now be prepared to give some information. Fisher, quite independently, had himself asked to see the police; it was then that he indicated he could give further information about the shooting of Davies. He also went on to say that he had taken part in a mock burglary of a public house for insurance purposes, and that he could and would name a police officer whom he claimed was corrupt. Now he wanted guarantees and a promise that he would be looked after. In return he said he was prepared to offer a good deal of information about Yorkshire crime and criminals, in particular violent ones.

Not surprisingly, Fisher had heard of what the police delicately called Resident Police Informers and clearly had in mind the possibility of becoming a supergrass. He was, it seems, told that subject to the approval of the Director of Public Prosecutions he might qualify, and that a new identity and address would be provided for him. Not surprisingly, the police wanted to hear something worthwhile before they put his case to the DPP. Matters were left in the air, with Fisher saying that he wished first to speak with his solicitor.

By 10 June when he was seen again, this time with his solicitor present, Fisher was convinced he had been promised immunity and a fresh identity, an idea of which he was swiftly disabused. It was made clear that the only time he would get immunity was with the approval of the DPP and that first he, Fisher, had to decide to supply the information in writing and agree to give evidence. Nor was there any change for Fisher in his suggestion that the *s*. 18 Offences Against the Person Act 1861 charge of wounding Davies (which carried life imprisonment) could be whittled down to a *s*. 20 OAPA offence which attracted a maximum of five years. Some of the police thought he was doing well not to be charged with attempted murder in the first place. Stalemate had been reached and Fisher decided not to proceed with the negotiations.

His trial at Doncaster Crown Court on 15 July was not a successful one from his point of view. Apparently given a short time to reconsider his position before he was sentenced, he failed to take heed and received eight years. Walker went down for five. On 20 July the police were back seeing him again in Leeds prison. Fisher had lodged an appeal and the length of his sentence was sinking in. Would the police help in his appeal if he gave the name of his employer for the Davies' shooting? He was nothing if not a trier. What about residency status? As for the first, the answer was that any help he gave would be mentioned to the Court of Appeal. As for the second, he had really burned his boats. In the experience of the police the Director had only been gracious enough to accord that status to the unconvicted. But there was at least one crumb of comfort still on the table, in that the DPP might agree that any other offence to which Fisher cared to admit might be written off. But he had to commit himself first. He hummed and hawed and eventually named Colin Widdowson as his contractor. He also went on to give at least some details of his own previous criminal activities, but sensibly he would put nothing in writing until he was moved from Leeds. Arrangements were made for him to be transferred to Liverpool in the next few weeks.

Whilst the police were speaking with Fisher, a message came that he had a domestic visit from his girlfriend Jenny.[1] He said that she would co-operate, and after her visit to him the police saw both her and another woman who told them Fisher had indeed said they were to help them. The police took Jenny back to Sheffield and learned that she was seeing Widdowson regularly, and that he had deposited some jewellery worth £5,000 as security for payment of the contract. The jewellery was recovered from the house of a third party. Sadly, Fisher seems to have been short-changed; the jewellery was found to be worth only half the amount he thought.

Now the police encouraged Jenny to continue to see Widdowson, surveilling the meetings and obtaining the money handed over. She was fitted with a tape-recorder. Keeping their part of the agreement, the police went to see a member of the staff of the Director of Public Prosecutions. The outcome was clear. There was to be no residential status for Fisher, but if a statement was taken, although he would not be granted immunity it was more than likely that no further proceedings would be instituted against him – if for no other reason than because of the eight years he was already serving.

In August and September Fisher made lengthy confessions about his involvement with Widdowson and other Yorkshire criminals. It was accepted that without his co-operation and that of his girlfriend there would be no real prospects of a successful prosecution of Widdowson. The police agreed that if the court permitted it an officer would tell the Court of Appeal about his help. It was now that, from everyone's point of view, things started to go wrong. The police wrote to the court and the DPP telling of Fisher's help. Fisher's application to a single judge for leave to appeal against his sentence was refused and, worse, the

1 A pseudonym.

various parties learned of this only through a piece in the local newspaper. The police went to see him to try to reassure him that so far as they were concerned there was no going back on the arrangements; they would, they said, be telling the full Court of Appeal about his assistance.[2] In any event there would be help after his release to re-settle both him and his girlfriend.

Fisher continued to show a measure of good faith. He persuaded another prisoner to turn Queen's Evidence and this man was granted residential status by the DPP, something which rankled badly. Unfortunately, however, Fisher had not come entirely clean, having omitted his involvement (with his brother-in-law and some others) in a nasty robbery in which an elderly lady was tied up and relieved of her possessions. It all came to light and when the matter was put to him specifically, Fisher admitted his part. Once more he was too late. Had he been more frank, this would have qualified for immunity.

The police now seem to have tried to persuade the DPP not to prosecute, but they were unsuccessful. After an inspector had outlined his help, Fisher received four years at the Sheffield Crown Court; this sentence was, however, made concurrent with his longer term. From his point of view there was worse to come. The police were not notified of the renewed application for leave to appeal and it was dismissed in February 1984. Once more the local press seem to have had better connections than the authorities, who learned of the dismissal only by reading the newspapers. Their attempt to have the appeal re-opened was unsuccessful. Fisher was effectively left with the Local Review Committee and the full Parole Board to do something about how long he actually served.

There were now complaints that the police had pushed

2 Generally the procedure is for a convicted person to apply to a single judge for leave to appeal against his conviction. This is done in writing and, if granted, there is a full hearing in which the prisoner is legally represented and legal aid is given. If the single judge refuses the application, the prisoner can renew the application which is almost invariably treated as the appeal itself. He can be legally represented if he has the money to pay for a solicitor and barrister. In these circumstances, however, if the application is again rejected he is at risk of losing some of his remission.

Jenny into helping them with Widdowson, something they vehemently denied. Fisher was also worried that she was having a hard time with the local faces. It was arranged that she should be moved to an address well out of the locality but she declined, suggesting a seaside resort more to her liking. Take it or leave it, she and Fisher were told. There would, however, still be the opportunity for help after his release.

In the end, some eight months before his sentence was due to finish, Fisher was told one morning to collect his clothes from the gate; he was being released. Apart from a payment of £500 and the provision of a new name, few arrangements had been made for any rehabilitation on his release; for some time he wandered about Sheffield, in theory under his new name but in reality mixing with his former friends. He and his girlfriend eventually left the area. Widdowson pleaded guilty and received an eight-year sentence; because he had pleaded guilty there was no need for Fisher to give evidence.

As for the metals case itself William Kelsey, a sixty-four-year-old managing director, was jailed for seven and a half years; Graham Storr, the detective sergeant mentioned by Fisher, received a five-year sentence and Bob Green, described as 'one of the blackest villains in South Yorkshire', received four and a half years for his crimes including a conspiracy to commit arson at a private school.

Mr Justice Glidewell told the jury, 'You must have wondered whether you were hearing about Sheffield or Sicily at times during this trial.'

The life of Williams *(private collection)*

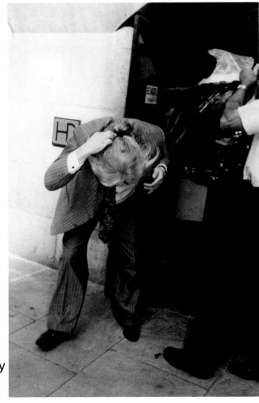

Ducking and diving - The life of O'Mahoney
(Enterprise News)

The four faces of Chrastney
("PA" Photo Library)

Nothing but the truth -
Joe Valachi testifies
(Camera Press Ltd)

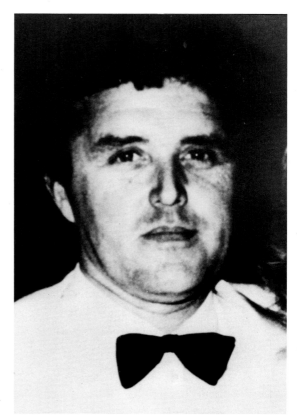

All dressed up - Roy Garner
("PA" Photo Library)

Well it's actually Leroy Davis
(Express Newspapers)

Fat Vinney
(Associated Press)

The Kray Consiglieri - Leslie Payne
(private collection)

At last Roger Dennhardt is happy
with things
(*Syndication International*)

Nipper Read brought the Krays to justice
(Popperfoto)

Keeping stumm
(S&G Press Agency)

Birth of a legend - Derek 'Bertie' Smalls flanked by
detectives *(London News Service)*

D.C.S. Jack Slipper and D.I. Peter Jones
return from Brazil - without Ronald Biggs
(Syndication International)

Still smiling -
Ronald Biggs in Brazil

(Syndication International)

8

The American Infiltrators

One of the earliest and most remarkable police-cum-private detective infiltrators was the Irish-born James McParland, who in 1873 managed to infiltrate and, effectively single-handedly, destroy the Irish-organised secret society – or terrorist group, say their detractors – the Molly Maguires, who were causing havoc in the coalfields of Eastern Pennsylvania. In a two-year operation he lived in the community, sending weekly messages back to the Pinkerton detective agency for whom he worked.

On 8 September 1867 McParland, an Ulsterman, arrived in America via England where he had worked in a factory in Gateshead. He worked throughout the Midwest as a stevedore, boxer, barman, labourer and bodyguard before signing up with the Chicago police, after which he joined Allan Pinkerton in his detective agency in the early 1870s. He was about 5 foot 7 tall, and weighed just over 10 stone, was a good card player, dancer, singer and one who could drink with the best.

It was through Pinkerton, often regarded as the father of undercover police work, that he was sent to infiltrate the Molly Maguires, who had taken their name from the apocryphal leader of an early Irish Land Reform group.[1]

---

1 In *The Pinkertons*, Richard Rowan suggests their name derives from their wearing women's clothing when carrying out raids. Trench, in his *Realities of Irish Life*, suggests that the name derives from their other habit of meting out duckings and lashings, traditional punishments for women, to their victims. The Maguires were also known as the Ribbon Men, the White Boys and the Buckshots.

At the time the conditions in the Pennsylvania coalfields under which the mainly Irish immigrants worked were some of the worst in America. Apart from the relatively short period of the Civil War when coal was needed urgently, miners in Pennsylvania rarely worked a full week. Their hours at the pits may have totalled fourteen a day, but they were worked for half a dollar. The general conditions were dreadful with a shack in a 'patch', a 'cluster of a few dozen company houses along a crooked, unpaved street, built within the shadow of a towering colliery'.[2] They were obliged to buy goods, usually on credit, at what was known as a 'pluck me', the company-owned store where goods had a 20 per cent mark-up. Given that many of the miners and their families were illiterate, there was considerable scope for further mark-ups. If a complaint was made, or if a miner declined to deal at the 'pluck me', then he would simply be blacklisted and there would be no work for him in Eastern Pennsylvania. A further torment and insult was the contrast of the clean and well-furnished three-storey home of the mine supervisor – almost invariably a Welshman or Scotsman.

The Molly Maguires, no more than a loose association of interests at first, was probably founded in a bar in Cass Township, Schuykill County, run by a Jeremiah Reilly. One story is that the organisation came about because Reilly's daughter and the local priest were roughed up by Welsh and English (and therefore Protestant) miners as the girl drove the priest through Yorkville home to Pottsville. There were reprisals in the form of a beating for the Protestant miners, and from there the communality of interests spread. By the 1850s the only group prepared, or capable, of taking on the mine-owners was the Molly Maguires. In many ways the structure was the same as in the Irish land troubles of two decades earlier. The mine-owners themselves were absent, as were the English from Ireland. In their place the oppressors were the Scots and the Welsh overseers.

2 Arthur H. Lewis, *A Lament for the Molly Maguires*, p. 7. He uses the spelling McParlan for the infiltrating detective, but the more usual is that given.

From 1862 to 1865 there were some 142 unsolved murders and 212 serious assaults, most of which went unpunished in Schuykill County. The victims were mine superintendents, supervisors, foremen and those known to be disloyal to the Mollies. By 1873 their grip on the six Pennsylvania counties appeared invincible, and it was the Molly-organised so-called Long Strike in 1874–75 which led the owners to determine to destroy them.

One of the people who stood to benefit most from the destruction of the Mollies was Franklin B. Gowen, a lawyer and former district attorney in Schuykill County. He was also President of the Philadelphia and Reading Railroad Company and, as such, was hostile to labour organisation – equating, not always incorrectly, crime with labour leadership. Coleman sees the double thrust by Gowen of the destruction of the Maguires and a blow to organised labour as a way of redeeming himself in the eyes of his stockholders, whose shares were not performing well.[3] Gowen is described as being:

Forceful, courageous, and daring with a personal magnetism that proved well-nigh irresistible even when his arguments were obviously preposterous; his greatest weakness was an incorrigible optimism and an apparent unwillingness to conform his larger projects to the practical necessities of the moment.[4]

Probably he recognised that the vast majority of the coalface workers were browbeaten and down-trodden, unable and unwilling to improve their lot. His wrath was reserved for those who sought to do so.

I say here, willingly and gladly that the great majority – I believe ninety-five out of every one hundred – of

3 J. Walter Coleman, *The Molly Maguire Riots*, p. 71.
4 Jules I. Bogen, *The Anthracite Railroads*, p. 51.

the men employed about the mines in the coal region are decent, orderly, law-abiding, respectable men; but there is among them a class of agitators . . . brought here for no other purpose than to create confusion, to undermine confidence, and to stir up dissension between the employer and the employed.

I have printed for your use a statement . . . of the outrages in the coal region . . . These outrages are perpetrated for no other purpose than to intimidate the workingmen themselves and to prevent them from going to work.[5]

Those men were the Molly Maguires, of whom their undoubted leader at the time was John 'Black Jack' Kehoe. Gowen recognised only too well that the collection of evidence sufficient to secure a conviction in the coalfield counties would be difficult, and he consulted Allan Pinkerton.[6] In Rowan's *The Pinkertons* there is a dramatic account of the meeting between Franklin B. Gowen and Allan Pinkerton, the head of the agency, which establishes the ground rules for an undercover agent. A high-flown passage sets out the qualities required of such a man:

He'll have to be Irish born, of course, and a Catholic

5 F. B. Gowen, *Argument before the Pennsylvania Legislative Committee*, pp. 78–86.
6 Allan Pinkerton was the founder of the celebrated detective agency. Born in Scotland in 1819, ironically he had fled to America in 1842 to avoid arrest for his part in labour reform agitations. An ardent abolitionist, he had helped to organise the underground railroad which smuggled runaway slaves to Canada. He joined the Chicago Police and, after destroying a gang of counterfeiters, had set up the agency. He continued to take part in the railroad movement and at one time sheltered John Brown and eleven runaway slaves. He saved Lincoln from an assassination plot he had uncovered, and during the Civil War was in charge of the Union secret service operations. After the war he was involved in an abortive effort to capture the James gang. After a Pinkerton agent was killed, the agency led a posse to the gang's hideout and killed James' eight-year-old brother. Pinkerton died in 1884 and the agency was carried on by his sons, William and Robert. The agency became increasingly active in anti-labour activities, and obtained a poor reputation following a number of unsavoury episodes including the breaking of the strike of Texas and Pacific Railroad in 1888. Once more, spies were used to infiltrate the strikers.

– brave, cool-headed, just about as smart a lad as ever
came over the seas. He'll need to work as a miner, and
that takes a strong constitution. And he must have his eye
peeled every minute to keep from betraying his purpose
to the cunning rascals he's sent out to get.

Pinkerton continues:

When the time comes for public prosecution, my operative
must not be expected to give testimony in court – unless
present circumstances are greatly altered . . . And since
we've no idea who's who in the Molly Society I urge you,
sir, to guard against spies. So many people are deathly
afraid of these ruffians, someone might turn informer to
curry favour with them.

Keep no record of this meeting, or of any future
dealings with me or the Agency. Avoid everything that
even suggests 'detective' – for at least one man's life,
and the whole outcome of our enterprise, will be staked
upon absolute secrecy. Whether my organisation is kept
on the job a week, a month, or a year or more, this sort
of caution must be maintained by us all to the end.[7]

Cover appears to have been arranged in the agency. The story
was put about that McParland was going abroad to England,
both for health reasons and to try to break a forgery ring.
Instead he went to Philadelphia, where he hung around the
dock area acclimatising himself until on Monday 27 October
1873, now using the name James McKenna, he took a train
to Port Clinton, Pennsylvania. It was from there that he was
directed to Tamaqua and Mahanoy City which was where most
of the state's coal was being produced. At a boarding-house
where he lodged, he was apparently warned to keep away

7 Richard W. Rowan, *The Pinkertons*, pp. 203–4.

from Pat Dormer's bar; Dormer, it was said, was 'captain of the Sleepers'. McParland appears to have made straight for the tavern where by his account he first danced and then played cards, caught one of the men cheating, took part in a bare-knuckle fight which he won in short order, and by using the phrase 'Here's to the power that makes English landlords tremble' indicated that he had been a Ribbon man back home and would like to re-join in America. It seems that when he was questioned about the Ancient Order of Hibernians, some of whose lodges were in the control of the Maguires – and about which, if genuine, he should know – he feigned drunkenness and slumped on a bench so putting an end to the questioning.

He was advised by Dormer, who seems to have been completely taken in by McParland, to travel to Shenandoah to see the powerful Mike Lawler. He made his way there in stages only to find Lawler had gone to Pottsville. It was 21 January 1874 before he met the bodymaster of the Shenandoah Lodge. His supply of cash was something to be explained and he gave out that he was peddling counterfeit Confederate money. His explanation brought him entry to the Lawler household, with whom he lodged from the next month, and he began work in the mines late in February.

In the first week of March he crushed his hand in an accident and was transferred to a shovelling job. Here he met Frank McAndrew, a man whom he admired and who was a rival of Lawler for the position of bodymaster. By the end of March 1874 men were being laid off and McParland was advised to go to Wilkes-Barre. He told Lawler, and was persuaded to stay on the promise of election into the Maguires in return for his support in Lawler's re-election campaign. McParland was also adroit at training fighting-cocks and was in charge of Lawler's stable. On 14 April 1874 he was initiated into the Ancient Order of Hibernians.

Quite apart from the initiation oath, the Order had all the trappings beloved by a secret society. A personal recognition was made by putting the tip of the right-hand little finger to

170

the outer corner of the right eye. The response was made by catching the right lapel of the vest or coat with the little finger and thumb of the right hand. If the sign was obscured, then an elaborate drinking toast was proposed: 'The Emperor of France and Don Carlos of Spain'. This must have served anonymity well in miners' bars in deepest Pennsylvania. The response was: 'May unite together and the people's rights maintain'. There were also passwords to be used when entering a division, and a bond phrase to prevent members who did not realise they were arguing with their own from actually coming to blows. 'Your temper is high' was to be answered with 'I have good reason'. It is amazing that they thought non-members would not realise something was up.[8]

McParland must have been a genuinely ingratiating man because when the election came up in July and was won by McAndrew, McParland became secretary to the illiterate bodymaster. It had taken him just over nine months since leaving Philadelphia to obtain this position of power. It appears that McAndrew was not the forceful person hoped for, and there was a campaign for McParland himself to become bodymaster. Before he achieved that dubious honour he would certainly have had to carry out a beating, if not an actual killing. He continued his pretence that he was unreliable in drink, indulging so much that he broke his health with bad liquor; his hair fell out and he bought a wig. Now he was excluded from every decent hotel and bar. Later his eyesight began to fail.

On 18 November 1874 six people were killed as the Maguires stepped up their campaign of intimidation and took reprisals against strike-breaking miners. Throughout the winter McParland appears to have done what he could to dissuade the leaders from this escalating campaign of violence and in April 1875, on the pretext of attending his sister's wedding, he returned to Chicago to see Pinkerton. Now more men were sent to the Pennsylvania coalfields, not as undercover men but

8 The phrases are from the testimony of James McParland reported in *The Pottsville Miner's Journal*, 9 May 1876.

as recruits to the Coal and Iron Police. One of them, Captain Robert Linden, claimed to be an old friend of McParland from Buffalo, now promoted to be in charge of the Shenandoah division of the Mollies, and was used as a go-between.

Part of McParland's undoubted charm seems to have been towards women and he had genuinely become involved with Mary Ann Higgins, whom he met at a Polish wedding. She was the sister-in-law of James Kerrigan, the Mollies' bodymaster at Tamaqua. In the summer of 1875 McParland's difficulties were compounded when Kerrigan ambushed and killed a policeman, Benjamin Yost, as he lit a street-lamp. McParland was also coming under increasing pressure to arrange the assassination of Gomer James, a Welsh miner who was believed to have killed an Irishman. McParland maintained that he sent messages of warning to James and delayed nominating a killer, together with a time and place, by pretending to be drunk.

On 2 June the striking miners paraded and marched towards those collieries still open. These shut down, not re-opening until August. On 14 August the men received their first pay and James was shot and killed. The real killer left the state, but the reward money of $10 paid for the murder was claimed by Thomas Hurley, a Shenandoahan.

In early 1876 matters came to a head. On 18 January two Mollies, Michael J. Doyle and Edward Kelly, were indicted with the killing of a John P. Jones, a manager who had treated one of the Mollies badly. Supervising the killing had been Kerrigan, who now elected to turn States' evidence. His line was that he had been something of a reluctant bystander drawn into the brotherhood, and afraid for his wife and family if he should try to leave. No, he had never taken part in any killing. As Doyle's trial proceeded to a 'guilty' verdict, Kerrigan began to sing loudly to the authorities; his statement ran to 210 pages.

On 5 February seven Mollies were arrested and charged with complicity in the murder of John P. Jones and that of patrolman Benjamin Yost.

172

According to Rowan,[9] Pinkerton had published lists of members of the Molly Maguires in local newspapers and rumour of a spy abounded in the organisation. Now was the time for McParland to be protected; his real identity was in danger of being revealed and he had been seen in Philadelphia, and there was the possibility that a priest also betrayed him. Pinkerton's idea was not, however, to pull him out of the danger zone but was for him to be arrested so that, with suspicion diverted, he could continue his operations.

When 'Black Jack' Kehoe called a meeting to denounce McParland, this precipitated the end of his work. It was arranged that this meeting should be at Ferguson's Hall in Shenandoah, where McParland would be given an opportunity to defend himself against the accusations. However, he saw it as a manoeuvre to keep him in the area and under observation. McAndrew, who had travelled back to the meeting to defend his protégé, suggested that they burn the books of the organisation, and this they did.

The next morning, 1 March, two men called at his lodgings saying they had arrived from Scranton. McParland realised that they were his appointed killers – the Scranton train was not yet scheduled. He drove with them in a sleigh to see Kehoe who, the story goes, was sitting down with his friends for a liquid breakfast to celebrate McParland's death. There he learned that it was a Father O'Connor who had put it about that he was a spy, and he demanded to go and see him and hear this from his own lips. The priest had gone to Pittston, however, and McParland now insisted on sending a telegram calling for an explanation. He went to the station, where he ostensibly began to complete a telegram while waiting for a train.

Other Pinkerton men were on the alert and Robert Linden had seen McParland at the station, suspected what he might be doing, and got on board the Scranton train to give help if he could. He could not, for McParland managed by himself. As

9 *Ibid.* pp. 218 *et seq.*

the train was drawing out, McParland said that he must go and see the priest in person and, making his escape, leaped into a carriage.

Another less dramatic version is that McParland went with McAndrew in a sleigh to confront Kehoe before the meeting, and after quarrelling with him turned his back on him and left in the sleigh before catching the train for Frackville, on which he met Linden in the smoking compartment.

> I knew there'd be no bullet in my back. Kehoe was a man even if he was a bad one. He really believed he was a kind of Robin Hood. Now I'm not tryin' to excuse what he did but maybe things'd been different, he could have been a leader of a decent group of miners fightin' for their rights instead of headin' a pack of killers.[10]

Whichever is the correct account, or if there is another somewhere between, amazingly – despite this extraordinary behaviour – the Mollies were not completely convinced of his deception. Kehoe stood his ground.

On 4 May 1876 the trial began of four Mollies – James Carroll, James Roarity, James Boyle and Hugh McGehan – charged with the murder of Yost. The next day John Kehoe, together with three Schuykill bodymasters and five other Mollies, was arrested. The organisation was broken.

McParland first gave evidence in the trial for the murder of Yost. It was, wrote William Linn, a trial observer, a complete shock when he walked down the aisle of the court.

> This was a complete surprise, not only to the Mollies, but to the public which had not hitherto known of his existence. This feeling of surprise deepened into one of wonder and amazement when . . . with perfect coolness

10 Arthur H. Lewis, *A Lament for the Molly Maguires*, p. 240.

and deliberation he told in detail the story of his career among the Mollies.

When he told of being suspected as a detective and related his interviews with his intended assassins, his escapes, etc., judges, jury, counsel, and audience listened with breathless attention; and so completely spellbound were all these by his recital of things the existence of which had not been thought possible, that at anytime the falling of a pin might be heard in the densely crowded room. Much of this narrative which was not relevant was not objected to by counsel for the defendants because of the intense interest they evidently felt.[11]

His evidence continued in a series of trials which led to the conviction of some sixty men including the leader John 'Black Jack' Kehoe. McParland's version of his participation was that he was a bystander who, although he knew of the proposed murders, could not warn the victims or his agency in case he himself was killed. Without success the defence lawyers put it that McParland was an *agent provocateur*. Looking back, Terence Powderley wrote:

> . . . that plague spot on American civilisation, the Pinkerton detective, had entered the council chambers of the workingmen of Schuykill County, and, under the guise of friendship, urged the men on to deeds of desperation and blood.[12]

Eleven of the Maguires were hanged and a further fifty-nine were convicted of various offences. One of them, Alec

11 Quoted in *ibid.* p. 240.
12 Terence Powderley, 'The Homestead Strike: A Knight of Labor's View' in *North American Review* 155 (September 1892), pp. 370–75.

Campbell, who owned a bar and was said to have been a bodymaster and to have supplied the gun which killed Jones, continually protested his innocence. On 21 June 1877, as he was taken from his cell in Maunch Chunk jail to the scaffold,

> . . . as if to impress the sheriff with the truth of his protest Campbell bent over, ground his right hand in the dust on the cell floor, and dragging his ball and chain after him took a long stride towards the wall. Then stretching himself to the full height, he smote the wall with his large hand. 'There is the proof of my words,' he said, 'that mark of mine will never be wiped out. There it will remain forever to shame the county that is hanging an innocent man.'
>
> They hanged Campbell that morning, but the imprint of his hand stood out from the wall like truth itself. In vain did the sheriff try to remove it. Succeeding sheriffs also failed. Campbell apparently was right.[13]

The imprint remained until the 1930s, by which time it had become a major tourist attraction. The cell was then replastered.

McParland subsequently travelled west to Colorado where he became head of the Denver branch of the Pinkerton agency. His work in infiltrating the Mollies was acclaimed throughout America and formed the basis of the first Sherlock Holmes' novel, *The Valley of Fear*. Over the years, however, his role has been substantially re-assessed. This began in 1906 with the trial in Boise, Ohio, of Harry Orchard, 'Big' Bill Haywood, George Pettibone and Charles Moyer, the last three of whom were leading members of the Western Federation of Miners.

13 George Korson in *Minstrels of the Mine Patch: Songs and Stories of the Anthracite Industry*.

Haywood went on to become a leading light in the Industrial Workers of the World.[14]

On 30 December 1905 Frank Steunenberg, a former governor of Idaho, had been killed by a bomb attached to his front gate. McParland found two informers, Steve Adams and Harry Orchard, whose confessions led to the arrest of Haywood, Pettibone and Moyer. Adams later withdrew his confession, insisting that his statement was false and had been Pinkerton-inspired.

Orchard, whose real name was Albert F. Horsley, maintained that he had received the bombing instructions from Haywood. Leaving aside the Steunenberg case, Orchard was a self-confessed killer. He had carried out a number of bombings for the Western Federation of Miners, including one in which fourteen non-union members died in an explosion in June 1904, and had probably been involved in other attempts on the Governor's life.

The great lawyer Clarence Darrow, appearing for the defence, created great inroads into Orchard's written confession in which corrections were probably in McParland's handwriting. There were good reasons for Orchard's killing of Steunenberg; in 1899 the then Governor had driven him out of Coeur d'Alene in Idaho, so depriving him of a one-sixteenth share of a mine which would have made him a millionaire. As for the implication of Haywood and the others, it is thought that this was either part and parcel of a power struggle amongst the leadership of the Western Federation

14 Known as the Wobblies, this early form of militant American trade union flourished in the first two decades of the twentieth century. The height of its fame came in 1915 with the execution by a firing squad in Utah of one of their leaders, Joe Hill, for murder. The IWW was able to mount international, if ultimately unsuccessful, support including a demonstration of 30,000 workers in Australia for clemency. Hill's last words were said to be, 'Don't mourn, organise.' After his death the influence of the IWW faded quickly and effectively disintegrated with the arrest of their leaders including 'Big' Bill Hayward for sedition in 1920 in the so-called Palmer raids. Haywood was released pending his appeal on bail of $30,000, but fled to the Soviet Union, where he died in the Hotel Lux, Moscow, on 18 May 1928. The Wobblies still maintain a small presence in San Francisco and Denver.

or, more likely, was inspired by the mine-owners. The three Wobblies were acquitted, with Orchard's death sentence being commuted to life imprisonment. Later he petitioned William A. Pinkerton, then head of the agency, to help him obtain parole. Rather contrary to the agency's usual practice of helping their informers whether a conviction had been obtained or not, Pinkerton refused, writing in a memorandum:

> I know that McParland always thought Orchard should have been released for testifying, but I still regard Orchard as a cold-blooded murderer who killed many innocent persons and who testified only to save his own skin.

In fact, Orchard was never released, dying in prison on 13 April 1954 at the age of eighty-six. By accounts he was treated as something over and above the ordinary prisoner. Early in his imprisonment he had a room fitted with electricity, and Charles Steunenberg recalled:

> Private parties gave him the money with which to buy machinery; the state permitted him to use convict labour for his own private enterprise in which he manufactured shoes for prominent people in Idaho and rolled up a cash reserve of $10,000.

By 1943 Orchard was keeping a chicken farm, although he would tell visitors that he 'just can't bring himself to kill a chicken'. He was described as still fat and sleek, oily-eyed and unctuous. He complained if anyone wished to clear up the 1905 record, and told Irving Stone: 'The trouble with you writers is that you never come here to write about me. You always want to use me to write about somebody else!'[15]

15 Irving Stone, *Clarence Darrow for the Defense*, p. 229.

The incident gets scant mention in Rowan's adulatory account of the Pinkerton agency, which suggests that Haywood and company were imprisoned. Indeed they were, although not quite in the way suggested by Rowan. Pinkerton agents had captured the men in Denver and put them on a special train to Boise, Idaho, where they were kept on death row until their trial. Nor is there any substantial reassessment in the rather more scholarly *The Eye that Never Sleeps*, in which Frank Morn drily comments: 'Third degree methods on Orchard soon produced enough evidence for McParlan [sic] to arrest the three labour leaders and spirit them away to Idaho.'[16]

One Pinkerton man, the stenographer Morris Friedman, was so disenchanted with the affair that he left the agency and wrote his own memoirs, *The Pinkerton Labor Spy*, in which he saw the Pinkerton management as a public menace masquerading as a public necessity and something not far from the Russian Secret Police.

His memoirs did not please the heads of the Pinkerton agency, and operatives who subsequently tried their hands at unauthorised and therefore unadulatory reminiscences found themselves in considerable difficulties. When Charles Siringo wrote *Pinkerton's Cowboy Detective*, he was forced to change the title to *The Cowboy Detective*; Pinkerton becomes Dickenson and Tom Horn, the range-rider and another operative, appears as Tom Corn. There was worse to come. In 1914 Siringo wrote *Two Evil Isms* and sent the manuscript to the agency for approval. Unsurprisingly, since one of the evil isms was Pinkertonism, the Pinkerton management disapproved of the whole concept, took Siringo to court and the printing plates were confiscated.

If the score between McParland and the mineworkers apparently stood at one-all, it was changed when, in January 1979, Kehoe was officially pardoned by the State of Pennsylvania.

16 Frank Morn, *The Eye that Never Sleeps*, p. 158.

As for McParland, the remainder of his life was not a happy one. Shortly after the Haywood fiasco he retired; he married twice and died in the Mercy Hospital, Denver, in 1918. In the last years of his life he had lost a leg and an eye, possibly through drink and diabetes. He had had high walls built around his Denver home and inside the walls had attack dogs always on the loose. Apparently he was in constant fear of being assassinated by descendants of the Molly Maguires:

> In addition, he had bars put on all the lower windows and has a hand gun on every table in the house. He also carried a gun constantly and got up frequently during the night to patrol the house.[17]

Whatever is the truth about the part McParland played in the year and a half when he was actively involved with the Maguires, his feat as an undercover operator – using his landlady's bag of dolly-blue to make ink and sending weekly messages back to Chicago – is one of the great feats of undercover detection and infiltration.

While he may have been the greatest of the early non-military infiltrators, McParland was neither the first nor by any means the last deep-cover man used by the Pinkertons. It was suggested that he was an *agent provocateur*, and it was certainly the case with other deep-cover men that they carried on their own trade side by side with the detective duties.

In 1888 Charles Siringo worked in the Denver office under the aegis of the former safe-blower Doc Williams, and the men cordially disliked each other. His preference was for outdoor investigation rather than office work; he became an undercover man in a Wyoming cowboy gang, and it was his testimony which later had them convicted. In 1889

17 Catherine McParland Schick, quoted by Patrick Campbell in *A Molly Maguire Story*, p. 187.

Eams, a senior man in the Denver office, was caught in a scam charging clients for work not done and pocketing the proceeds. The agency then brought in the gunfighter Tom Horn as an operative.

In 1892 Siringo went deep under cover and, under the name of C. Leon Allison, infiltrated the mining unions in the northern Idaho minefields, becoming a friend of George Pettibone and yet – as McParland had done a decade earlier – all the time sending reports on the union plots. His double role was discovered and he escaped to the hills, returning to town only to give evidence.

One of the mine-owners, John Hammond, recalls Siringo's reappearance.

[He and Siringo] walked together down the middle of the road, each of us carrying two pistols in our coat pockets. There was a running fire of comment from miners on the sidewalk as they expressed their hatred for Siringo in no uncertain language. As he walked, Siringo kept his hands in his pockets. The outline of his guns could clearly be seen as he swayed ominously from side to side.[18]

Eighteen union leaders including Pettibone were jailed.

Siringo had long been a master undercover man. In his younger days he had chased Billy the Kid, losing him when he was cleaned out of his money in a card game, and also had travelled through Indian territory to claim a suspect. In New Mexico he contracted smallpox, which left his face badly pitted. He had posed as a wanted man to persuade Elfie Landusky, a Hole-in-the-Waller, to tell him where Harvey Logan was hiding. After he retired, apart from the indictment of the Pinkertons he wrote a number of fairly

18 John Hays Hammond, *The Autobiography of John Hays Hammond*, Volume 1, p. 195.

successful cowboy thrillers, but died in what were described as poor circumstances in Los Angeles in 1928.[19]

Tom Horn was another of the undercover agents, but this time one whose personal interests were not at odds with those of the agency. He had been an Indian fighter and army scout before he arrived in Denver in 1890 with what were described as impeccable references. For the next few years he was the Pinkerton's Rocky Mountain operative, making a number of arrests of train robbers and cattle-rustlers, killing a number as well. He took time to commit a robbery for himself in Nevada, and was protected by the agency. Siringo wrote:

> . . . on one of his trips to Denver, William A. Pinkerton [one of the sons] told me that Tom Horn was guilty of the crime but that his people could not afford to let him go to the penitentiary while in their employ.[20]

Despite the protection, let alone the salary the agency offered, Horn felt tied down and resigned in 1894, becoming a freelance detective and hired gun of the Wyoming Cattlemen's Association. He is described as a tidy, patient and skilful murderer. He would wait hours in driving rain, chewing bacon fat, to ensure he had the one necessary clear shot at his target. After each killing he would leave a stone under the head of his victim so there was no doubt as to the killer. However, in 1901 he made

---

19 Located in Wyoming, Hole-in-the-Wall was one of the best-known Western safe hideouts. A Hole-in-the-Waller was synonymous with being a member of the Wild Bunch. Harvey Logan, better known as Kid Curry, a notorious member of the Wild Bunch, was widely regarded as one of the more vicious killers of the West. In 1904 he broke out of Knoxville jail after strangling one of the guards and, according to the Pinkertons, formed a new gang in Colorado. He is said to have travelled 1,400 miles in a twelve-day period before being cornered in Glenwood Springs, where he shot himself. He was identified by Pinkerton agents, although the identification was hotly disputed by other agencies including the Union Pacific. His photograph was sent back to Knoxville, where the recognition was confirmed. The alternate and more romantic theory is that he did not go to Colorado but rejoined Butch Cassidy and Harry Longbaugh in Columbia. C. Sifakis, *The Encyclopedia of American Crime* (1982), p. 394.
20 C. Siringo, *Two Evil Isms*, p. 46.

what proved to be a fatal error when he killed fourteen-year-old Willie Nickell, the son of a sheep-farmer, mistaking him in poor light for his father.

For two years, partly because of Horn's powerful protectors, the murder remained unsolved. His eventual undoing was another semi-undercover man, Joe Lefors, a deputy US marshal who became Horn's confidant and, when the latter was well in drink, obtained from him a bragging confession which he took the precaution of being noted by a hidden shorthand-writer and another witness.

Despite his pleas for help from his former employers and a donation of $5,000 to his defence fund from an unknown admirer, Horn was convicted of murder in 1903. He had tried to impugn the confession, suggesting that what he said was just a tall tale and that the stenographer had added pieces of his own. Whilst awaiting execution he escaped from prison but was quickly recaptured and was hanged on 20 November 1903. In recent years efforts have been made – as has often been the case with outlaws – to rehabilitate Horn. It is said that the confession should have been ruled inadmissible and that, indeed, he was not the youth's killer.[21]

Another of the early infiltrating Pinkerton men, A.W. Gratias, managed to infiltrate the Western Federation of Miners so successfully that he became chairman of the union relief committee in a year and president of his local union a year later. He even attended the annual convention, faithfully returning reports on the union activities to the Denver office. It is hardly surprising that the Pinkerton agency was regarded with both fear and loathing amongst the mineworkers of the West. Their talents did, however, provide an example for any self-respecting infiltrator of the twentieth century.

One of the great success stories of twentieth-century police infiltration was that of Mike Malone, who managed to snuggle

21 Dean Krakel, *The Saga of Tom Horn*.

up close to the great Chicago gangster Al Capone and lived
to tell the tale. In 1930 Capone was under investigation by
the Internal Revenue Service in an operation led by Frank
J. Wilson, and was also being attacked on his flanks with no
greater success by the 'Untouchable', Eliot Ness.

Malone is described as being 'black Irish' and coming from
Jersey City; 5 foot 8 tall, barrel-chested, weighing 200 pounds,
with jet-black hair and a brilliant friendly smile, he could easily
pass as Italian, Jewish or Greek. He and his wife had separated
after the death of their young daughter in a road accident,
and after that he seems to have had little interest in anything
but work.

A long and elaborate cover story was invented detailing his
crime history from Brooklyn. He took a room in the Lexington
Hotel next to one of Capone's bodyguards. Malone, using
the name De Angelo, hung about the hotel lobby until he
was approached and asked his business. He was, he said, a
promotor. Did anyone wish to buy gold bricks?[22]

Malone claimed to have been a member of the feared Five
Points Gang and, it appears, just as the punter who is offered the
chance of taking the gold brick to the jeweller for examination
never does so, his story was never checked out. He obtained
a job in one of Capone's casinos, graduated to head croupier,
drank and played with Capone's men and all the time made

---

22 The gold brick confidence trick has long been a part of American swindles and
survives even today. Indeed 'to gold brick' has passed into slang as meaning to
malinger. The basis of the trick is that the mug punter buys what he thinks are
gold brick ingots and ends up with worthless brass or lead. The trick almost
certainly started in the Californian Gold Rush and there is some evidence that
Wyatt Earp and Dave Mather were involved in the swindle in Mobeetie, Texas,
in 1878. The con was probably brought to New York in 1889 by the talented
Reed Waddell; his bricks were marked in the manner of a regulation brick from
the US Assayer's Office and the mug was always given the chance – or believed
he had the chance – to take the brick to a jeweller of his choice. Thirteen years
later Waddell was still working the trick with a partner Tom O'Brien. Eventually
in 1895 the two fell out and Waddell was killed by O'Brien. A similar scam
is the Green Goods swindle, another well-known confidence trick in which the
mug punter sees banknotes being 'produced' by a machine. He is then given
the choice of purchasing either a large quantity of banknotes at a substantial
discount on the face price or the machine itself. Although very popular in the
late nineteenth century, it is still occasionally practised today.

reports back to Wilson, including a detailed one on Capone's hit-man Frank 'The Enforcer' Nitti. Shortly after this Malone was invited to attend a banquet at which Capone would be present. At a previous such occasion Capone had beaten one of the guests with a baseball bat; now Malone feared that his cover might be blown and he was to be the next. In the event he thought he was being poisoned when he was served spiced steak which burned his mouth; he called for water and was mocked for not drinking champagne until he explained that he had an ulcer. The rest of the dinner passed without incident and Malone was given a friendly pat on the shoulder by the great man.

Shortly after this, Malone was joined by another agent under the pseudonym of Graziano and they learned of the imminent attack on Wilson who was staying at the Sheridan Plaza under an assumed name. Wilson and his superior feared that Malone had indeed been identified and that his life was in danger. Malone insisted it was not, and that both he and Graziano wished to stay under cover. It was fortunate that they did so, because Malone was able to confirm to Wilson that there was indeed a plot against him and that he and his wife must leave the hotel immediately. Later, when Capone had been indicted and was on bail for the revenue frauds and other offences for which he would eventually receive seventeen years, Malone sent another message that Wilson was again under immediate threat.

Malone met Capone one more time. On Saturday 24 October 1931, when Capone was sent to Leavenworth penitentiary on the night he was sentenced, he met Malone in the lift and recognised him – or at least this is the legend. 'The only thing that fooled me was your looks,' he is reported to have said. 'You look like a Wop. You took your chances, and I took mine.'[23]

---

23 E. L. Irey and W. Slocum, *The Tax Dodgers: The Inside Story of the T-Men's War with America's Political and Underworld Hoodlums*, p. 65. They had some snappy titles in those days.

But what of Eliot Ness, the man who according to criminal mythology was the one who really brought down Al Capone? Sadly for Wilson, who never had a television series of films made about him, and sadly for Ness, who didn't bring down Capone, he played a much lesser part than has been accorded to him over the years. Was he an infiltrator or even a major figure in the destruction of the crime czar?

Not to any great extent, according to Laurence Bergreen in *Capone*, his biography of the gangster. He considers that Ness was very much a second-division player compared with Wilson in bringing about Capone's downfall. He was a member of the 300-strong staff of the Prohibition Bureau in Chicago and certainly from time to time posed either as a corrupt Prohibition agent or a bootlegger, drinking in a Chicago Heights saloon known as Cozy Corners. It seems he was at one time paid $250 a week by racketeers – something he faithfully turned over to his superiors – but it was, to use a pun, strictly small beer. It was not necessarily without danger, however. Shortly after Ness, along with Italian-speaking agent Burt Napoli who was posing as his chauffeur, paid a business call on Joe Martino, then head of the Unione Siciliano, Napoli was murdered. A suspect was arrested, but the man hanged himself in his cell before he could be effectively questioned. Ness's cover was blown and his undercover work came to a halt.[24]

The Capone era abounds with stories of cross and double-cross. One of the more interesting is that of the double life played out by newspaperman Alfred 'Jake' Lingle, a police reporter for the *Chicago Tribune* who was murdered on

24 The career of Eliot Ness, full of promise and now fictionalised probably beyond recognition, never quite achieved the height to which he aspired; throughout much of his life he was overly attractive to women, with the consequent difficulties that brings, and a drink problem to match. After the Capone trial he became the chief investigator of Prohibition violations in Kentucky and Tennessee, and in 1935 the Public Safety Director in Cleveland. He is credited with ridding the town of the Mayfield Road Mob which at that time controlled prostitution and bootlegging. Unfortunately his heavy drinking involved him in a hit-and-run accident on 5 March 1942. He escaped prosecution, but resigned on 30 April 1942. After the war his career slid further into the depths until he died of a heart attack on 16 May 1957 at the age of fifty-four. Laurence Bergreen, *Capone*, pp. 346–9.

9 June 1930. Known as a courageous reporter who had waged a fearless war against the Underworld, Lingle had left the *Tribune* offices saying that he was going to try to get a story about the Moran gang. He was seen a short time later at the corner of Randolph and Clark, and then heading down Randolph to catch a train to the race-track. His movements are well documented; he stopped to buy a racing paper and then headed for the tunnel to the station. A well-dressed young man walked behind him and shot the reporter through the head; he died still clutching cigar and racing paper.

There was an immediate outcry. Lingle was named as a 'first line soldier' in the fight against crime, and rewards of over $50,000 were posted by his paper and local groups. But things were not quite the way they seemed. It transpired that through his police connections he had the ability to award beer-selling and gambling rights, also that he was into demanding money from brothel-keepers and at the time of his death had been wearing a diamond-studded belt given him by Al Capone. His stock slumped and the *Tribune* was reduced to writing articles denouncing other newspaper reporters, notably Julius Rosenheim of the rival *Chicago Daily News* who had been shot to death a few months previously. He, too, had been blackmailing brothel-keepers.

A year later a penniless small-time gangster, Leo V. Brothers, was charged with and later convicted of shooting Lingle. He was expensively defended with a battery of five counsel led by Louis Piquett, who later defended Dillinger, and received fourteen years. 'I can do that standing on my head,' he is said to have announced after the verdict. Over the years there have been persistent suggestions that he was not the killer at all but had been paid to take the rap. He was released after eight years and died in 1951 without disclosing who had paid him either for the contract or for going to prison, whichever was the case. Brothers had been unearthed by a private detective, John Hagan, who had infiltrated the Moran gang and later Egan's Rats in St Louis to do so.[25]

A rather more honourable part in undercover work was played by Jerry Thompson in July 1979 when he was sent by his editor, John Seigethaler, to work on Nashville's *The Tennessean* to infiltrate the Ku Klux Klan. After a decade of dormancy it became clear that at the end of the 1970s the Klan was staging a resurgence in rural communities near Nashville, and Thompson was sent undercover for a few months. This followed the traditional pattern of undercover work, with Thompson leaving his home and setting up a new life in another town.

As with many undercover operations which are intended to last only for a few months, it extended itself in this case to nearly a year and a half. He and his family paid a high price for the investigation, which ended with Thompson returning to his home more as a guest than a family member, an armed guard, and a lawsuit – claiming $1 million – which he successfully defended. In an afterword to his book his wrote:

> It has been almost a decade now since that story broke, and we are still trying to resolve some of the issues which were raised during that turbulent period of our lives.
>
> From a journalist's standpoint, there is the issue of where my commitment to my job – to a story – begins and where it ends. From the standpoint of being a husband and a father, there is the question of when my responsibilities to my family outweigh my responsibilities to search out and expose the truth.[26]

25 Little is known of Jack Hagan, but Egan's Rats were founded in about 1900 by Jack 'Jellyroll' Egan, principally as strike-breakers. By the 1920s, with unions more firmly established, the members turned to safe-breaking and, once Prohibition was announced, entered the game with enthusiasm. It is suggested that one member, Fred Burke, took part in the St Valentine's Day Massacre in 1929. The gang did not survive the end of the era. Their leader, Dinty Colbeck, was shot and the gang split up in the late 1930s.
26 Jerry Thompson, *My Life in the Klan*, p. 321.

The extended length of successful deep-cover investigations is a problem for all investigators. In more recent times there has been a welter of officers who have gone long-term undercover and who have lived to tell the tale. Reading between the lines, particularly of Joe Pistone's autobiography, *Donnie Brasco*, the name he used in his five-year undercover stint with the New York Mafia, there are long-term deep-cover agents working in most cities in the United States.

His is, perhaps, the most interesting of all the stories, if only for the length of time he spent during a period when techniques for the protection of the agent had not been refined in any way and he was at daily, if not hourly, risk of discovery by the highly volatile crowd with whom he mixed. He had originally been part of a relatively minor FBI operation in Tampa in 1975, working on a ring of car and lorry thieves. How the FBI came to be involved is yet another example of how an informant is born. A teenage boy had been arrested on an unrelated charge and his father volunteered, in return for a non-custodial sentence for his son, to blow the whistle on the team who were operating all over the south-eastern United States, stealing bulldozers, Lincolns, Cadillacs and occasionally aeroplanes. In February 1976 the entire ring, consisting of thirty people, was arrested. From there Pistone became part of the Truck and Hijack Squad in New York and it was only a short, but large, step to take to become Donnie Brasco, jewel thief, looking to hang out with the Mafia.

It took him several months of frequenting a local bar, offering to sell stolen jewellery to the barman, before he was gradually accepted into the milieu. He moved on to a knock-out shop dealing in stolen clothing, and from there was taken up by rival mobsters. In the end he was more or less selected by Benjamin 'Lefty Guns' Ruggiero, connected to the Bonanno family, and groomed by him if not for stardom then at least as high as an outsider could rise in the Mafia. After he left and testified against leading lights in the organisation, a contract of $500,000 was put on his head. The people to whom he was closest in the organisation were also under threat. Tony Mirra, who had at one time wanted to use him on a more permanent basis, was murdered in New York in 1982 six months before Brasco began to testify. Then there was Sonny Black, to whom Brasco admits to having had:

> some uncomfortable feelings . . . I felt a kind of kinship with him. But I didn't feel any guilt of betrayal, because I'd always maintained in my own mind and heart the separation of our worlds. In a sense we were both just doing our jobs.[27]

Black was found, handless, in a hospital body-bag in the Mariner's Harbor section of Staten Island, some five months into the trials of other *mafiosi*.[28]

27 J. D. Pistone, *Donnie Brasco*, p. 365.
28 There have been many other accounts of the lives of former undercover agents. They include Derek Agnew's *Undercover Agent – Narcotics*, and Michael Detroit's *Chain of Evidence* which tells the story of a woman police officer who infiltrated bikers in Southern California. This is particularly interesting because it tells the story not only from her point of view but from that of her handler.

9

Infiltrators – England

There is little doubt that infiltrators have been used in Britain in political and religious intrigues since the Tudors. The use of the infiltrator in the criminal Underworld for non-political purposes is more recent. So far as the former is concerned, the playwright Christopher Marlowe may well have begun his career as a spy by himself being the victim of an informer. His atheism had been reported to the authorities and he may well have taken up the offer to work as a Government spy in order to avoid punishment.

Shortly before the establishment of the New Police, there was another outstanding example of the use of the spy and a cover-up of his operations by the authorities. The history books may show that the Cato Street Conspiracy of 1820 was instigated by Arthur Thistlewood who had fallen under the spell of Tom Paine, the great Republican, and, whilst he lived in France, of Robespierre. A closer examination will also indicate the crucial role played by a government spy to bring the conspiracy to fruition and its disastrous conclusion. Thistlewood had risen in the Army to the rank of lieutenant, and married a lady of some wealth; she died, and possibly he soon gambled away her fortune. Other accounts are that he lost his money by an injudicious loan to a friend. His great desire in life, it seems, was to assassinate the members of the Cabinet

191

and then seize power. The attack was timed for Wednesday, 23 February 1820, when Lord Harrowby was entertaining the Cabinet in Grosvenor Square. The idea was that one of the members of the conspiracy should go to the house to deliver a parcel and then, when the door opened, the others were to rush the premises and kill the members of the Cabinet. The plan was for Lord Castlereagh – then Prime Minister – and Lord Sidmouth to have their heads cut off. However, the plot had been infiltrated by a government spy, George Edwards, who ran a shop near Eton School in which he sold models of the headmaster which the boys could then use as targets. He was also employed by Sir Robert Birnie and the Bow Street magistrates.

Sir Robert Birnie himself led the disabling raid on the conspirators. One Runner, Smithers, was stabbed by Thistlewood and the conspirators – excepting Edwards, who managed to disappear – were arrested. At their trial they endeavoured to make him give evidence and sent depositions indicating his guilt to Viscount Sidmouth, who refused to issue a warrant. Edwards escaped, it is said with Government assistance, and fled first to the Channel Islands and then to the Cape.

There was never likely to be much chance of an acquittal on the charges laid of high treason, but such as there was disappeared with Edwards. The defending lawyers argued that the jury should draw the conclusion from Edwards' absence that the plot had no foundation in reality, and that if it could be properly investigated the affair would be shown to be that of a spy and informer. It was said that the idea of attacking the Cabinet at dinner was that of Edwards. In his speech before receiving the death sentence, Thistlewood roundly denounced the absent Edwards, who he said had

a plan for blowing up the House of Commons. This was not my view: I wished to punish the guilty only, and therefore I declined it. He next proposed that we should attack the Ministers at the fete given by the Spanish Ambassador.

192

This I resolutely opposed . . . there were ladies invited to the entertainment – and I, who am shortly to ascend to the scaffold, shuddered with horror at the idea of that, a sample of which had previously been given by the Agents of Government at Manchester . . .[1]

If Thistlewood was right, and there is much to support his view, here was an *agent provocateur de luxe*.

Three years earlier Samuel Bamford, the eighteenth-century North Country radical, had devised a method to thwart the spy system. He and his fellow prisoners had coached themselves to give a single agreed version of events. Then

> if government brought them to trial, it would have to unmask its spies and informers, instead of making them fall by their mutual contradictions, mistrusts and jealousies which as it seemed to me, the government would prefer doing.[2]

Unfortunately, as is so often the case, one of the defendants, Robert Adams, to save himself from the scaffold broke ranks and gave evidence for the Crown. On 28 April the plotters were found guilty of the conspiracy and of the murder of Smithers, and on 1 May they were hanged by James Botting. Much to the disgust of the crowd, who had been kept behind barricades well away from the scaffold to prevent any rescue attempt, they were then decapitated.

When within the decade the New Police marched forth it was never the intention of their founder, Sir Robert Peel, that there should be such a thing as a police spy in his force. The very idea of such a continental device was abhorrent. Nevertheless,

1 Quoted by E. P. Thompson, *The Making of the English Working Class*, p. 772.
2 Samuel Bamford, *Passages in the Life of a Radical*, p. 93. Thistlewood clearly had a death wish. He had previously been acquitted of high treason following the Spa Fields riot in South London in December 1816.

spies there were from a very early stage. Within a few years there was a disaster when the police clashed on open ground in an area between Holborn and Clerkenwell known as Coldbath Fields. One police officer, PC Culley, was killed and an inquest jury later returned a verdict of justifiable homicide. An inquiry followed swiftly.

At the same time as the inquiry into the Coldbath Fields disaster, another inquiry was set up. This stemmed from the behaviour of a former schoolmaster, Sergeant William Stewart Popay, of P division and latterly of the Walworth and Camberwell 'class' of the National Political Union. The Government was highly suspicious of the Union and Lord Melbourne instructed the commissioners to keep him informed of its movements. In turn Popay had been instructed by his superintendent M'Lean to attend the meetings and, as it was found, had interpreted this to mean he should infiltrate the organisation. From 1831 to 1833, masquerading as a coalman put out of work by the Coal Act, Popay did just that.

His radical speeches soon ensured that he was elected to office in the Union. In late April or early May 1833 his cover was blown when he was recognised by a Union member, John Fursey, at his station desk at Park House police station.[3] For the time being he managed to explain away his presence, and indeed he marched with the members to Coldbath Fields, but later – in the course of the defence of another rioter, George Fursey – Popay's behaviour came under scrutiny.

Fanned by the oratory of William Cobbett, author of *Rural Rides*, the House of Commons responded to a petition organised by John Fursey and others including a Frederick Young:

---

3 The early police forces seem to have had only a rudimentary idea of undercover work. As has been demonstrated throughout police history, others did not learn from the salutary lesson of Sergeant Popay. In 1840 a PC Barnett of the Birmingham City police infiltrated the Chartists in the city. Unfortunately his superiors required him to work in uniform when he was not busy infiltrating, and it was not long before he was seen in a theatre. His explanation that he was working in a private capacity for the theatre manager (an early example of police moonlighting if it was true) was not accepted. (B. Porter, *Plots and Paranoia*, p. 74.)

That he used to urge the members of the Union to use stronger language than they did in their resolutions and other papers, which he sometimes altered with his own pen, in order to introduce such stronger language; that in his conversation with one of your Petitioners particularly, he railed against the Government, damned the Ministers for villains, and said he would expel them from the earth; that he told one of your Petitioners that he should like to establish a shooting-gallery, and wanted some of them to learn the use of the broad-sword, and did give one lesson of the broad-sword to one of your petitioners.

It was the end for Popay who protested, as well he might, that his plain clothes were for his own protection. It was found that:

. . . he complained to several members of the misery to which he and his family had been reduced; he paid frequent private visits to their leaders and never failed to address them as friends; arm in arm with another member he marched to a meeting to celebrate the French Revolution. More serious still he took part in discussions, supporting resolutions, sometimes even proposing that their wording should be strengthened, and encouraged the establishment of an arms depot offering to give members of the Union sword practice.[4]

His conduct was described as 'highly reprehensible' and he was dismissed the force with ignominy. His superiors, who in turn argued that they had employed Popay at the request of the Home Office but only to watch the meetings of the Union, were criticised for not keeping him under closer control. Whilst the Select Committee accepted the need for a plain clothes force, it deprecated 'any approach to the Employment of Spies, in the ordinary acceptance of the term, as a practice most abhorrent

4 Report from Select Committee on Metropolitan Police (675) 1833 Parl. Papers (1833), vol. 13, pp. 401, 409.

to the feelings of the People and most alien to the spirit of the Constitution'.[5]

Looking back, there is little doubt that poor Popay was the sacrificial goat, but were there others like him who remained unmasked? Yes, said Young and others, who maintained they had seen men 'whom they knew to be policemen, disguised in clothing of various descriptions, sometimes in the garb of gentlemen, sometimes in that of tradesmen or artisans, sometimes in sailors' jackets'.[6]

No, replied the police. Popay was a rogue, an original bad and sinful apple, not the tip of an iceberg. Of course, it is now unbelievable that for two years Popay led this double life without the knowledge of any of his superiors. Did no single one of them ever ask how he came by his detailed information?

After the Popay affair, however, the Commissioners were keen to avoid a repetition and in 1839 a Metropolitan Standing Police Order prohibited officers from attending private meetings of any sort. Nor were officers encouraged to adopt a subterfuge to obtain evidence. Indeed, policing in plain clothes was considered unsporting and, with the exception of the small detective branch set up in 1842, all policing was done in uniform. It was something regarded as abhorrent to right-thinking British people generally.

Over the years, however, a number of instances have come to light. On the 'tip of the iceberg' principle it may be that, as with the Special Branch, there was a far greater number of cases when a police officer had donned a disguise than the authorities would care to admit. After all, Rowan, the Police Commissioner, had been an Army officer serving under Wellington in the Peninsular campaign, where he would have became thoroughly versed in infiltration.

In 1845 a constable who had pretended to be a cobbler in order to arrest a counterfeiter was severely reprimanded; as was another who, six years later, hid behind a tree in Hyde Park to

5 *Ibid.* pp. 409–10.
6 *Ibid.* p. 411.

observe an 'indecent offence'. When these scandals broke, the Home Office was at pains to play the matters down.[7]

On the other hand, the detective force led by Field was happy to discuss its success and exploits in disguise with the novelist and social commentator Charles Dickens, who, until he fell out with the police over the actress Ellen Ternan, was their great champion. Dickens was told of an exploit concerning the arrest of silk thieves involving one of the young officers, Henry Smith, who disguised himself as a butcher's boy:

> Never, surely, was a faculty of observation better brought to bear upon a purpose, than that which picked out this officer for the part. Nothing in all creation could have suited him better. Even while he spoke, he became a greasy, sleepy, shy, good-natured chuckle-headed, unsuspicious and confiding young butcher. His very hair seemed to have had suet in it, as he made it smooth upon his head, and his fresh complexion, to be lubricated by large quantities of animal food.

This facility was not altogether unsurprising. Dickens omitted to write that Smith (whom he cleverly disguised as Mith) had been a butcher before he joined the police.[8]

One of the earliest of police officers to put pen to paper, Chief Inspector Andrew Lansdowne, was at pains to correct the view of the newspaper-fed public that a policeman spent his days in donning and shedding disguises with the celerity of a quick-change artist: 'Now all this is fudge. During the

7 B. Porter, *The Refugee Question in Mid-Victorian Politics*, pp. 114–15. There was quite clearly a great deal more undercover work going on than the police cared to admit. Officers could be put into civvies for particular operations. See also G. Thurston, *The Clerkenwell Riot*, for an account of the demonstration in Coldbath Fields and the death of PC Robert Culley.
8 Charles Dickens, 'The Detective Police' in *Miscellaneous Papers*, pp. 60 *et seq.* The incident to which Smith referred may have been the arrest of a Richard Elliott and Richard Vincent for breaking and entering and stealing 460 yards of silk and 461 yards of white linen. They appeared at the Central Criminal Court, where Vincent was acquitted and Elliott sentenced to transportation for fifteen years (*The Times*, 12 March 1845).

Whitechapel business a zealous stripling certainly did put on women's attire one night, but he was not commended for his detective instinct in so doing.'

Lansdowne did admit to two other occasions on which a disguise had been worn. Apparently one officer had enterprisingly dressed himself in a baize cloth to resemble a statue in order to catch a thief at the Great Exhibition of 1862. The second time was when an inspector he refers to as 'G' dressed as a clergyman so as to catch a shopkeeper selling indecent prints. Lansdowne was not pleased: 'It was scarcely a credit to the cloth that a clergyman's attire was considered the best disguise, but it was.'[9]

Other officers were more prepared to admit to the use of disguise in run-of-the-mill criminal cases. Detective Inspector J. G. Littlechild maintained that a clergyman's outfit was a favourite with detectives, since it was both easy to put on and it disarmed suspicion. In his time Littlechild had disguised himself as a surveyor and a sanitary inspector as well as a cab-man. Acting was clearly in his line. To win a private bet he had dressed as a minstrel and had been thrown out of a public house.

In the fight against one of the lesser-known aspects of English criminal behaviour – arson, animal maiming and poaching in East Anglia in the nineteenth century – a Superintendent English was hired from the Metropolitan Police in 1844 for the West Suffolk area. Writing on the period, John Archer describes him as: '[to] be considered as the outstanding policeman of the period. He was the forerunner of the plain-clothes policeman, for he dressed and worked as a labourer in order to gain working people's confidence.' English was responsible for the trials of five principals and received an award of £100 and a watch for his effort.[10]

9 Joan Lock identifies the clergyman-officer as G. H. Greenham. In his memoirs, the Chief Inspector mentions the instance as the only occasion on which he wore a disguise. Joan Lock, *Scotland Yard Casebook*; G. H. Greenham, *Scotland Yard Experiences from the Diary of G.H. Greenham*.
10 J. E. Archer, *By a Flash and a Scare*, p. 156; *Bury and Norwich Press*, 11 September 1844 and 30 April 1845.

Much of the dislike of disguise can be traced to the attitude of the Commissioner of the time, Sir Charles Warren, who on taking the post relinquished the Governorship of the Red Sea Littoral.[11] He took over from Colonel Sir Edmond Henderson following rioting in Trafalgar Square in February 1886.

Warren lasted two and a half years, during which time there were more troubles on the streets and he quarrelled bitterly with the Home Secretary over the duties and powers of the Commissioner. He also came under severe criticism for the failure of his officers to solve the so-called Jack the Ripper Whitechapel murders, attributed over the years to a wide variety of suspects from the Duke of Clarence downwards. Indeed, one of the more farcical aspects of the Ripper case was the hiring of two bloodhounds from a Mr Brough in Scarborough at the amazing cost of £100. The dogs managed to lose themselves.

There is little doubt that the CID was having a really bad time in the latter part of the 1880s. According to the *Pall Mall Gazette*, whose gadfly-like editor W. T. Stead stung the authorities whenever possible, it had collapsed by October 1888. The reasons given were numerous. First, there was a rule that all officers had to be over 5 foot 10 in height. The *Gazette* also complained that all CID men had to serve two years in the uniform branch, so giving the criminals a chance to get a good look at them and, worse, by the time they did become detectives they could only walk with the characteristic Scotland Yard 'gait' and so were even more readily recognisable. More serious were the limitations on payments to informers and the rule that an officer could not leave London on a case without the permission of the Chief Commissioner. 'Under these circumstances it is not surprising

11 For an account of his early career, see W. Melville Lee, *A History of the Police in England*.

that our detectives do not detect,' chortled the *Gazette* happily.[12]

By November 1887 James Monroe, the Assistant Commissioner head of the CID, was complaining that his department was overworked and under-manned: 'The result has been that Mr Williamson has broken down, and that I am in a fair way to break down also.' Frederick Williamson, the then head of the Detective Branch, was granted three months' sick leave in February 1888. Nor was the CID getting much support from Warren. He believed it was a 'drop in the ocean' compared with the uniform branch, as he wrote in *Murray's Magazine*, adding insult to injury when he concluded that the original function of the police had been prevention and that detective work was not suited to the 'genius of the English race'.[13]

As Bernard Porter says, Warren thought that:

. . . policing should be open, visible and by the book, rather like cricket, where everything was governed by the rules of fair play. Plain-clothes policing was like taking off the bails at the bowler's end without a warning whilst the batsman was backing up. It was also a constant temptation to corruption as history showed very well. This sort of attitude from a superior was clearly difficult for a dedicated detective like Monroe to live with. Detectives knew that life was not like cricket, and especially among the criminal fraternity. Corruption was the risk you had to run to be effective, and not half so dangerous as the stultifying effects of red tape. This was really the hoary old dilemma of the British

12 *Pall Mall Gazette*, 8 October 1888, p. 3. William Thomas Stead was one of the great crusading English editors campaigning amongst other things against child prostitution. In 1883 he procured a child, handed it to social workers and then wrote an article. Prosecuted, he was imprisoned for three months, but his campaign led to the passing of the Criminal Law Amendment Act 1885. Later he embraced peace and spiritualism, writing a book, *If Christ Came to Chicago*. He died in 1912, a passenger when the *Titanic* sank.
13 Watkin W. Williams, *The Life of General Sir Charles Warren*, pp. 587–90.

police since its earliest days: how to reconcile purity with results.[14]

The first woman undercover worker employed on more than a casual basis was almost certainly a Mrs Garner (or Gardiner):

> In 1916 at the request of the Admiralty, we trained and supplied a selected policewoman for anti-espionage work, and to help tackle the problem of the drug traffic, which was then growing to very dangerous proportions amongst soldiers back on leave from the Front . . . Our unit disguised herself as a prostitute, got to know all her supposed colleagues, moved in circles where she was in constant danger from the drug-runner, and obtained information of a most important kind, both in connection with drug-running and spying.[15]

> . . . who, a florist before the war, developed a positive genius for detective work. She was lent to Commander Paget, who was engaged in special intelligence work for the navy and some very important evidence on cocaine was obtained through her, leading to further legislation. She was the only woman on the staff of the Metropolitan Observer Service for the detection and location of enemy aircraft, the only woman who understood all the complicated machinery used for the purpose.[16]

In February 1920 Mrs Garner was awarded an MBE for her work with the Metropolitan Observer Service.

Women had been used on a more casual basis before Mrs Garner, however. In what amounted to an almost classic

14 Bernard Porter, *Origins of the Vigilant State*, p. 84.
15 Mary Allen, *Lady in Blue*, p. 38.
16 Mary Allen, *Pioneer Policewoman*, p. 132.

example of the *agent provocateur*, one undercover woman was possibly the wife of a police officer (reports vary) who was used to ask the advice of a chemist, Thomas Titley, about her pregnancy. He had long been suspected of being an abortionist, but there was no evidence to go before the Grand Jury (the rough equivalent of examining magistrates). In 1880 an inspector wrote to Titley explaining that he had seduced a young woman who was now pregnant and wished to procure an abortion. Titley was asked to supply the necessary drugs. At first he seems to have been reluctant to do anything without, at least, seeing one if not both of the parties. A police sergeant and a 'female researcher' called at his house in the assumed characters of the seducer and the mother of the unfortunate girl. Medicines were supplied and so the evidence was now in place. The Grand Jury was invited to consider the position in December 1880 and the Recorder of London set everything out before them. The first problem they had to overcome was that it was admitted that the story told to Titley had been baseless from beginning to end. There was, as the Recorder pointed out, no young man, no mother and no young woman. In law the transaction was complete the moment the sale was effected, but the Recorder had some strong things to say about the conduct of the police.

What they did is to be justified only on the assumption that all means are fair which lead to the detection of crime. But even this is not a sufficient excuse for the means employed in the case before us. Thomas Titley was suspected, but no more than suspected, of having given his help in genuine cases before. What if the suspicion is unfounded? What if the temptation held out by the police had induced Thomas Titley to take his first criminal step? The law knows nothing of suspicions. It presumes innocence until guilt has been produced. Is it the duty of the police to do all they can to lead innocent men into crime and then to turn around upon them and denounce them for the arranged offence?

There had to be a true bill against Titley, but the Recorder also invited the jury to return one against the police and their witnesses for fraud and conspiracy, and this they did.

The Times was convinced the police had behaved badly. It was in good, thundering form:

> Whether the phantom charge against Thomas Titley can be sustained or not is a matter which concerns himself. The charge against the police is of much more general consequence. We must undoubtedly assume that the police and their associates believed that they were doing right. It is even said that they acted under direction which would go far to absolving them from personal liability. But whatever may be the issue of their trial, the result it cannot fail to have will be a clear laying down of the rules by which they are to be guided for the future. Within what limits is it allowable for the police to tempt men to the commission of crime? There are certainly some cases in which the thing in question may be done. The police-constable who is served with drink at forbidden hours or in an unlicensed place does not thereby expose himself to the charge of conspiracy. To send letters by the post containing marked coin is a common practice enough where a letter-carrier is suspected of dishonesty, and, possibly to lead him into an offence of which he may never have been guilty before. But to convey letters with money in them is, it may be urged, one of the regular duties of a letter-carrier. He is subjected to no unfair trial by being set to do what he had undertaken to do and what he may be called on to do any day.
>
> . . . In Thomas Titley's case the whole crime from one end to the other is the mere concoction of the police. He is found engaged in his lawful occupation as a chemist,

and he is urged to an unlawful course outside his regular business. There is more here than the detection of crime. The initiative is with the police and not with the offender, each subsequent step is the result of a distinct suggestion on the part of the police. What should we think of a police-constable who instigated a man to open a booth for the unlawful sale of liquor, who then bought liquor from him, and who finally dragged him into court for his breach of the Excise laws? What if a letter-carrier were told of a valuable packet about to come into his charge, and were urged to steal the contents and divide the spoil with his informant? If such courses as these are held to be justifiable, they will cover Thomas Titley's case, as it appears in the charge of the Recorder, but they will hardly more than cover it. If the police have really done what the Recorder's charge implies, and what the finding of the Grand Jury endorses against them, the proceeding is described none too strongly as very greatly to be reprobated in itself and for the abuses to which it obviously lends itself.[17]

Then as now.

It did Titley little good. Two days later the police officers were discharged and Titley was sentenced to eighteen months' hard labour. A series of memorials raised on his behalf were sent to the Home Secretary. One was from his wife, the second was signed by 286 neighbours and the third by 3,800 people from London and the provinces. They did the chemist no good either. Writing to Titley's solicitors, the Home Secretary said that he had examined the allegations by Taylor and Morgan, whose complaints had led to police intervention in the first place, and found there was no ground for interference in the man's sentence.[18]

The so-called golden age of a crime-free Britain of the

17 *The Times*, 14 December 1880.
18 *The Times*, 14 March 1881.

1930s may have been something of a myth, but there is no doubt that the Second World War irrevocably changed the face of British crime. Before the outbreak of hostilities there is little doubt that the ordinary public eschewed crime. They probably saw their involvement as little more than fending for their families, but now new doors were opened for old and new criminals alike. Now, with bomb-damaged shops and buildings open to looting, all kinds of goods came on the black market and into receivers' hands. There was a steady trade in stolen ration books. Under cover of the blackout the smash-and-grab raid proliferated and Billy Hill, for one, found that small post offices were a profitable target for safe-breaking expeditions. By the end of the war it was estimated that there were 20,000 deserters in London alone.

It was in this climate that on 31 December 1945, shortly after the end of the war, one of the more curious and relatively short-lived of Scotland Yard's innovations, the Special Duty Squad, was created. Under the aegis of Sir Ronald Howe, then the Assistant Commissioner (Crime), and Percy Worth, then head of Scotland Yard's CID, four young officers – John Capstick and Henry 'Nobby' Clark, both of whom were then detective inspectors, and Detective Sergeants John Gosling and Matthew Brinn – were given the task to 'carry the war into the enemy's camp'. Each of the men had specialist knowledge of the criminals of a part of London, and their brief was specific. They were to use their extensive knowledge of London's Underworld and live amongst the criminal fraternity. Later they were joined by Detective Sergeant George Burton.

Neither you nor your men will give evidence in court. As far as the Underworld is concerned, you will have no more material existence than ghosts. How you manage it is your affair but we want results – fast!

From those remarks of Worth the squad took its name. Its official title may have been Special Duty Squad, but it was known to everyone as the Ghost Squad. There were good reasons for its introduction.

> Against the depleted ranks of the police was ranged a new type of criminal, cunning, ruthless and well informed. Many had served in the armed forces – some with distinction – and many more were deserters. They were younger, fitter, harder, more resourceful and more energetic than the pre-war criminals.
>
> All Britain was the province of these new criminals. Time, money and distance were no object if the pickings were good. They swooped almost every night. Lorryloads of tea, sugar, butter, clothes, cigarettes and whisky disappeared from the streets or were stolen from warehouses. Jewellery and cash vanished from private houses into the pockets of thieves who worked like phantoms. Fur and rings, clothing and petrol coupons, carpets, lipsticks, typewriters, razor blades, shoes – anything with a ready cash value was loot for the army of the underworld. The figures of stolen property rose to astronomical proportions.[19]

There had been at least one forerunner of the Ghost Squad, recalls Capstick.[20] 'Squibs' Dance, along with his brother Alf, was a member of the Flying Squad:

> A rough diamond, he always wore a cap and scarf, like a labouring man, and rolled his own cigarettes from a virulent brand of shag. He never took a cigarette out of his mouth once he had lit it. When the stub was an eighth of an inch long he spat it out, and he didn't care much where it landed. It was never a good idea to stand within a couple of yards of Squibs for that reason.
>
> He more or less lived with thieves in the public-houses,

19 J. Gosling, *The Ghost Squad*, p. 20.
20 J. Capstick, *Given in Evidence*, p. 91 and pp. 53–4.

and was usually accepted by them as a particularly cunning member of their own fraternity. He worked different areas in rotation, and was never tumbled. Drifting into a tavern in South London, cigarette dangling from his lower lip, he would be greeted: 'Blimey! Where have you been?' To which he would mumble, 'Well, I only came out of stir last week.' Then he would work in the far west of London and when asked, 'Been having a lay down for six months?' replied shortly, 'Nah, four.' If somebody ventured to inquire which prison he had been in, and what he had done, Squibs would glare and mutter that he didn't talk. No wonder the underworld looked upon him as a real fly thief.

Another of his favourite disguises was that of a seaman, a common and useful one for police officers generally: 'We paid a visit to a dockland slop shop and emerged as three of the roughest, most drunken seamen who ever lurched ashore from the K. G. Five dock.'[21]

John Gosling describes the early days of the Ghost Squad which lived in an office – something which was, he says, the nearest approach to a cell he had seen outside prison.

> Our office was spartan: four walls, two tables, a telephone, and a door with a key in the lock; that was all.
>
> Only one policeman, apart from the members of the Squad, had access to that room during our tenancy. He was Archie, a bald-headed policeman who was the essence of discretion. He was a wonderful character. He brought us cups of tea and sandwiches and sometimes meals. We called him 'the Butler'. He was also invaluable as a 'base camp' man. We were nearly always out and Archie took the phone messages which arrived while we were on the job.

21 Robert Colquhoun, *Life Begins at Midnight*, p. 59.

The members had a *carte blanche* with which to work. They would meet between ten and ten-thirty in the morning, depending on when they had gone to bed the night before, and at six o'clock they would telephone John Capstick to tell him how their day had been spent. At first he sent a weekly report to the Home Secretary, but with the Squad functioning more than satisfactorily this requirement was dropped after three months. For transport the Squad shared an old and dirty Austin 16 which Gosling recalls he once managed to coax to a dramatic fifty-five miles an hour. Perhaps he was a poor driver – Capstick recalls the car as 'super-tuned'.

The Squad had a spectacular success in February 1947, when information was received that a team from North London would raid the Midland Bank in Kentish Town. This was to be one of the earliest examples of kidnapping a manager, stealing his keys and then raiding the vault. The Ghost Squad could find out when but not where the manager was to be snatched. The information was passed to the then head of the Flying Squad, Bob Lee. It shows what dangers lie in undercover work even when precautions are taken.

Lee decided to substitute an officer for the bank manager, and a DS William Davies took the part. Wearing spectacles and a bowler hat, he left the office and travelled towards the manager's home on the Northern line to Woodside Park; he was followed at a discreet distance by two other detectives. As he walked along a footpath by the then semi-rural station, he was attacked and coshed and the officers saw him being bundled into a van. Once the gang had the keys he was thrown out into the snow, still bound and blindfolded. Half the team began an unsuccessful search for Davies; fortunately for him, he was seen by a motorist who drove him to a doctor. The other half kept watch on the bank and when within an hour a man arrived and let himself in, the Ghost Squad swooped. Neil Darbyshire puts it delicately: 'The terrified robber, a window cleaner by day, was in no position to demur and immediately told the furious detectives all they wanted to know.'

At the Old Bailey the team received between three and five years. Davies was awarded the King's Police Medal.[22]

A similar exercise took place the following year when a team of robbers were thwarted in their desire to steal some £250,000 from the BOAC warehouse at London airport. An informer tipped off the police, and fourteen detectives substituted themselves for the guards, mechanics and other staff in the warehouse. The arrangement had been for the guards to be given drugged tea, but the warehouseman who had been approached had contacted the police. When the robbers arrived they found the guards apparently asleep. Fighting broke out and at the end eight robbers were captured. Some reports say it was the whole team, but Underworld legend has it that at least one escaped by hiding under a lorry.[23]

By the late 1940s there were serious doubts about the wisdom of operating the Ghost Squad. The money paid to informers was considerable, and the law of diminishing returns was beginning to apply. Even more seriously, there were fears that accusations could be made that the police were acting as *agents provocateurs*. The original officers had become too well known to the criminals, and officers from the Flying Squad were drafted in and out. Now some officers were thought to be getting too close to their criminal counterparts for their and the force's good; there were also suggestions that reward money was being shared by some officers and their informers.

One of the casualties of the Ghost Squad was Detective Sergeant Robert Robertson who, whilst seconded to the Squad,

22 Neil Darbyshire and Brian Hilliard, *The Flying Squad*, pp. 83–4. Since the 1970s, kidnapping and hostage-taking has become a much more common form of crime. Examples include the 1976 Dunstable bank robbery, when a manager's family was held hostage, and the £1 million Security Express robbery in Millwall when a security guard and his family were taken hostage. The aim is to force the key-holder to co-operate and usually the hostages are released relatively unharmed. One of the most highly publicised in recent years was the kidnapping of Elizabeth Kerr, whose husband managed Barclays Bank in Sale, Greater Manchester. It followed an attempt the previous week when Tony Bosson-Williams, the kidnapper, had gone to the wrong house. He received a total of fourteen years at Chester Crown Court on 14 January 1994.
23 Shifty Burke, *Peterman*.

met Morris Page. He was a hanger-on to the notorious Messina brothers – Maltese pimps who had had a grip on vice in Soho over nearly a twenty-year period – and their brother-in-law, Tony Micalleff. Robertson's downfall came as late as 1955 when he was involved in the case of Joseph Grech, charged with housebreaking. The solicitor in the case was Ben Canter, one of the lawyers who had acted for the brothers. Grech seemingly had an unshakable defence. Part of the evidence against him was that the key to the burgled premises had been found on him, but he maintained that it fitted his own front door and therefore was of no significance. However, the jury found that it was and, from his cell where he was serving three years, Grech subsequently unloaded a series of legal bombs.

He had, he said, given Page around £150 to hand to a Detective Sergeant Robert Robertson, the officer in charge of the initial case, who made the key to the burgled premises available so that a locksmith could make a lock to be fitted to Grech's front door. There was to have been a further £150 given to Robertson on an acquittal. He also alleged that Robertson had coached Ben Canter about the questions to be put at the trial.

When Robertson, Page and Canter appeared at the Old Bailey charged with conspiracy to pervert the course of justice, Grech unloaded even more bombs. His conviction, he said, had been brought about by perjured evidence of other officers acting on the instructions of an Inspector Charles Jacobs attached to West End Central.[24] Jacobs, he said, had asked him for £2,000 so that none of his flats or brothels would be raided. After negotiations, the terms had been set at £500 down and £30 a week. Canter, said Grech, had been the bagman, taking £100 to give to Jacobs. According to Grech, Canter came back saying, 'He wants £500.'

24 In February 1956 Jacobs was dismissed the force, having been found guilty by a disciplinary board of assisting a prostitute to obtain premises, of failing to disclose in court a man's previous convictions, and of failing to account for property taken from an arrested man. His application to the High Court for an order quashing the verdict, on the grounds that by reason of his mental health at the time he was unfit to prepare his defence, was rejected.

When he came to give evidence Canter was in difficulties over his relationship with Micalleff, who had been accepted as a surety in the original case by Robertson:

—Can you imagine any honest policeman agreeing to take Micalleff as a surety for this man Grech?
—That is a difficult question to answer.
—I think it is a simple question. Try to answer it . . .
—It depends on the circumstances.

Canter received two years' imprisonment, as did Robertson – who for many years continued to protest his innocence, consulting various firms of London solicitors to try to have his conviction overturned. The intermediary, Morris Page, went to prison for fifteen months.

In September 1949 the Ghost Squad was closed down by Sir Harold Scott. During the three years and nine months of its existence, members arrested 789 criminals, solved 1,506 cases and recovered property worth more than a quarter of a million pounds. Despite this undoubted success the autonomy given to the officers, for the best of motives, can be seen as the beginning of the period when the Flying Squad began to operate 'a firm within a firm' which would lead to the great police corruption trials of the 1960s and 1970s.

The Squad may have ceased officially to exist in 1949 but according to the former Commissioner, Sir Harold Scott, in 1954 'a little group of officers continues to act in this way'.[25] This was the Criminal Intelligence Branch, serving the whole of the CID and not merely the Flying Squad.

Although ten years later officers were still being used to infiltrate gangs and carry out jobs with them, it was by no means common practice. According to Leonard 'Nipper' Read, former National Co-ordinator of the Regional Crime Squads:

25 Sir Harold Scott, *Scotland Yard*, p. 168.

Before the Regional Crime Squads, there wasn't the money available and anyway there were considerable dangers for the officers. Without careful handling there is also the danger that the officer seeing money vastly in excess of his salary and pension may be turned.

This has certainly been the case in America.

Whilst there are now numerous accounts of in-depth undercover infiltration by police officers in America, there are few documented examples of English work. Nevertheless, over the years they have taken place.

One recent American example is of a northern Californian officer who went 'deep cover' riding for eighteen months with a group of Hell's Angels. The operation was a great success resulting, as it did, in a very large number of arrests of high-level dealers who until then had been regarded as almost untouchable. The officer was highly praised but the cost to him was a high one. He became personally involved in drugs and fighting and slid into alcoholism; his family life disintegrated and after resigning from the force he took part in a number of bank robberies and received a term of imprisonment.[26] In another case a Chicago police officer who posed as a pimp and infiltrated a prostitution ring became so enamoured with the life that he took it up himself after the investigation.[27] In a third case another officer, a member of an elite drug enforcement unit in Boston, became an addict.[28]

What makes a good undercover officer? Joe Pistone, one of the most successful of all time undercover agents, is clear:

You have to have a strong personality. Strong means

---

26 Laurence Linderman, 'Underground Angel' in *Playboy*, July 1981, quoted by Gary Marx in 'Who really gets stung? Some issues raised by the New Police undercover work' in *Crime & Delinquency*, April 1982, pp. 165–93, as are the next two examples.
27 *Chicago Daily News*, 24 September 1975.
28 *Boston Globe*, 26 October 1979.

disciplined, controlled, confident. It doesn't mean loud and abrasive or conspicuous. It means your personality can withstand the extraordinary challenges and temptations that routinely go with the work. It means you have an ego strong enough to sustain you from within, when nobody but you knows what you're really doing and thinking.

You have to be street-smart, even cocky sometimes. Every good undercover agent I have known grew up on the street, like I did, and was a good street agent before becoming an undercover agent. On the street you learn what's what and who's who. You learn how to read situations and handle yourself. You can't fake the ability. It shows.[29]

In Britain senior officers look to what Detective Chief Superintendent Roy Ramm calls natural attributes:

By natural attributes I mean their size, shape, colour, gender. Nobody too physically outstanding is selected, and we expect them to have some special skills that we think might be useful in their undercover role, such as speaking a foreign language. We then take them on a training course for two weeks, which gives them a lot of basic about the law, making sure they know how to avoid overstepping the mark.

We are keen to make sure that the officers keep their feet on the ground, that they don't think they are part of Miami Vice, that they don't start to live their undercover role.[30]

Back in 1966, Bobbie James,[31] an officer from a North Country force, was deputed – almost at a moment's notice and certainly

29 J. D. Pistone, *Donnie Brasco*, pp. 98–9.
30 R. Fleming with H. Miller, *Scotland Yard*, pp. 112–13, 115.
31 A pseudonym.

untrained – to infiltrate and report on a London gang of robbers. He had joined the police in Wales before coming to the North where he became a beat officer and then transferred to the CID after some six months. He was seconded to the Regional Crime Squad in April 1965 when 'in those days they were still selling themselves to local forces'.

I came to know a Hungarian who was obviously a true villain with an English wife who was working as a prostitute. He'd been very active in London on smash and grab raids. He was giving me information and I got to know him over a period of time when he was trying to establish himself as a decent member of the community, apart from the prostitution that is. Of course people like that can't. Money is the root of all evil. With a good class villain no matter what money he gets he gets rid of it easily so the villain's wife went on the game in Hull. Some of his pals kept coming up to see him. His name was now Joe and he knew I was a police officer. Initially he tried to soft-soap me and passed me information. He was working as a handyman ferrying other prostitutes.

Then one of his friends, Tibor,[32] another Hungarian successful smash and grab artist, came up to see him. Joe went back down to London with him and rang me and asked if he could see me. I met him at the station and he took me for a drink and five or six of the gang came in. I was passed off as a mate. I was never called by my name – just Taff. Stayed overnight and saw him again the following day. It took a period of time for me to be accepted and gradually I let it be known that I was an escapee from Walton and was willing to assist in anything they did. I had no written guarantee from my superiors. It was never even mentioned. The prime object was to put them away as best you could.

32 The names of all those who were not convicted in the subsequent case are pseudonyms.

The first job was a clothing shop in the Seven Sisters Road in North London. It was led by a Brian Scrivens. He was an absolute charmer, a man who could mix in any circles. He was also totally paranoid. He was speechless before a job – he did nothing but think about it. He'd been on the run for two years after escaping from a six-year sentence for armed robbery and was paying a detective in Fulham weekly rent for his freedom. He would go to the toilet with him to bung him. He used to say, 'Here's another fucking payday for him.'

Another member of the team was another Brian [Johnson] also on the run after two out of four years. A third, Legos Trestyen, had got out of Hungary at the time of the uprising and it was said amongst them that he was wanted for murder back there, but I've no idea if it was true.

The Seven Sisters job was just because someone wanted clothes. We wore the suits for months afterwards but the basic jobs were smash and grab raids on furriers all over the South of England as far as Bournemouth. We would steal a Jaguar and then leave it in a car park for four or five days. There would be four of us on a job. There would be the driver, the one who went for the window, and two on either side would be on the pavement ready to fend off any spirited citizen who wanted to intervene. I would usually be one of those. The m.o. was to circle the place and do it any time of the day when we thought that it would be less busy. Early hours of the morning or mid-afternoon on half-day closing were really best. The men had no fear. If anyone was in our way they'd have no hesitation in carting them on the bonnet.

We'd steam up to the premises, pick-handle through the window and pull the grille out, hit the glass below. There could be thousands in the window. For example the Hull jewellers, Carmichaels, had £220,000 on a pad in the window and that was in the 1960s.

215

The funniest episode was in Russell's Antiques in Richmond Hill in Bournemouth. We did it in the early hours of one summer morning. We'd broken the window grille and taken £20,000 in jewellery in that time. Then the Borough Force came up the arcade in a vehicle. I was off like a shot. I ended up in the toilet in the centre of Bournemouth. I was actually standing on the ledge of the door when the dog came sniffing around, and if there's one thing of which I'm frightened it's dogs. I stayed in that lavatory for about two hours before I went to catch a train back to London. I was frightened they'd do a second search. I was regarded as quite a hero for getting away. I got back before Tibor and was surreptitiously blaming him, 'How can there have been so many bastards', and so on. Very often the people who got caught seemed to get the blame for the failure.

Of course, they were basically bloody evil people. We were living in Bayswater and Joe took his wife and used her as a prostitute there. In turn he befriended a girl from an approved school and got her on the game. Some of the time I lived with yet another Hungarian. I can't remember his name. He had two girls living in a place off Fulham Green with Scrivens and his girlfriend.

The team loved bragging together saying what they'd done and talking in derogatory fashion about Old Bill, how they'd been caught on the job but hadn't had their collars felt because the stuff they'd stolen had been stuck in the back off the police car and away. The gang was on the fringe of the Richardsons and things went in their direction. The firm got 25% of the proceeds if they were lucky. There was a shareout for those who were on the raid and we blew it all in a few days. If you were out of cash it was a treating situation. If you weren't on the job you got a backhander. It meant the man who was treated was now a 'friend' or a 'pal', someone who wouldn't squeal. It proved an affinity. If he was bunged then he was as near a trusted friend as he could become. Whoever was around when the job came up was invited. What we did depended on how much money we had, if a job was coming off or if we were planning one. Work came to us rather than our going out looking. Someone had heard . . . someone had suggested . . . it was easy to do . . . a lot of money . . . jewellery somewhere. We would look at local newspapers to see who was appearing in court and for what. Were the local police up to dealing with us?

There were about thirty who came and went in the gang. There was no team leader. Scrivens wasn't trusted anymore than anyone else. I had to show I wasn't trusting the others without actually saying it. I had to get with Joe without actually seeming to do so.

If we were between jobs things were relaxed. We would get up very late and go to the pub to drink, go for a meal in a café and then back boozing. It was rare we ever ate at the flat. Sometimes the men would stay with a girl for a week or so and then discard her. A number of them had girls on the game, so it was a question of collecting money from them in an evening and possibly going to a nightclub. I was amazed how much the girls earned. They handed it all over. They were far too terrified to hold any back. Once we gatecrashed a party – Scrivens could easily talk his way in somewhere like that. It was quite a society party with everyone swapping partners so no one knew who was with who. Coats and wraps all over the place. Suddenly Scrivens says, 'We're off.' The back seat of the car was laden with coats, jewellery, a couple of pieces of silver. There was never an opportunity missed. He'd obviously done it over a long period of time. He liked to take the piss out of the Establishment and to have a pay day at the same time. It satisfied his ego.

Part of the time I lived with a man known as the Chinaman in N11. He kept a collection of firearms in his place. Then I moved and I lived with Scrivens in the upstairs flat in Fulham Green. I drove the car for him on one occasion. We also did an electrical shop, car radios were packed in oblong boxes. They were piled high along the wall. This was security money for a good Christmas. The women who lived with Scrivens were terrified. They'd take a thumping and next minute be in bed together. The flat was piled high with clothing. We'd wear a different suit every night. A lot of the gear never got taken out of its boxes.

One thing I'll never forget was watching a young girl procured for prostitution in Hull. This lass, she'd dyed jet-black hair. She was married to a fisherman but separated. The fishing fraternity was then very localised. She was very pretty but common as muck. Joe's wife, Tricia, befriended her. A Hungarian came up and took her out, gave her cash which she spent, thinking it was a present. She got a good hiding when she couldn't repay, and he took her to London and put her on the game. There was nothing I could do to stop it.

James's life with Scrivens and his friends wasn't the only problem:

During this time I was liaising with a DI on the Flying Squad. There was an attitude of disbelief that a lad from the sticks was telling them what was happening. We'd heard there was a hell of a lot of bent coppers in London. It was just as well I didn't know too much about them. They could have pressured the people I was living with, and what they'd have got by whispering in their ears who I was. I'd have been a body in the Thames.

I'd spoken to him two or three times before I met him which was about a week after the first job – the clothing shop in the Seven Sisters Road. We'd done it basically because someone wanted some clothing. I passed the information back but no one was ever pulled. I went to

218

the Yard and my contact and his sidekick took me out for a few pints. I had to have some wheels and he took me to a car hire shop and I got a grey Morris 1000 which to my knowledge I've never paid for. We never got a bill for it up here. My story to the boys was that it was a ringer.

With Scrivens and his friends, once there was plenty of money about no one was attached to you. On the other hand, if there was a job you were always chaperoned. It was strange the way they manoeuvred without saying anything directly; two were never left alone together. 'I'll go with X.' 'I'll go with Y.' There was no internal trust. Once it started to be planned, then there was just no way you could get away.

My difficulty was in trusting the Flying Squad.

There were two fraudsmen called Tony and Harry on the edge of the gang. They would take a luxury flat, pay the initial rent and get an extra three months' living. The next thing was they'd hire a chauffeur-driven Bentley, get some stolen credit cards and cheque books, pull up outside stores, always on a Friday afternoon, and have a ball filling the boot. I'd hardly seen credit cards used up to this time.

I went with them this one Friday and we literally filled the boot. They couldn't be served quick enough. We went back with stuff to the flat and there must have been £10,000-£15,000 worth of gear. That particular night we went boozing. It was the time of the purple heart scene. The gang weren't addicts; they used to drink a fair bit and were pushers rather than addicts. Then around 2 a.m. they started on the hearts. Early next morning I got in touch with the D.I., went to Bow Street Magistrates' Court and we got a warrant at 10 a.m. before the court started.

There was a café at the gates of Scotland Yard and I sat there reading a paper whilst a D.I. and his mate went off to turn the flat over. I knew the boys were out to the world. At 12 they came back. I had arranged to meet them at a pub on the corner. They said there was nothing, just a few cheque-book stubs. I was absolutely flabbergasted. The gear was positively there. Even with the answer, 'just a few cheque books', they should have had their collar felt for that.

By the Autumn things were getting difficult. My job was to get information back and not to be involved in a prosecution. There were always people being caught on or after the robberies and there were always people getting away, but I began to think that I was getting away too much and someone would notice. In London my work had put seventeen people away in six months:

The end came in Hull in the December. Joe came back up, and I'd been away from the team for a couple of weeks when Tibor came North. When he saw Carmichaels' window he had eyes like organ stops. When we were all back in London Tibor was telling the group about Carmichaels. There was no problem he said about security. There really wasn't any. The difficulty would be getting out of the city. He'd got a local paper to read the crime and to see what the police were used to. Had they facilities to deal with robbery? The truth was they hadn't. There was another recce, this time with Johnson and Tibor, and it was decided we would come up and do it.

I told them I knew the area because once I had been released from Hull prison and had to make my way home. I said I'd go and find a flat. I could then telephone and tell them where I was, which was going to be in the east of the City. By this time I was pretty well trusted and I was the first of the team to arrive. Johnson, Scrivens, Trestyen all came up in a stolen Austin Cambridge. Some of us were going to get out of the City by train and so one had a ticket to Sheffield, one to Birmingham and so on. Tibor was to be at the station.

Meanwhile Joe had gone back down to London and I got a telephone call from Dover to say he was in the nick for some petty crime. He'd been locked up after he'd come across on a ferry. He wanted to see an officer straight away as he'd found out that there was a pile of cannabis coming into Dover. Thomas Smith, a DS from Yorkshire, and I waited up that day and were told that yet another Hungarian, Peter, would be met by two coloured fellows and we stayed in Dover that night.

I was told the man was a big dealer, Alexander, who had a shop in the Finchley Road and a flat in Golders Green. We went to the Drugs Squad C1 and there a DC and a detective sergeant were assigned to us. We got warrants for both the shop and the flat. On the Wednesday there was a half-day closing and the shop was shut. I went with the detective sergeant to the flat. Who should be there but Tony and Harry.

Not a word of recognition. But as we were searching, a Jag pulled up and Peter shouted something in Hungarian down to an elderly gentleman and a lady. Off they went. Then a couple of minutes later up came another Jag with two coloured lads. Peter yelled, 'Fuck off, Old Bill,' and they were away. We should have moved him from the window.

We took him across to the jeweller's shop and there was nothing. It was just a front, watches, inexpensive stuff. At the back it was virtually empty but there were cement bags and in those bags were polythene bags of cannabis as well as stolen cheque books and passports.

Peter asked to speak to the DS. He came back and said, 'He's just offered me an open cheque.' Walt asked, 'What are you going to do?'

'Bail him under the Magistrates Courts Act.'

Walt said, 'Christ, you can't do that.'

But we were on their midden. We came back disgusted. We kept ringing up and were told the substance had to be tested but the other stuff was obviously stolen. I've no idea whether it ever reached the security lockers. After about six weeks we got in touch with the DS. He'd refused to charge Alexander. 'Why?' 'Insufficient evidence.'

I had to put up with that the whole time. A little later Peter was locked up in Hertfordshire over a load of stolen art treasures from some stately home and started to sing. One day I was in the Crime Squad and the telephone went and who was it but the DC from London. He asked if I had been questioned and indeed I got a call from a DI at Scotland Yard. The DC wanted to know what I'd said and I told him I'd spoken to John Bliss who was then the National Co-ordinator of the Regional Crime Squad when he'd visited our area. So had Thomas Smith. Neither of us heard any more.

The prime object was to put them away as best you could, but the object of some officers in the Met at that time seemed to be to keep them out as long as they were paying. There was no question of my acting as an *agent provocateur*. That kind of person lived by committing crime.

In the meantime I'd told the powers that be and I had my left arm put in plaster to protect me against the police dogs when they arrived. When the team asked what had happened I told them I'd had a long wait at Doncaster to get the connection and so I'd done a job. I told them I'd fallen off a wall whilst doing a screwing. When the police came round I was on my bike and away. They thought this was great. It was the beginning of December. In the flat in Williamson Street there was a provision for open fires. I got a couple of bags of pre-packed coal. I told the men I'd nicked the coal from a shop up the road. Nicking coal, in a strange sort of way, was as good as a high-class burglary. What I was doing was copying the bravado they often showed.

We stayed in the flat six days. Every day we would case the place and we were also looking for a Jaguar as a getaway car. We went miles for the thing – as far as Harrogate. Then came the news that the higher-ups thought it would be too dangerous to try and capture us as we did the robbery. On 6 December 1966 the flat was raided and we were all locked up. When we were nicked a nice fire was glowing.

One of the first things was a de-briefing and I told them about the slaughter in Fulham Green. We kept ringing but for hours and hours there was no reply. Eventually we got through, gave the message and then more hours later the reply came back. There was nothing there. My cover went when I wasn't seen in the dock. It was only then that I learned two of them really were prison escapees.

Within the next year a man who had been serving a sentence for armed robbery was released six months after I had finished. He was a bouncer at the 51 Club and said, 'How's your arm, Taff?' What had happened was Stocken was an escapee and he had spoken with the man who had put two and two together. I said, 'What are you on about?' and he just shrugged. I never had any repercussions. I saw Joe about three years later. He was back with his wife in Hull and now she had two children.

We put away about seventeen people in six months or so on my information, which wasn't bad. As for fear, I don't think I knew fear then. I was young and the adrenelin was flowing.[33]

33 On 12 December 1966 David Johnson, Brian Scrivens and Legos Trestyen appeared before Mr D. N. O'Sullivan, the Hull stipendiary magistrate, and pleaded guilty to receiving a car knowing it had been stolen. The police case was that they had been keeping watch on the car and had seen combinations of the men pass it nine times. Johnson had escaped twice after thirty months of a four-year sentence for possessing forged notes and an automatic pistol. The first escape had been in 1964 and in December 1965 he had escaped from Wormwood Scrubs. Scrivens had received four years in 1962 for office breaking and possession of housebreaking instruments and explosives. Thirteen days later he had received a further six years for armed robbery. He had escaped in 1964. Trestyen had five previous convictions and had been recommended for deportation. All were committed to Leeds Quarter Sessions for sentence. The magistrate told DI Williams, 'I commend you in particular and the Crime Squad generally for your action in causing the apprehension of these three men. I regard this as an important case and it is obvious that a great deal of thought, care, intelligence and powers of observation went into this operation.'

In rather more structured circumstances a Metropolitan officer, Frank, was able to infiltrate the team who planned to rob the KLM warehouse at London airport. On 9 October 1992 Peter White and Carl Harrison were jailed for twenty and sixteen years respectively. White – who, using false references, had obtained a job in the KLM warehouse – and Harrison had planned to kidnap and torture Ann Blake and her daughter, so forcing Ian Blake, a KLM cargo supervisor, into opening the Heathrow strong-room which was said to contain up to £40 million in banknotes and diamonds. It was a thoroughly professional job, with Blake being watched and timed in his movements.

White contacted a former cellmate whom he wanted to fly his share of the proceeds from an airfield at Elstree to Switzerland for him. Unfortunately for him the cellmate had turned informer and a police *Operation Daedalus* was put into effect with Frank being introduced to White as a professional robber. He and Harrison were taken to prearranged venues such as Heston Service Station and the Hounslow East tube station, where up to 40 hours of incriminating tapes were recorded. Later a second officer was introduced as a driver.

On 8 December 1991, armed with handcuffs, wire ties, an imitation revolver and a CS gas canister, Harrison – wearing a balaclava and with Frank in tow – went to Blake's home in Staines, Middlesex, to find more than fifty officers waiting for him. White was arrested later in the day. The surveillance operation had lasted five months.

Detective Chief Inspector Toby Child said of Frank:

He put his life on the line in order to get us the result that we wanted. It is unusual for criminals in this type of offence to plead guilty. The operation was so successful that up until the arrest and even subsequent to the arrest, neither Harrison nor White suspected anything.[34]

34 *Today*, 10 October 1992.

Commenting on his role as an undercover officer, Frank said that the first fifteen minutes were the worst: 'I learn the background of the other person and I live that during the course of the operation.'

Undercover work is now recognised as extremely dangerous and stressful, and officers are now given an 'uncle' to whom they can speak freely without management barriers and paperwork. Although a number of officers have been injured, fortunately in this country none has been killed.[35]

One of the other problems an undercover officer faces is having to stand by and watch the beating of another person rather than break that cover. In 1990 an undercover officer watched a fight in a Newcastle nightclub following which the late Newcastle hardman, Viv Graham, received three years for wounding Stuart Watson, the doorman at Hobo. At the end of the trial the doorman said he was sorry for what had happened, and went on to accuse the Regional Crime Squad of using him as bait to get Graham and the others. There had been an undercover officer posing as a customer when the incident had taken place, who had been under orders not to intervene. Unsurprisingly he came under heavy fire from the defence lawyers and was asked whether, when he realised one of the men had a spiked weapon, he should have stepped in. 'No,' replied the officer. 'I had been briefed and instructed not to.'[36]

One of the most successful long-term operations was *Operation Julie*, the code name – after one of the women officers, a twenty-eight-year-old Detective Sergeant – given to a drug surveillance operation in the late 1970s which ended in trials at the Bristol Crown Court in March 1978 and led to the jailing of Richard Kemp, a brilliant chemist studying nuclear magnetic resonance for his doctorate, who had started the operations with Dr Christine Bott, daughter of an Army officer and sister of a

---

35 R. Fleming and H. Miller, *Scotland Yard*, pp. 117–18.
36 Graham was shot dead on New Year's Eve 1993. No one has been charged with his murder.

Scotland Yard officer. They met at Liverpool University and, according to her, he 'turned her on to cannabis and LSD'. Early in his career he produced LSD for both an American operation in Paris and a mobile suitcase operation which moved peripatetically around Europe.

Originally there was one laboratory – the Cambridge Connection – run by Kemp, Bott, an American author (a disciple of Timothy Leary, the drug propagandist) and Henry Barclay Todd. It operated from 1970 to 1973 and then, when Kemp and Todd fell out, one laboratory became two. Kemp and Bott moved to Wales, where amongst other things she bred goats and he turned out LSD tablets. The second, larger laboratory was at 23 Seymour Road, Hampton Wick, run by Todd with the assistance of Andy Munro and Brian Cuthbertson, the chemist and general assistant in charge of distribution respectively. Export was undertaken through Amsterdam by Richard Burden, who ran a restaurant in Chelsea.

Operation Julie became a worldwide operation, with the American DEA running a simultaneous operation known as Syntac 10. It was discovered that Bott, alleged to be the group's banker, had a deposit box containing £45,000 in Switzerland, and it was thought there was a supply route to West Germany where another of the defendants had a deposit box. There was also a supposition that supplies had percolated through the Iron Curtain. In February 1978, the Soviet delegate at a narcotics conference in Geneva had proposed a resolution condemning LSD, and none of the other delegates could understand why he had done so.

In 1975 a raid had accidentally been thwarted when quite innocently the wife of a local police officer let slip to bricklayer Alston 'Smiles' Hughes – so-called because of his piano-key teeth and an engaging grin – that her husband was going to visit him. When the detectives, including Martyn Pritchard, went back to Aberystwyth police station, the officers began gossiping and the name of Kemp was mentioned. His name had been on record when earlier that year a man arrested by the Mounties in Montreal had bargained his way to freedom by giving information about drug manufacturers and dealers both in America and in Britain. Kemp had recently been involved in a fatal accident when his Land Rover knocked down a vicar's wife; the vehicle was still in the police garage and it was decided to check it out. Amongst a pile of slates some torn scraps of paper, one with the words 'hydrazine hydrate', an ingredient in LSD, were found. In February 1976 *Operation Julie* was launched, and from then on Kemp and Bott were under surveillance. A detective sergeant and a woman officer rented a cottage near the Kemp home for a two-week fishing holiday. Dick Lee, the acting Chief Inspector, posed as a London businessman recovering from a heart operation and was joined by another officer. Although they spent their time in the pubs, they made no progress with the locals and Lee said: 'I suddenly realised that they thought we were two homosexuals and that was why nobody would accept us.' A young policewoman was hastily summoned as a live-in secretary, and relations with the community improved dramatically.

Meanwhile Pritchard, who had lived five years as an undercover cop on the streets and had been 'arrested' for buying cannabis, returned to London and later to Devizes where again Hughes' name turned up. Now a connection was made, wrongly linking Hughes with Kemp and Bott instead of with Todd.

Two officers, Eric Wright and Steve Bentley, spent eight months, part of the time camping in a van, living amongst the hippies in the village of Llandewi Brefi, targeting Hughes who had been pushing drugs since the 'swinging sixties' in the Kings Road. They met him in the New Inn, Llandewi, public house and became friends, losing £90 to him in a card-game. At first Hughes was suspicious of them and accused them of being officers. Wright grabbed him by the throat and threatened to beat him up. Bentley increased their cover by rowing with the local constable about drinking after hours.

After four months they moved out of the van and began sending messages on a radio transmitter from the loft of their cottage. This stopped abruptly when Hughes told them that when he could not sleep at night he liked to listen to ham radio wavelengths. As the months went by Wright drank and took drugs with Hughes, baby-sat his children and, he says, developed such a friendship that he came close to tipping him off that a raid was pending.

Meanwhile Todd was targeted by a surveillance team of eighteen officers camping out in a three-bedroom house in Hendon. A tail was put on him and when he led the officers to Seymour Road the house was put under constant observation. Even now the police were divided as to whether there was more than one laboratory. Dick Lee was convinced the manufacturing was done only in Wales and said categorically, 'No way is there a lab at Seymour Road.' Later, on his retirement, he would be presented with a plaque:

NO WAY

ITALASR

On 25 March 1977, 800 police made swoops in Wales and Seymour Road. In Wales they found nothing, and it was not until shortly before Christmas that Kemp revealed his hiding-place beneath the quarry-tiled floor of the lounge at his home. The laboratory equipment had been hidden down a well.

Shortly before Christmas 1977 another raid produced a haul of 13 million tablets of LSD worth, it was said, £100 million. In a titillating sidebar to the raid, it was made known that on a previous raid a hippy had been found having sexual intercourse with his girlfriend on the floor of an old caravan: 'The couple were on a "trip" and the man had hammered a six-inch nail through his nose "for a new kick".'[37]

37 *Daily Telegraph*, 24 December 1977.

Kemp received thirteen years, as did his rival Todd, and Cuthbertson eleven, Bott nine and Hughes eight. To the annoyance of many of the officers involved in the surveillance, most of the defendants were paroled after serving half their sentences. Kemp and Bott returned to live together after their release.

An interesting side-note appears in the *Sunday Mirror* for 12 March 1978. Chief crime reporter Norman Lucas writes: 'Many top detectives believe that politicians are closing their eyes to Britain's drug problem.'

One officer claims that

> Successive governments have condoned the fiddling of Home Office drug statistics. It could be that only the death of sons or daughters of prominent politicians through drug addiction will start a crusade against those who deal in the dirtiest crime racket in the country.

As is so often the case after a successful operation, jealousy and in-fighting – which had more or less been held at bay during the previous months – now burst out. The hope and belief of Dick Lee was that *Operation Julie* would lead to the formation of a National Drugs Squad, but his hopes were misplaced and instead he soon found himself back in uniform. He resigned, wrote a book on the operation and bought a tobacconist's in the North of England. Six others resigned almost immediately over various criticisms of the way they were treated when they went back to their forces, and there were calls for a Home Office inquiry. Twenty-two members of the squad remained in the force.

> What I will say is that the morale in the squad during the operation could not have been higher. Members of the squad lived in filthy, wet accommodation, ate and slept when they could, worked tremendously long hours

229

and were away from their families a hell of a long time. I just hope someone remembers all this.[38]

In his account of *Operation Julie*, Lee remembers that:

> . . . within months he and five of his men, Johnny McWalters, Martyn Pritchard, Paul Purnell, Alan Buxton and Eric Wright resigned from the police. They found the work they had done and the experience gained was not considered by the Chief Constables to be of any value.[39]

After the Thames Ditton raid three officers ingested drugs through the skin and wound up in hospital fearful that they would be sent to the psychiatric unit, something which would appear on their records:

> We were laughing and smiling about anything . . . When we got to hospital we asked for beds well away from windows in case it might give us that feeling which has affected others that they could fly. It was that scaring.[40]

In his book *Busted!* Pritchard recounts that he was obliged to visit his mother after dark so as not to shame her in front of the neighbours. Some time later he resigned and became a publican in the Midlands. Later, the eponymous Julie left the force to marry a fireman. Wright was one of the officers who left the force soon after the operation was completed.

Short-term undercover officers in *Operation Swordfish* were successful when they posed as the licensee, head barman and a barmaid for six weeks in 1989. The Cauliflower pub in Upminster Road, South Rainham, had been going through managers at the rate of five within eighteen months before the police went behind the bar to flush out a protection team.

38 *Sunday Telegraph*, 26 February 1978.
39 Dick Lee and Colin Pratt, *Operation Julie*, p. 348.
40 *Daily Express*, 9 March 1978.

In July 1990 the leaders, Donald Hoey and Leonard Sherwood, received six years apiece for counts of blackmail.

The dangers for an undercover officer are obvious, as policewoman Elaine Manson[41] discovered about the same time.

In what the police described as the first serious outbreak of protection racketeering – apparently they had already forgotton *Operation Swordfish* – Frank Salmon, a market trader from Dagenham, was gaoled at the Old Bailey for seven and a half years. He had been convicted of blackmail, affray and an attack during which ammonia was squirted in a victim's face. Robert Mitchell, said to be Salmon's right-hand man, was sentenced to three years for blackmail, affray and possession of a firearm, whilst Gary Pollard received four and a half years and Donald Meason twenty-one months.

Salmon had reigned over a part of the East End and Essex for a little over a year, trying to obtain protection money from twenty-three wine bars, clubs and saunas. He had shot up one bar and pressed a gun under the nose of a barman. In 1989 disc jockey Russell Holt, who played the East End pubs, had forty-two stitches in his head and hand following an assault by four masked men. His ankle was broken by a pool cue and he too went to the police, telling detectives he had been asked to pay Salmon £1,500 as a share of his earnings.

The police used Elaine Manson as the person to trap Salmon. Acting as the friend and business associate of Holt's wife, Denise Seaga, who ran a dress-shop, she met Salmon on five occasions, paying out a total of £800. It was thought that Salmon, known as a womaniser, would be less suspicious than if a male officer had acted as a decoy. On one meeting she was patted down by him for wires when he came to suspect that she was a police officer. His antennae were sound. Another time he accused her of being a policewoman and she told the court, 'He started at me and flicked his fingers . . . He shook his arm and a knife slid down inside his left palm.' On a third

41 A pseudonym.

occasion when she was with him she noticed a bulge in the leg of his trousers and remarked that it looked like the outline of a knife. 'Brains of Britain . . .' he replied. 'In this business you get wankers who don't play ball.'

On 22 May 1989 Manson handed over £600 in marked notes and asked Salmon why he referred to the cash as a present. 'I am not going to shout out it is protection money, am I?' he replied. Shortly afterwards he was arrested.

Operation Motion, hailed as the way ahead in British policing and launched in October 1994 by West London Drugs Squad, involved three women police officers going under cover and posing as prostitutes in a brothel in Queensway.

> We were trying to create the image of tarty street girls. We didn't wash, we left our hair dirty and matted and we deliberately chewed our nails.
>
> We had an AIDS poster, packets of Durex lying around and bottles of water which addicts use to smoke.
>
> If you are playing the part of a prostitute you have to prepare for the worst.
>
> Some would grope you but you just had to grit your teeth.
>
> We had to be very careful not to ask for cocaine directly because that would have been entrapment and they could have got out of it in court.

The thirty-five dealers who were filmed on video pleaded guilty and received sentences of between four and six years.[42]

Undercover work and informers go hand in hand. Here is an old-time criminal recounting his involvement; if it is accurate, it nearly amounts to another instance of the work of an *agent provocateur*.

In 1985 I was sitting indoors when Harry Brand,[43] the kid

42 *Sun*, 11 August 1994.
43 A pseudonym.

who lived next door, came round. He was really the local bully and he'd offered me bits of crooked gear from time to time. Usually I declined because it wasn't the stuff I dealt in. If there was any gear I wanted for myself I did a deal with him. Sometimes he wanted a bit of advice and sometimes he told me a few lies but I'd taken them in my stride. Now he wanted to know if I could get him any counterfeit £50 notes. I said I wasn't interested in anything like that. There were too many of the notes about at that time and people were being nicked. A few days later he came back again saying he had a friend in Nottingham who wanted to lay out ten to twenty thousand pounds for £50 notes. This should have stopped me right away because he offered £10 a note when the going rate was £4.

I eventually agreed to go and meet this fellow on the Saturday morning, 22 June 1985. I was with him and another man Jackie 'Tinker' Taylor and I arranged the meet under the flyover at Brent Cross. There were three men in the car. One was a young man in his late twenties who said he was Tony Offord. The second was a very coarse and very nervous Irishman, Paddy Flynn, who was dripping gold and who said he was the purchaser, and their driver. I took them for a drink well away to a pub on Highgate Hill, The Woodman. We had a few drinks and I wouldn't talk business and from there I split them up. I suggested we leave Harry Brand, Offord and the driver there but Paddy insisted his driver stays with him. I decided I'd take them to a pub over Hackney and I'd got bad vibes about this meeting. On the way Paddy asks us if we'll pull into the forecourt of the Archway pub. I said, 'This is a bit peculiar. You come all the way from Nottingham yet you want to go to the Archway.' He made a remark that there wasn't a Paddy in the land that didn't know the Archway. From there we went to The Swan in Kingsland Road. We had a drink and he pulled me aside and said would I sell him some fifties. I asked him how it was to be done and he said he'd bring £20,000 next week but it would have to be the Saturday. He asked if I'd give him a sample and I gave him a straight note. He wanted to keep it but I wouldn't let him.

Jackie and I decided to give it a miss. He didn't feel right about it either; he reckoned the driver was a copper. Paddy and the driver then went back to The Woodman and got Harry Brand to phone us to ask if we'd do business and we said no.

When I got home that night Harry came round and spent two hours trying to persuade me that he'd known Offord for many years and that I should do the business because it meant a good drink from both sides.

I told him we were under the impression it was a set-up and to keep away from it. Every day for the next two weeks he came in begging and pleading for me to do the business. Eventually he asked if I would speak to the Irishman on the phone and come to some arrangements as he'd upped his purchase to £40,000.

From what he said I got the impression the money was for the IRA and I had a talk with Jack who said, 'I can't see the kid next door setting you up, neither can I see his mate Offord setting him up.' So out of greed we decided to do the business.

So, at short notice, we managed to scrape together £110K at face value. It cost £2 a piece. Then we sat down and worked out routes in case it was a ready-eye.

The stuff was taken to Highgate Hill and early on 6 July my nephew put it in black rubbish bags outside a private garage by some shops. There was no danger of anyone picking it up by accident. We'd already given it the once-over and there were no collections that day. I'd spoken to Offord and to the Irishman once on the phone. Now I think he was speaking from a police house.

When I knocked for Harry that morning he said he

couldn't come as his brother had just rung him up and told him he wanted him to drive a lorry. I said to Jackie we'd better swallow it. He didn't think the boy would put it on us and anyway Offord was to be there.

I decided we would go to the meet and I sent my nephew down to a place about two miles from The Woodman and told him once I was satisfied to bring the stuff to me. The Irishman, Detective Constable Valentine O'Rourke, and the same driver, Detective Inspector Roger Hazell, were at The Woodman. Offord wasn't. O'Rourke asked if I had the stuff. He had the cash and we could go round the corner and count it. I wasn't having it. I still had bad vibes and I was afraid of being shot.

So we went to Marler's Wine Bar at the bottom of Highgate Hill. We sat outside giving my eyes a chance. The wine bar was my choice to put them out of position if anything was wrong. I asked to see the cash and Paddy said he wanted to see the notes first. I went to have a world with Jack in the toilet to do a detour round the block and bring back about £10K. I didn't want them to see my nephew.

Roger went and sat in his Volvo. Paddy sat drinking with me as though Scotch was going out of fashion. Jack and I were drinking lemonade. Paddy agreed that he go and pick the cash up. He came back three-quarters of an hour later with a flying bag over his shoulder and I shouted out to Mike to go and get the stuff as everything appeared to be all right.

Next moment Mike brought the stuff up, handed it to Jackie Taylor and the next thing I can remember is being hit over the head with something. There was a Scotsman shouting, 'Where's my piece' and men were jumping on me. I screamed to people sitting outside the wine bar, 'These bastards have fitted me up.' Everyone was herded into the pub and I was taken to Holloway Road police station. When it came to it I was charged with £50K.

Now I know Brand was a police informer. He never gave evidence but his name did come out. While I was in the Scrubs waiting trial Harry came up to see me and said he hoped I didn't think he'd had anything to do with it.

When I got bail though I got him, put a knife to his throat, laid him on the floor and said that if I found he had done it I'd kill him. This bully of the neighbourhood was crying out, 'Please, Mick.'

I wanted to be sure and I went to have a meet with a Chief Inspector I knew and said I'd give £5,000 for the names of the people who'd fitted me up. The message came back two weeks later that there were to be no names but all I had to do was look outside my own front door so I never paid over the money.

Brand used to ring me up crying down the phone, but I had to be very careful with him because I was under twenty-four-hour observation and eventually he was sent to Canada.

I got three years and he came back eighteen months into my sentence. When I came out his family put the house up for sale and then one day the 'For Sale' notice was taken down and I found they'd sneaked out of the back door in the middle of the night. They must have taken all the furniture out that way. That's the last I ever saw of the family. The whole thing cost me £4K and three years.

Even later I learned Brand had stuck up a number of other guys.[44]

44 Some of the police statements in the case appear as the Appendix, and provide a somewhat different account of the incident.

10

The Attitude of the Courts

What then has been the attitude of the courts to the informer, the cell snitch, the undercover agent and the entrapper? Certainly as far as the entrapper is concerned, in Britain and the United States they have followed two differing lines. In one case entrapment was literally that, when a Gary Dawes climbed into a car thoughtfully left by the police for the purpose of luring such people as Mr Dawes who might want to steal from it or take it for a ride around the block. When he shut the door the car locked, and there he was when the police arrived a few minutes later to arrest him. Charged with the offence of aggravated vehicle taking and convicted, he appealed and the Divisional Court said that, on the facts, the process had been a perfectly lawful one. Their Lordships did, however, foresee problems if the officers did not arrive within a short time after the suspect was trapped, and suggested that a recorded message could automatically inform the suspect why he had been arrested.

Entrapment together with the use of informers, both here and in the United States, has always provided problems for the police in terms of just how far the courts in either jurisdiction will admit evidence obtained by such methods. America has always been much stricter in excluding such evidence. There entrapment is in effect a defence, provided it is a relatively innocent person and not an unwary professional criminal who is trapped. The stage was set in the *Sherman v United States* case.

Professional criminals can, at times, be judges. John M. Murphy was an associate county court circuit judge in Illinois from 1972 until 1983, when he was charged with accepting bribes to fix the outcome of hundreds of cases from drink driving to felony, theft and battery. He was assigned to the traffic courts for the first eleven years of his tenure, during which time Judge Richard LeFevour was the supervising judge of the traffic court and the man who had the authority to decide which judge would hear which case. His cousin James LeFevour, of the Chicago police, was assigned to the traffic court throughout almost all that period and organised the movement of cases to Murphy, who would dismiss them or give a supervisory sentence. Money would then pass from the successful lawyer to James for onward transmission to Richard LeFevour. The going rate seems to have been about $100 a case, with 10 per cent in addition for the police officer running the traffic court list.

The state prosecutors expected to win as much as 90 per cent of their traffic cases against public defenders but none against a group of lawyers known as 'miracle workers'. In one drink-driving case the prosecutor asked a woman defendant, 'And don't you think it is fair to say that you were under the influence of intoxicating liquor?' The woman, who had failed the roadside tests and admitted drinking, replied, 'Yes, I guess that is a fair thing to say.' Judge Murphy called a recess, suggesting that the defence attorney have a word with his client. As he left the bench he was heard to call out, 'You won't believe this. The State's Attorney just got the defendant to admit she was drunk.' When the court sat again the defence lawyer asked his client if she was drunk and this time she said she was not. The defence lawyer made no closing argument. Murphy said, 'I still have a reasonable doubt. Not guilty.'

An *Operation Greylord* was set in place in which agents

of the FBI lied on oath about made-up cases. Murphy had an ingenious defence to the allegation that by his bad behaviour he was depriving the people in his jurisdiction of his honest services. It was impossible, he argued, for there to be 'honest services' because these cases involving the FBI were themselves frauds on the court.

The United States Courts of Appeal disposed of this quite simply: 'In the pursuit of crime the Government is not confined to behavior suitable to the drawing rooom.' The FBI and the prosecutors had, the court found, behaved honourably in establishing and running *Operation Greylord*. They had notified the presiding Judge of the Circuit Court's Criminal Division, the State's Attorney of Cook County and the Attorney General of Illinois. The *Greylord* cases did not interfere with the smooth operation of the local courts. In this respect they were less offensive than 'sting' operations in which the existence of a well-paid fence may induce people to steal goods. Here no stranger was at risk. *Operation Greylord* only harmed the corrupt.[1]

Evidence obtained by the use of entrapment has gone down two sharply divergent paths in America and in these courts. In the United States, where entrapment has been shown the courts have, in the past, rigorously excluded that evidence where the behaviour has actively encouraged the commission of a crime.

One of the old American cases, *Grimm v United States*,[2] points up some of the difficulties and actually sets out the distinction the courts have often made in these cases and the thin line they have often walked to uphold or quash a conviction. Mr Grimm was convicted of mailing information to a Herman Huntress as to the terms of sale of what were engagingly described as 'obscene, lewd or lascivious pictures'. I doubt they would cause a blush on the face of the proverbial

1 *United States of America v John M. Murphy*; 768 Federal Reporter, 2d Series, p. 1518.
2 156 US 604.

maiden aunt nowadays. Unfortunately for Mr Grimm, however, Herman Huntress was the pseudonym, or perhaps *nom
de chasse*, for Mr McAfee, a post office inspector and an agent
for the grandly named Western Society for the Suppression of
Vice. The US Supreme Court held that McAfee was merely
seeking to discover the nature of Grimm's business, as opposed
to endeavouring to induce the commission of a crime.

In another example, *Sorrells v United States*,[3] a conviction
for selling a half-gallon jar of whisky was overturned. The
prohibition agent had posed as a tourist and – something
which seems to have aggravated matters, it appears – had
either served or pretended to have served with the defendant
in the same regiment in the First World War.

In *Sherman v United States*[4] the Supreme Court took a similar view. Here the court roundly condemned the behaviour of a
government agent, Kalchinian, who whilst awaiting sentence
for drug offences made friends with another man who was
trying to wean himself off a drug habit. He was eventually
persuaded by Kalchinian's repeated appeals to supply him
with drugs. Worse, he went back on to drugs himself. The
Court said:

> The case at bar illustrates an evil which the defense of
> entrapment is designed to overcome. The . . . Government
> plays on the weakness of an innocent party and beguiles
> him into committing crimes which he otherwise would
> not have attempted. Law enforcement does not require
> methods such as this.

Over the years, as crime and criminal have become more
sophisticated, we can see the American horror of entrapment
weakening. There are two essential issues in an entrapment
defence, says Professor Alan Dershowitz:

3 287 US 435.
4 356 US 369.

The first is whether a government agent *induced* the defendant into committing the crime. If he did, then a second issue arises: the defendant cannot be convicted unless – and this is a big unless – the government can prove that the defendant was *ready and willing* to commit the crime and was just waiting for an opportunity. If the government can prove that the defendant was thus 'predisposed' to commit the crime, then it can convict him even if its agents 'induced' him into committing it on that occasion.[5]

Now in *United States v Williams*,[6] convictions for mail fraud have been upheld even though Federal undercover agents embossed blank credit cards supplied to them by the defendant at their invitation. The courts seem to have had no trouble with undercover agents who run a pawnshop as part of a 'sting' operation or who buy stolen cars. There are, however, American jurists who take the view that an undercover agent may buy but not sell drugs.

The current American position can perhaps be summed up by the case of *United States v Murphy*.[7] Here a conviction for an escape from a Federal prison was upheld notwithstanding a due process claim based on the alleged conduct of prison officials who were said to have encouraged and possibly assisted the escape. The court took the view that even if the allegations were true they failed to establish a due process defence because the government had not engineered the crime from start to finish and its involvement in the crime had not risen to the level of 'creative activity'.

The entrapment defence known to American lawyers as the 'defense of last resort' works only rarely if there is anyone approaching a professional criminal in the dock. They regard it as a defence which can be used only if there is no other chance

5 A. Dershowitz, *The Best Defense*, pp. 236–7.
6 1986, CA9 Cal.
7 1985, CA7 Ill.

241

of acquittal. The thinking behind it goes that prosecutors can use inducements on the basis that any jury will take the view that organised crime leaders will be predisposed to committing any crime and are just awaiting the opportunity to do so. Entrapment is, therefore, in no way unfair.

Over the years there have been various attempts – mostly unsuccessful – in the English courts to limit the damage to a defence by the use of a police spy or *agent provocateur* as opposed to a co-conspirator or co-accused.

In *Dowling*,[8] a jury was advised to treat with caution the evidence of a man who had entered into a conspiracy in order to betray it. Both the judge, Mr Justice Erle, and another judge, Mr Justice Maule, in *Mullins*,[9] another case that year, were sure that an infiltrator was not an accomplice about whose evidence the jury had to be given a specific warning.[10]

The next step was to try to have the evidence excluded on the grounds that it had been unfairly obtained, so putting it on a par with an improperly obtained confession. In a Courts-Martial case, *Murphy*,[11] the defendant had been convicted of giving information regarding security at a barracks to men whom he believed were Irish terrorists but who were, in fact, undercover agents. Lord Parker, C.J. had said in an earlier case, *Callis v Gunn*:[12]

That discretion [i.e. the 'overriding discretion' to exclude admissible but unfair evidence], as I understand it, would certainly be exercised by excluding the evidence if there was any suggestion of it having been obtained oppressively by false representations, by a trick, by threats, by bribes, by anything of that sort.

8 (1848) 3 Cox C.C. 509.
9 (1848) 3 Cox C.C. 531.
10 J. D. McLean, *Informers and Agents Provocateurs* [1969] Crim. LR 527.
11 [1965] N.I. 138.
12 [1964] 1 Q.B. 495.

It was now argued that the behaviour of the officers pretending to be members of a terrorist organisation was a trick. The Courts-Martial Appeal Court would have none of that. Oppression would not be satisfied by mere deception by the police which was 'as old as the constable in plain clothes'.

The next tack to be tried was that, as a mark of its disapproval of the conduct of the police, the court should refuse to convict. This is a line which, if raised sufficiently delicately, may appeal to a jury but received no change from the Divisional Court. In *Sneddon v Stevenson*[13] the defendant had spoken to a plain-clothes officer and was subsequently convicted of soliciting for the purposes of prostitution. The argument, which had no success at all, was that the police officer was acting as *agent provocateur* and the court should quash the conviction to show its disapproval. The court said that the police officer had 'merely placed his car so that she [the defendant] could solicit *if she so desired*'. The case would seem to be a relatively early example of what might be described as passive entrapment, as opposed to active entrapment as is exercised in vice cases in America. There a game of cat-and-mouse is played when the undercover officer endeavours to get the girl to make a fatal proposition before she discovers his real identity. As the cases of Titley, Birtles and Macro showed, even active entrapment has only counted towards sentence, and in the first of those cases not even then.

Four years after Birtles in December 1973 the question of law, reality and Northern Ireland all meshed neatly into one case to the eventual benefit of no one. Jeremiah Mealey and Philip Michael Sheridan appealed against their conviction at St Albans Crown Court of conspiracy to rob. The allegation was that they had conspired with a number of other people who lived in Luton to rob a bank and send the proceeds back to Ireland for the benefit of the Republican interests there. They were probably talked into the enterprise by an Irishman,

13 [1967] 2 All E.R. 1277.

Lennon, who at the very least was an informer and probably an *agent provocateur*. With some skill he put together the robbery, but at the last minute pleaded he had a sick child and could not leave the house. On the way to the robbery – surprise, surprise! – Mealey and Sheridan, along with two others, were arrested. They received ten years' imprisonment for their pains.

So far so good, or bad, depending upon one's attitude. The next stage was that Lennon went to see the National Council for Civil Liberties and began to make a statement to the secretary, Larry Grant, part of which made criticisms of the police for forcing him to become an informer. Unfortunately, although he said sufficient for Mr Grant to make a reconstruction from his notes, Lennon did not live long enough to sign a complete statement. He was shot dead in Surrey.

The Court of Appeal was not sure that Lennon was an *agent provocateur*, but that he was an informer they had no doubt. Nor did the Lord Chief Justice mind that he was so.

> . . . It must be accepted today, indeed if the opposite was ever considered, that this is a perfectly lawful police weapon in appropriate cases and common sense indicates that if a police officer or anybody else infiltrates a secret society, he has to show a certain amount of enthusiasm for what the society is doing if he is to maintain his cover for more than five minutes.
>
> . . . it is, in our judgment, quite clearly established that the so-called defence of entrapment, which finds some place in the law of the United States of America, finds no place in our law here.[14]

The appeals were dismissed.

The discretion of the courts to exclude what could be seen to be unfairly obtained evidence was largely clarified by *Sang*.[15] In this case involving forged US notes, the defence was that

14 *R. v Mealey and Sheridan*, 60 Cr. App R p. 62.
15 [1979] 2 All E.R. 1222.

his conduct was the result of behaviour by a police *agent provocateur*. The House of Lords unanimously rejected the decisions which had favoured the discretion of a judge to exclude evidence gained as a result of entrapment.

The question of improperly obtained evidence was to a certain extent codified in the Police and Criminal Evidence Act 1984 *s.* 78 (1). It provides that in any criminal proceedings where the court is asked to allow evidence on which the prosecution proposes to rely to be given, if it appears to the court that, having regard to all the circumstances, including the circumstances in which the evidence was obtained, the admission of the evidence would have such an adverse effect on the fairness of the proceedings, the court ought not to admit it.

It was not long before appeals were being lodged after convictions where the trial judge had refused to exclude evidence. First, however, there is a 1986 Home Office circular to be considered: '. . . No member of a police force, and no public informant should counsel, incite or procure the commission of an offence.'[16]

In *Harwood*[17] the defendant and two others were convicted of conspiracy to evade the prohibition on the exportation of counterfeit currency. It was suggested that X, the person to whom the currency was to be delivered, was either an *agent provocateur* or an informer. The trial judge held that he was not but, even had he been, *s.* 78 was not designed to exclude entrapment evidence. The Court of Appeal observed, *obiter*, that since PACE was an Act dealing with evidential matters it could not be used as another route to abrogate a rule of law that entrapment was no defence.

In *Gill and Ranuana*[18] the defendants were convicted of conspiracy to murder. They alleged that X, through whom they had met undercover police officers, was an *agent provocateur*,

16 Home Office Circular No.35/1986, *Informants who take part in crime.*
17 [1989] Crim.LR 285.
18 [1989] Crim.LR 358.

something the trial judge rejected. The Court of Appeal expressed doubts about the observations in *Harwood*, reverting to *Sang* by saying: 'we have no doubt that the speeches in *Sang* and the import of those speeches are matters to be taken into account by a judge when applying the provisions of *s.* 78.'

It was clear the Court of Appeal was going to have to reconcile these decisions and in effect lay down some guidelines, and it had the opportunity to do so in some domestic undercover operations.

A recent phenomenon – or if not recent, one which has newly surfaced – is that of the disgruntled spouse or lover, usually the former since there is often insurance money involved, who, tired of his or her partner, seeks out a hit-man or woman to remove the incumbrance. Since it is said that the price for disposing of an unwanted lover is around £1,500 it is not surprising that the trend is growing. In a twist to the tale, the hit-man turns out to be an undercover police officer and the enterprise ends in tears and prison. It appears that some officers specialised in these productions, travelling outside their area to assist in the undercover operation. One regional crime squad detective was found to have posed as a contract killer on three occasions.

Barrie Irving, Director of the Police Foundation, said on the Channel Four television programme *Dispatches* which highlighted this line of business:

> The undercover policeman acts the part well, but perhaps too well. The target genuinely believes that the hit-man is a professional killer prepared to murder for a relatively small sum of money.
>
> That generates a high level of fear. The 'hit-man' may then put pressure on the target saying things like, 'Make your mind up – have you got me all the way here for nothing? You're wasting my time.'[19]

19 Quoted in *Police Review*, 15 October 1993.

It was not long before the matter was resolved. In two cases which came before the Court of Appeal in the autumn of 1993, *Smurthwaite* and *Gill*,[20] the court considered in what circumstances evidence obtained by undercover officers should be excluded. Both cases concerned defendants who had been convicted of soliciting to murder. The prosecution case had been that each defendant had tried to arrange the murder of his or her spouse but, in fact, the 'contract killer' turned out to be an undercover policeman. Should the court allow the evidence obtained in what was undoubtedly a trap?

The Lord Chief Justice, Lord Taylor, after emphasising that *s.* 78 of the Police and Criminal Evidence Act 1984 had not afforded a defence of entrapment, set out the considerations the judge should take into account in exercising his discretion in excluding evidence as unfairly obtained. Questions in a not exhaustive list included: Was the officer acting as an *agent provocateur* in the sense that he was enticing the defendant to commit an offence he would not otherwise have committed? What was the nature of the entrapment? Does the evidence consist of admissions to a completed offence or does it consist of the actual commission of the offence? How active or passive was the officer's role in obtaining the evidence? Is there an unassailable record of what had occurred or is it strongly corroborated?

This, it was thought, might have settled the undercover contract killer policeman situation once and for all, but it did not.

In the case of Harbel Mann, who received a six-year sentence at Oxford Crown Court in 1992, he said his marriage had been breaking up and his wife was seeing someone else. A police informer approached him at a club and offered to find a hit-man, who turned out to be an undercover policeman. In the case of Paul Dixon, who received five years at Plymouth Crown Court, also in 1992, the court was told

20 *New Law Journal*, 5 November 1993.

he was having a nervous breakdown and gambling heavily. He was approached in a casino by a man who offered to deal with his wife for him.

The would-be contractor might wish to withdraw but, as in the case of Alan Bainbridge who received seven years in 1989 at Chelmsford Crown Court, they found themselves unable to do so, saying that after meeting the undercover officer he or she was too terrified to do anything but go ahead with the plan. Concerted appeals were launched and the Court of Appeal heard an application for leave to appeal in the cases of Mann and Dixon.[21] The idea was to show that the third person, the one who had contracted the police, was an informer and because he had not given evidence in the trial it was unfair. An informant might have purposes of his own (indeed they all do), and by the time the undercover officer had been introduced, the husband or wife had been incited to commit a crime that would never have been contemplated but for the informer.

Bainbridge's solicitor, John Bacon, had told Duncan Campbell in the *Guardian*:

This is a nebulous point of law . . . with the undercover police masquerading as hit-men. If you place someone in submissive circumstances their free will will be overborne and they provide evidence against themselves.

The Court, with the Lord Chief Justice presiding, would have none of this.

One of the main reasons for using undercover police officers in such cases was to avoid having to rely on informants of bad character, who might be regarded by the jury as unreliable witnesses.

In many cases, moreover, there were other good reasons of public policy for not calling informants. They, or

21 Their appeals were dismissed.

their families, might be put at risk of reprisal and their value as informants in ongoing or future cases might be destroyed.[22]

The attitude of the officers involved in these contract killer cases is typified by 'John' in *Scotland Yard*:

> What I will never do is talk them into it. But I don't talk them out of it either, because I worry that if I talk them out of it, a week later they'll go and ask someone else.[23]

In *Christou*[24] the Court of Appeal had already decided that discussions between suspects and undercover officers, not overtly acting as police officers, were not within the ambit of the codes under the 1984 Act. Then in *Smurthwaite* the Lord Chief Justice added a proviso that officers should not use their undercover pose so as to circumvent the code. In *Bryce*[25] the court had held that the undercover officer had done just that and acted outside the code. The judge, in deciding whether to admit the evidence, must then consider whether he has abused his role to ask questions which ought properly be asked by a police officer and in accordance with the codes.

Given the law as set out by the Lord Chief Justice, it is easy to see how Mr Justice Waterhouse came to exclude the evidence in the case of Keith Hall. On the other hand, if the defendant is an experienced criminal this may count against him even if there is a deliberate breach. In *Allardice*[26] the defendant had been refused access to a solicitor and then made a confession. In his evidence at the trial, he said that he was well aware of his right to remain silent, and so his confession was given in evidence.

22 *Guardian*, 18 July 1994. *Dixon* (Paul): *Mann* (Harbel); *The Times*, 31 December 1994.
23 R. Fleming and H. Miller, *Scotland Yard*, p. 122.
24 [1992] 4 All E.R. 559.
25 [1992] 4 All E.R. 567.
26 [1988] Crim. LR 608.

Then in 1994 came two cases which set post-crime undercover work on its head.

Patricia Hall, the mother of two young boys who disappeared
from her home in Pudsey, Yorkshire, in January 1992, has
not been traced. On 10 March 1994 her husband Keith was
acquitted of her murder at Leeds Crown Court. The prosecution
case was that Hall, who ran a mobile grocery, had confessed
to an undercover policewoman 'Liz' that he had strangled his
wife and then incinerated the body. The policewoman had
been planted on Hall after he replied to a 'lonely hearts'
advertisement in his local paper. All their meetings and
telephone calls had been tape-recorded, and when Liz was
discussing marriage and expressed a worry that Patricia Hall
might return, Hall was alleged to have said, 'I was sleeping
downstairs, then I woke up. I strangled her. It wasn't as simple
as that, there were voices in my head telling me to do it. I'm
sorry. Does that change anything. Do you still want me?'

At the trial the judge, Mr Justice Waterhouse, refused to
allow the jury to hear the tape, saying that the questioning by
the policewoman had driven a coach and horses through the
Police and Criminal Evidence Act 1984 which was designed
to protect suspects in interviews. After the verdict he did,
however, allow the publication of the contents of the tape.
Hall had maintained that his wife, who had had psychiatric
treatment, had simply walked out on him after the marriage
had deteriorated. He appealed to her to return so that their
relationship could be renewed. She does not, so far, appear
to have done so.

Perhaps the most gross example of an attempted entrapment
to garner a confession came in the case of Rachel Nickell who
was savagely killed, stabbed to death on Wimbledon Common
in July 1992. There was the usual police sweep of suspects
and men living in the area who had convictions for indecent
assault or indecent exposure. Amongst them was Colin Stagg,
then twenty-nine, who had, it appeared, a compulsive hatred of
blonde women whom he told friends were wicked people with

loose morals. Many of the women to whom he had exposed himself were blondes. He lived in a poorly furnished council flat in Roehampton near Wimbledon Common, and had a collection of fairly soft-core porn girlie magazines. He was a survival fanatic, and a committed pagan who said he wanted to be thought of as a white witch. What he also craved was a long-term relationship.

He fitted the profile drawn up by Paul Britton, a clinical psychologist, who had been called in to assist the police. Other aspects of the psychological profile concluded that the killer would have a fantasy of using a knife to physically and sexually assault a young submissive adult woman, and sexual excitement from anal and vaginal assault coupled with the victim's fear and submissiveness. Stagg at some time wrote letters to a woman who had placed a 'lonely hearts' advertisement; she told the police that they were 'totally disgusting'. Britton was now invited to mastermind a honeypot trap, using a young policewoman to insinuate herself into Stagg's emotions and so, it was hoped, obtain a confession. A policewoman who was identified as Lizzie James began a correspondence and purported friendship with Stagg.

Guided by Britton, she wrote to him of her fantasies which were described in court by William Clegg QC as 'just about the most hard-core pornography one could imagine'. It was suggested by Mr Clegg that the police and Mr Britton operated a carrot and donkey routine in which Lizzie would 'punish' Stagg by not replying immediately to a letter which was considered not to have gone far enough, and to reward him with a quick response if the letters he sent were suitably deviant. Letters which would probably have been 'rewarded' included those he wrote saying he had never had a sex life, and those containing fantasies such as having sex in the garden and one of having sex in a car.

His rewards included a letter which read, in part:

You write really well, if I close my eyes I can feel you

sitting astride me and pressing me into the grass. I believe this is only the tip of the iceberg. I'm sure your fantasies know no bounds.

In a reply to a letter in which he thought he might have gone too far, she wrote:

My fantasies know no bounds, sometimes my imagination runs riot, sometimes this worries me. I hope I'm not sounding unnatural; but sometimes normal things are just not enough and my demands are much greater, not just straight sex, there is so much to explore. God, don't think I'm a weirdo.

Her later letters contained hints of her past experiences of ritual sexual abuse, her desire to be dominated and, later, of sado-masochism. It was now thought that she must speak to Stagg on the telephone. He was not as forthcoming as was hoped and she offered to take him on holiday. By May 1993 she brought the subject round to murder, and he talked of using a knife in his sexual fantasies. They met for lunch in Hyde Park and he then handed over a letter which contained what were seen to be the common key ingredients – a local common, sunny weather, trees and a knife used to trace marks on the victim. To help things along, Lizzie claimed she had taken part in a satanic murder of a baby and a young woman. 'In certain ways I wish you had [killed Rachel] because it would make things easier for me,' she told him.

Four days later he told her a completely invented story of how he had strangled a young woman in the New Forest and had buried her. At their third and last meeting, Lizzie threatened to break up the burgeoning relationship.

'There can't be anything between us, Colin,' she said, and added in reference to the Rachel murder 'if only it had been you'. According to her evidence Stagg continued to deny the murder but admitted being close to the scene. He started to show signs of sexual arousal and spoke of another fantasy in which on Wimbledon Common he would creep up on Lizzie with a knife. 'If only you had done the Wimbledon Common murder it would be great,' she enticed.

By now, however, Stagg was clearly suspicious and contacted the *Daily Star*. He told Lizzie that he could have admitted to the murder, but that to do so would have been a lie. The operation was wound down, the letters dried up and within weeks Stagg was arrested and charged.

The prosecution's argument was that the psychological profile showed a man who had a sexual fantasy of inflicting anal injuries and who lived near Wimbledon Common in similar circumstances to Stagg. There was a negligible chance of two men with those fantasies being in the same place at the same time.

On 14 September 1994 Mr Justice Ognall refused to allow the evidence of Lizzie James to be given in evidence:

> Any legitimate steps taken by the police and the prosecuting authorities to bring the perpetrators to justice are to be applauded, but the emphasis must be on legitimate. A careful appraisal of the material demonstrates a skilful and sustained enterprise to manipulate the accused, sometimes subtly, sometimes blatantly.

He went on to say that the transcript of the interviews showed an attempt had been made to seduce the accused into exposing his innermost fantasies.

Almost immediately there was a bitter argument between the police and Crown Prosecution Service over where the blame lay for the exclusion of the evidence. On the face of it the rift was healed when Sir Paul Condon, Commissioner of Police for the Metropolis, and Mrs Barbara Mills, Director of Public Prosecutions, metaphorically held hands on television and said the criticism had been misplaced.

Curiously enough, two days after the Hall decision a case

at the Swansea Crown Court showed that the informer-*agent provocateur* is alive and well, albeit having in this instance fled to Greece, and that however gross an entrapment there may be to commit a crime there is still no defence. A police informer, Graham Titley, run by a Midlands Regional Crime Squad officer, managed to persuade a gang to forge £18 million American Express travellers' cheques. He is said to have netted around £100,000 from Amex by way of rewards.[27]

In August 1990, Titley was arrested by the West Midlands police in possession of £10,000 of counterfeit currency. He came under the wing of Detective Constable Alan Ledbrook and began to talk. At his trial in February 1991, Detective Superintendent R. Beards, then second in command of the West Midlands Regional Crime Squad, sent a letter to the judge saying that Titley could help to smash 'major criminals throughout the United Kingdom and Europe . . . who are engaged in the large scale distribution of drugs and counterfeit currency'. It was also thought that he could expose paramilitary organisations in Northern Ireland who were using drugs sales to finance their activities. Titley, who had a string of relatively minor convictions going back to 1970, was sentenced to eighteen months' imprisonment of which he served seven. As befitted a good officer, Ledbrook kept in touch with Titley during his sentence. By the end of the year and now relocated in Staffordshire, Titley was used in a target operation.

The target was sixty-one-year-old David Docker, who said that until he met Titley he was conducting a successful business in factoring and buying and selling end-of-range goods. An undercover operation was set up. First there was an attempt to persuade him to buy a container of drugs from Holland; the undercover police buyers said they would buy it from him. An attempt by Docker to persuade the police to pay up front failed. He made no attempt to contact the 'sellers'.

This operation was not a success and in March 1992 the

27 David Rose and John Merry, 'Scandal of police "fit-ups"' in *Observer*, 25 September 1994.

254

director of casework at the CPS headquarters, C.W.P. Newall, authorised the police to obtain and try to supply Docker with fake travellers' cheques. Immunity would be given to Titley and an undercover officer known as Mickey for offences they might commit along the way to their target. On 16 May 1992, Docker and some friends were lured to a hotel on the M1 where there were £4 million fake Amex cheques in the boot of a car. Seven men including Docker were arrested. Titley received £37,000 for his efforts.

Nor was the trial a success. Defence lawyers spent a considerable amount of time and effort in trying to get disclosure of documents from the prosecution, including the amount paid to Titley as a reward. In turn he disappeared. When it came to it, Ledbrook did not attend the trial either: he had, said the police, suffered a nervous breakdown. Judge Richard Gibbs dismissed the charges in July 1993, saying that the case was an abuse of process. He was particularly unhappy that the prosecution had not complied with his order for disclosure of documents. He kept an open mind, he said, on why Ledbrook had failed to appear.

What might have been disclosed if the documents had been produced was the sum of £50,000 also paid by Amex to Titley in May 1993 for the Swansea case. By now Titley had been resettled in South Wales and was in contact with a printer, Bernard Wilson, trying to persuade him to print forged Equity cards, MOT certificates and cheques. Wilson, facing bankruptcy with the failure of his business, agreed to print the cards but not the other items. Titley brought pressure on Wilson to go ahead with the whole deal. Wilson claims that threats were made to ensure his full co-operation and, with £5,000 supplied to the police by Amex and handed on to Titley, the necessary equipment was bought. The South Wales police were tipped off and when Wilson and seven others were arrested the raids discovered a world record of $26.6 million forged cheques. Judge Hugh Williams, criticising the conduct of Titley and Ledbrook, said that the eight men arrested were victims of 'scandalous, corrupt incitement' which led them to being 'fitted up to commit crimes which none would have ever dreamed of committing otherwise'.

At least one serving police officer from the Midlands Regional Crime Squad knew or believed that the informer was acting as an *agent provocateur*. Not only that, but he was doing so when he was being handled by a serving police officer from the Midlands. Despite his comments, the judge refused to allow the men to change their pleas to 'not guilty', saying that he was not considering imposing a custodial sentence.[28]

In late October 1994 a third trial involving Titley collapsed when no evidence was offered at Leeds Crown Court against two men, neither of whom had convictions and who had been accused of trying to sell fake travellers' cheques, a situation into which they had been lured by Titley. The Police Complaints Authority began an investigation into all three cases.

Then came a drug importation conspiracy in the Court of Appeal in which, if ever there was a case of entrapment, this was surely it. The facts were simply that a man named Honi, a Pakistani informer used by the United States Drug Enforcement Agency, brought 20 kilos of heroin into this country at the request of Shahzad, a Pakistani dealer, and with the knowledge of at least one customs officer. Honi was then installed in a hotel room and for several weeks tried to persuade Shahzad to come to England. His friend, Latif, arrived the next day, and when both men went to see Honi they were given six bags of Horlicks made up to look like heroin. Both men were promptly arrested. On appeal they claimed first that it was an abuse of process to lure them here, and secondly that Honi's evidence should have been excluded under *s*.78 Police and Criminal Evidence Act 1984.

The Court of Appeal was particularly impressed by the fact that for once a major operator had been arrested. All too

28 *The Times*, 17 September 1994.

often it is the small mule who is caught; sometimes with the connivance of the bigger operator who sacrifices a pawn to enable a smarter move to be made. If on occasions the bigger fish were lured here and then hooked, there was no abuse in that.

There still remained the overall question of whether Honi's evidence would have such an adverse effect on the fairness of the proceedings that it should be excluded. Their Lordships had little sympathy with the argument that *s.*78 of the Police and Criminal Evidence Act 1984, which was designed to protect the innocent, should be invoked on behalf of an importer of £3.2 million worth of drugs into the country. They thought Parliament might be surprised to hear that the protection of the section extended to such a man. Nor were they impressed with the argument that the evidence should be excluded on the grounds that he was encouraged by an agent of the British Government.

They did not accept that the admission of Honi's evidence had such an adverse effect that it should not have been admitted, and they reiterated that it was for the trial judge to decide; they could not begin to say he was wrong. The appeals were dismissed.

It would seem that once again the court has hardened its heart against the professional criminal and, given there was no bad faith, in future it will take a great deal of persuasion before evidence in such a case would be excluded. Nevertheless the exclusion of evidence under *s.*78 is a matter for the discretion of the trial judge, and for the present officers should not rely on judges always taking such a robust view. However, overall the heartening part of the appeal from the viewpoint of the police is that it appears the Court of Appeal was, at least obliquely, strengthening the resolve of judges against excluding such evidence. It might seem, however, that the court had rather gone against the principles of *Smurthwaite*.

However, not all cases in which the defence has tried to have evidence excluded under *s.*78 have gone against the police. In

Bailey[29] a little psycho-drama was acted out for the benefit of the defendant. The inquiry had reached a stage where there could be no further questioning because charges had been brought; now the officers and the custody officer played out a little charade to fool the defendant. The investigating officers pretended they did not want the defendants put in a cell together, but the custody officer said he was going to do so. The cell was bugged and the defendants then made damaging admissions in their conversations with each other. The Court of Appeal upheld the inclusion of the evidence.

What is to be made of these varied cases? It seems clear that professional criminals may find themselves treated less favourably than the ordinary defendant. There are great dangers in the use of entrapment evidence, and from the point of view of the police it is difficult for them to know when evidence obtained by such means will be admissible. Perhaps it is time for the Court of Appeal to lay down more detailed guidelines.

If sometimes it is difficult to distinguish between the decisions of the Court of Appeal, if one compares *Bailey* and *Mason*, then a line can be drawn. Whilst almost always bad faith will cause the evidence to be excluded, the courts will not intervene when defendants have hanged themselves of their own accord and where by a trick the police have encouraged them to do so. In *Mason*[30] the investigating officer told the defendant (and his solicitor) that his fingerprints had been found near the scene of the crime. This was quite untrue and the subsequent confession was then excluded. Lord Lane did however say that 'if the police had acted in bad faith, the Court would have had little difficulty in ruling any confession inadmissible'.

In *Williams and O'Hare v DPP*,[31] the defendants were summoned for interfering with a motor vehicle with intent to commit a theft contrary to s.9 (1) of the Criminal Attempts

29 [1993] 3 All E.R. 513.
30 [1987] 3 All E.R. 481.
31 [1993] Crim. L.R. 775.

Act 1981. They based their defence on the entrapment by police officers who in a high crime-rate area, at least so far as vehicle theft was concerned, had left an unattended and open Ford Transit van with what appeared a valuable load of cigarettes apparently there for the taking.

Initially the magistrates found that there had been no communication with the defendants. The justices found the police had not been *agents provocateurs* and that the defendants had been caught through their own dishonesty. The Divisional Court heard the case by way of case stated and concluded that the justices were right to admit the evidence. It was unimpressed by the argument of 'irresistible temptation'.

In the earlier case of *Christou and Wright*[32] it was said that not every trick that produced evidence against an accused would result in unfairness. In this case undercover officers had set up a jeweller's shop in an attempt to recover stolen property and collect evidence against thieves and handlers who took the property to the shop for sale. The appellants had argued that the evidence of fingerprints (they had to sign receipts), conversation which had helped the police trace the owners and general banter should have been excluded either under *Sang* or *s.* 78 of PACE. Further, the claim was that a three-month sting operation such as had been carried on was contrary to public policy. The Court of Appeal would have nothing of it.

In *DPP v Marshall*[33] plain-clothes officers had bought a can of lager and a bottle of wine from a shop licensed only to deal in bulk purchases. The Divisional Court regarded that as a wholly legitimate exercise by the police. It is difficult to see how there could have been any very different ruling. The purchase of drink by police officers in undercover operations in bars and nightclubs has been standard practice for decades.

A slightly different line of cases is where, after the offence has been committed, the police then use a trick to obtain a

32 [1992] 3 W.L.R. 228.
33 [1988] 3 All E.R. 683.

259

confession. In *Payne*[34] a driver charged with drunken driving was induced to see a doctor to see if he was ill, on the understanding that the doctor would not examine him as to his fitness to drive. The doctor subsequently gave evidence, based on that examination, on his fitness.

When in *Mason*[35] a suspect was induced to confess because of the lies of a police officer, in the presence of the defendant's solicitor, to the effect that the man's fingerprints had been found on a piece of glass, the Court of Appeal, in overturning the conviction, had some harsh words to say on the subject. Curiously these seemed to relate to the deception practised in part on the solicitor rather than the suspect. In *Christou and Wright*, the Court of Appeal was able to differentiate the situation in *Mason*, saying the present case was not a trick within a trick but part of the whole. The fingerprints could have been obtained from dusting the shop counter, and this itself appears to have gone to the overall fairness of the trick.

In *Edwards*[36] undercover police officers offered to buy drugs to provide evidence of an existing conspiracy. The Court of Appeal found, as it was really bound to, that this necessarily involved deceit but in Edwards' case it did not have such an effect on the fairness of the proceedings that it should be excluded. Possibly the *Mason* and *Payne* line of thinking by the court can be justified on the basis that those suspects were in custody when the deception was practised on them, whereas *Edwards* and *Christou and Wright* were out and about.

All this may seem to leave the police with no clear path to tread. Obviously bad faith will count very much against the admission of a confession, but even without this aspect every case is going to be dealt with on its own merits. Senior police officers will have to be involved at an early stage to determine just what is permissible in the way of undercover evidence. Unless great care is taken in difficult cases, then the courts

34 [1963] 1 WLR 637.
35 (1988) 86 Cr. App. R.349.
36 [1991] Crim. L.R. 45.

may not hesitate to exercise their discretion in favour of the accused with what may then seem to the police and public to be bizarre results.

What good judges do like to know are the circumstances of the case, and they get quite het-up when they are kept in the dark. In 1968 Macro was charged with robbing a sub-post office with a man unknown. Quite wrong. The man was definitely known; he was an informer who with the police had warned the impending victim of the proposed raid. The police staked out the premises and the victim went through the charade of allowing himself to be tied up. The court was not pleased when it discovered the true circumstances.

One of the more curious aspects of criminal court procedure has been the use of the cell fink or snitch – the murderer, child rapist or general lowlife – who shares a cell or takes exercise with the defendant against whom there is often not a great deal of evidence, and apparently is able to obtain his confidence to such an extent that he can wheedle a complete confession out of him. The snitch then appears in a shining white shirt at the trial and, having given his evidence, walks off with a much lighter sentence for his own crime.

In fiction, there is now no American thriller in which the defending lawyer does not warn his client against the dangers of self-incrimination in this way. In real life the annals of British and indeed any other nation's criminal cases are littered with notable examples, including success stories for the Crown in, for example, the case of James Hanratty, temporary success in the Luton Post Office murders, and failure in those of John Bindon and the killing of Arthur Thompson junior, the son of Glasgow's King of the Underworld who was shot whilst on home leave from prison as he made his way back to the family fortress after an evening in the local Indian restaurant. Two men were shot to death prior to young Thompson's funeral and in 1992, after a trial lasting fifty-four days, Paul Ferris, suspected of being one of Thompson jnr's murderers, was acquitted.

Much of the evidence against Ferris was from a fellow-prisoner and supergrass Dennis Woodman, a Geordie, who told the jury Ferris had confessed to him in prison. Woodman and his then common-law wife and her brother had been involved in the nasty kidnapping of a farmer in Dumfriesshire in an effort to get him to withdraw money from his bank accounts. How had Ferris made the confession? Shouting through the bars of his cell to Woodman, conveniently in the next cell, whom he had never seen. How had Woodman been placed in the next cell? Well, apparently when in another prison he had been found with escaping tools in his cell, something which he (Woodman) said had been planted by the authorities, and as a result he had been transferred. Woodman, cross-examined by Donald Findlay, told of the tragic death of his children in a road accident, something for which everyone had sympathy for several days until it was revealed that the children were alive and well and living in England and, indeed, Woodman had sent them a Christmas card from prison after their 'death'. Most of his evidence about the case could be traced, almost word for word, to pages from the Scottish editions of the *Sun* newspaper. As the trial went on the normally pro-active Findlay quietly demolished Woodman, who became more and more wild in his allegations, including a suggestion that Ferris's solicitor had endeavoured to bribe him. It was evidence which badly backfired on the prosecution for Woodman was not believed, something which by the end of his two weeks in the witness box surprised few experienced observers.

Sometimes the cell snitch does not have to give evidence. The Flying Squad detective who recruited the man he referred to as the 'Ice-Cream' soon put him to work. He had been informing on receivers at the weekend market in Petticoat Lane in the East End of London with such alacrity that police officers were beginning to rebel against Sunday-morning work.

But it was on a murder in Hackney that the 'Ice-Cream' really proved his worth. It was a sad job, even as murders go. A gang of hooligans about fifteen strong had set out from Islington intent on wreaking revenge on a rival mob in Hackney with whom they had had some previous altercation. They boarded a bus in Essex Road and on arrival at the end of Mare Street they had spotted their intended prey. Mob-handed they left the bus and with knives, hatchets and an assortment of other implements they attacked the luckless Hackney team who seem to have been caught completely unawares. In the fighting an eighteen-year-old boy – from Hackney – was stabbed in the chest with a stiletto-type weapon and drowned in his own blood in the Mare Street gutter.

It was a shocking and quite mindless murder, but happily there was no shortage of witnesses. There were a number of the Hackney mob who knew the names of the Islington gang, and there was the bus conductor as well as some passers-by. There were, however, two problems: no one was giving even the slightest indication as to which one of them had done the actual killing, and certainly no one was admitting the stabbing himself.

Over a period of days we took ten or twelve Islington youths into custody and they were all held in Hackney police station.

Drastic situations need drastic measures and it was agreed we would introduce the Ice cream. The double-cell passages each contained about six cells, and they were full to overflowing even without our hooligans and the nightly stream of drunks and so on who were waiting to go to Old Street court. With the story he had been . charged with robbery we planted the Ice cream in one of the cells with one of the suspects. He was an older man and far more experienced and street-wise than any of his cell-mates. Within a relatively short time he had a couple crying on his shoulder. We moved him to other cells with the Islington prisoners – in fact we had him dodging about from cell to cell for a couple of days. By the time he was 'due to go to court' he was able to tell us exactly who had done what in the fight. All the youths he had spoken to had come up with the same name and story about the killer, who we then interrogated at length and who confessed. The Ice cream pulled the whole job down for us.

Occasionally the cell-mate was a police officer, or at least a Pinkerton agent, in disguise. In 1888 David Henderson had been elected Chief of Police in New Orleans, running on a reform ticket at a time of considerable industrial dispute and gang wars with the Provenzano gang then seeking to control the longshoremen. Two years later, on 15 October 1890, he was assassinated and the New Orleans police appeared powerless to do anything until they had 'heard from Pinkerton'.

Frank Dimaio was sent to Louisiana, his reputation being that '[there was no] man in the Agency who is his equal in regard to work among Italians'. Placed in the cell of Emmanuel Politz, he was able to cozy up to him and obtain a confession implicating the Mafia. Despite Dimaio's efforts, amidst allegations of jury tampering, the men were found not guilty. It did them no good, for on 14 March 1891 under the leadership of New Orleans lawyer W.S. Parkerson the jail was stormed and the suspects either lynched or shot.

Dimaio later went on the hunt for Cassidy and Longbaugh before becoming the head of the Pinkerton operation in Pittsburgh.

At one time the judges tended to encourage juries to believe these sinners who repented, giving as they did so the most facile explanations for their assistance in an endeavour to cover the fact that they wanted out as soon as possible. In Bindon's case, the cell-mate was a William Murphy.

Bindon, armed with a machete, had come to the aid of his friend, Roy Dennis, who was being attacked by Johnny Darke, one of a well-known London family, at the Ranelagh Yacht Club in Putney on 21 November 1978. This was not the version of the prosecution, who maintained that Darke's death was a contract killing by Bindon for a fee of £10,000 said to have been put up by a John Twomey. The evidence that it was a contract killing came from the familiar source of a cell-mate to whom Bindon was said to have confessed. The £10,000 was the story of prisoner William Murphy, also on trial for murder. Asked why he grassed Bindon, he piously replied, 'I don't think it's right people should go around killing other people and getting paid for it.' Murphy was convicted.

One of the cases in which it did go right for the police and which involved cell-informer evidence was that of Dudley and Maynard, the so-called Legal and General gang in the Epping Forest murder of Micky Cornwall and Billy Moseley. In two connected gangland killings there still seems to be no general consensus of opinion as to why the victims were executed, nor for that matter is there complete certainty amongst the cognoscenti that the right men were put away. The Legal and General murders was the last major case investigated by Commander Bert Wickstead and concerned the deaths of two top-of-the-second-division robbers – the gaunt, gangling Billy Moseley and his close friend, Micky Cornwall,* the first of whom disappeared in the autumn of 1974 and the second in the spring of the following year.

The Legal and General gang[37] was headed by Reginald Dudley – a hardman who had served a six-year sentence for slashing his first wife – together with a most unlikely villain, Bobby 'Fat Bob' Maynard, a roly-poly amiable man with little in the way of previous convictions, who had a terrible speech impediment caused (it was said) by being severely hit over the head in a fight in a club in Tottenham Court Road. He spoke extremely slowly, with long gaps between words, and was seemingly unaware of this problem because if interrupted

* A pseudonym.
37 The sobriquet 'Legal and General gang' came about when Dudley and Maynard appeared in a Kentish Town public house wearing identical overcoats which resembled a popular television commercial for the Legal and General insurance group.

by the recipient of his telephone call with a 'Hello, Bobby,' he would reply, 'How-do-you-know-it's-me?'

By the middle 1970s Dudley had become a professional receiver and possibly – accounts differ – a police informer. He had, on his own account, been approached by a top London officer to perform that small service. As for receiving, 'He didn't mess about with anything except high quality stuff,' dealing with the Underworld and the police alike. According to one police officer who knew him:

> He was well respected in the fraternity. I always thought he could go as far as the Krays and the Richardsons. He had a team and he had the ability and the sense of purpose to do to North London what the Krays did to East London.

There was also a story that Dudley was working with the notorious officer, Alec Eist, shaking down robbers and relieving them of their stolen goods.

On his release from prison in September 1974, Moseley was horrified to find that his old school-friend Maynard had teamed up with the man.

On 26 September 1974 Moseley set off for a meeting at 6.30 p.m. with Ronnie Fright at the Victoria Sporting Club in Stoke Newington. He had been having an affair with Frankie, Ronnie's wife, while Fright was serving a seven-year sentence for armed robbery, and the meeting was to clear the air between them. Moseley was never again seen alive. Parts of his body started to surface a week later in the Thames near Rainham. Although the head and hands were missing, it was possible to make a positive identification of the body since Moseley had suffered from a rare skin disease. The autopsy also showed that he had been tortured; his toenails had been pulled out and he had been burned.

Moseley's other great friend, Micky Cornwall, was released from prison a fortnight after the bits started floating along the river. He was tied in to Dudley through a short liaison he had been having with Dudley's daughter Kathy. Kathy had once been married to a John Dann, known as 'Donuts' – possibly because he had worked in a bakery, but also because it was said that he cut holes in people who offended him. That marriage had broken down and she had taken up with a Ray Baron. When he in turn went to prison, she took up with Cornwall. In theory this was just as heinous a crime as Moseley's affair with Frankie Fright, but neither Baron nor the paterfamilias Dudley seems to have objected.

Cornwall, along with any number of criminals before and after him, was looking for a 'big one'. He now had a new girlfriend, Gloria Hogg, and was looking for sufficient money to buy a place in the country. Again like many other criminals, he lacked discretion and confided his plans to John Moriarty, hardly the best person because Moriarty later turned supergrass after being shot in the leg for the second time. Cornwell left Gloria for the 'big one' on Sunday 3 August. He had been renting a room from another police informer, Colin Saggs, and left shortly before two men came looking for him. Sharon Saggs, his daughter, would identify them at the trial as Dudley and Maynard. Moriarty saw him at a bus-stop in Highgate on 23 August, and that seems to have been the last sighting of him before his body was found in a newly-dug grave at Hatfield, Hertfordshire. He had been shot in the head.

Wickstead's last swoop was on 2 January 1976. Seven people out of eighteen taken were charged; they had been interviewed over a period of four days[38] and included Dudley and his daughter Kathy, Maynard, and Ronnie Fright. During the period in custody they had made admissions which amounted to evidence against them. Dudley was alleged to have said of Cornwall, 'I told him if he had sex with her,

---

38 The effective implementation of the Police and Criminal Evidence Act 1984 was nearly ten years away. At the time suspects in serious cases could be interviewed almost endlessly. Then such protection as was available to suspects was the informal Judges' Rules, which did not include the right to the presence of a solicitor during interview.

I would kill him.' Maynard allegedly admitted going to the Saggs' house looking for Cornwall. 'It was business,' he said. As for the question put to him that he had told Fright to be late for the rendezvous at the Victoria Sporting Club, he is said to have replied, 'I'm not answering that, otherwise I'm finished.' Apparently, Wickstead had had a tape-recorder fitted into his desk at the police station but had never switched it on. Why not, asked the defence?

'I am a police officer who believes in police methods and tape recorders are not used in police interviews,' replied the Commander.

The prosecution's case as to motive was convoluted. The killings had occurred because (1) Moseley had had an affair with Frankie Fright; (2) he had fallen out with Dudley ten years earlier; (3) Moseley had been suggesting Dudley was a grass; (4) he, Moseley, was sitting on the proceeds of a large jewellery robbery; (5) out of sheer sadism; (6) Cornwall had set out to avenge Moseley's death; (7) he had discovered Dudley and Maynard were the killers and so (8) had had more than a brief liaison with Kathy in order to find out the truth. It was said that Moseley had been shot with a single bullet. The case against Ronnie Fright was that he was deliberately late for his meet with Moseley outside the Victoria Sporting Club and so had lured him to his death.

Much of the rest of the evidence was the rag-bag of serving prisoners who, having seen the light, were able to give evidence against their former cell-mates. One of them was thirty-year-old Tony Wild, who asked the judge if he could sit down as he had a fissure on his anus.[39] He had, he said, been homosexually raped as a young man and, apart from contracting syphilis, he had this permanent reminder of the experience. He had served his apprenticeship in crime as shoplifter, car thief and office breaker; from where it was a

39 I am most grateful for the help I have received from Duncan Campbell and for his permission to quote extensively from the chapter 'The Grass' in *That was Business, This is Personal*.

268

short step to armed robbery and a series of attacks on Securicor vehicles. The money disappeared into the funds of the Golden Nugget casino in Piccadilly, major London hotels and on a series of presents to himself including a £1,200 fur coat.

In February 1976 he was caught after an attack on a Securicor vehicle which had temporarily netted £7,274. Wild had fired at pursuing Securicor men and escaped in his Volvo, but he crashed and was found hiding in a field. He was fortunate not to be charged with attempted murder and became a grass, receiving the semi-statutory five years for his troubles compared with eighteen for fellow-robber Tony Cook. Wild, it seems, did not want the luxuries accorded notables such as O'Mahoney. He was quite happy in his cell, keeping a diary of his conversations with other inmates such as Oliver Kenny, a publican and old friend of Dudley, and sending selected extracts to the police. Initially they were not impressed with his information and Wild wrote:

> Although I have passed on information that I believe would be useful to your inquiries, I have received from your office not even an acknowledgement of the receipt of my letters let alone a routine questioning as to the validity of their content. Perhaps you feel that I am trying to work a ticket or something.

Now he offered them Reggie Dudley, writing to Wickstead:

> I hope you will appreciate that I have been very forthright in this letter and that in itself will indicate to you that I have other more serious matters to impart to you.

When he was finally allowed to make a statement:

> It's almost a relief to be in the police cell and get it off

my plate. I am caught and am going to spend a long time in prison. When I come out I want only to spend the rest of my life quietly with those I love.[40]

Wild told the police that Dudley had boasted about killing Micky Cornwall, saying, 'He went up in the fucking air, didn't he, boys?' He added his threepenceworth against Maynard who, he said, had commented, 'I didn't know guys would squeal like a pig.' But perhaps the most damaging remarks he quoted related to Olly Kenny and the Horse and Groom pub in Brighton. Dudley, he said, had brought a head into the pub one night and the publican had nearly died of fright when he saw it.

In the witness box Wild, carrying a copy of the criminal legal textbook, *Archbold*, was at least the equal, if not the master, of the legal talent ranged against him. When asked if he was eating in the witness box he replied, 'I am eating wine gums. Like all the jury, all the defendants and half the police in court. Can I carry on?'

The burden of the cross-examination by luminaries such as Michael West, for Dudley, was that as a disgusting homosexual, real men such as Dudley would not have anything to do with a man like Wild and therefore would not have given him the time of day, let alone what amounted to a confession. Wild would have none of it.

I have been to bed with literally hundreds of women and I could call five hundred into this court to testify to that fact. I have also had dozens of jobs of a masculine nature. I cannot bear men touching me. My crimes, I know, have got progressively more serious, ending up with armed

40 This is a common enough and probably, at the time, genuine thought. I recall defending one man on a bank robbery. 'If I get chucked I'm going to give it all up,' he told me shortly before the trial. 'I'm going to go away and live in a little town which has a supermarket. That's all I need. Well, make that two supermarkets.'

robbery. I would interpret that as an attempt – or at least a subconscious attempt – to regain my manhood.

Apart from the confessions and the liaisons between the various dead and accused there was not, as the judge, Mr Justice Swanwick, told the jury 'evidence on which the Crown could ask you to convict'. The police had stated on oath that they were accurate and the defence had said they were fabricated. Whom were the jury to believe?

In the end Ronnie Fright was acquitted, as was another defendant, whilst a third had been acquitted at the direction of the judge. Bobby Maynard was found guilty on a majority decision on the third day of the jury's retirement. He and Dudley were sentenced to life imprisonment; Kathy received a suspended sentence along with an old-time villain, Charlie Clarke. Olly Kenny died before his trial. Six weeks later Moseley's head, wrapped in a plastic bag, was found in a public lavatory in Barnsbury, North London. Perhaps significantly the copy of the *Evening News* wrapped around it was dated 16 June 1977, when the jury had been in retirement.

Some facts emerged from the inquest. Professor James Cameron, who had undertaken the initial autopsy, told the coroner that the head was in 'extremely' good condition. Traces of car paint indicated it had been in a garage for some of the three years since Moseley had choked on his own blood; that removed one of the pillars on which the Crown had based its case. It had also been in a deep-freeze, for it was on the thaw when it was discovered.

In 1980 Wild retracted his evidence. He told the *Guardian* crime reporter Duncan Campbell in a pub in Hove that he had made up the evidence about the head, saying that the police had given him a scenario which he had followed. Campbell reported the interview in *Time Out* and was later interviewed by the Serious Crimes Squad. Wild was soon rearrested for another armed robbery.

On 23 April 1982 Anthony Wild was sentenced to ten

years' imprisonment for a series of five raids in Cheltenham and Croydon between April and October 1981, as well as a bank in Uxbridge. During the raids he had fired several shots, maintaining that he only did so to frighten people. Mr Justice McCowan said he did not regard Wild as a vicious or ruthless man and accepted his story that whilst firing the shots Wild had no intention of harming anyone.

His capture had come about in a none too dissimilar way from his previous escapade. On 9 December 1981 the police received information that he was travelling in a taxi on the A27; a road-block was set up and Wild tried to shoot himself before he dived out into an icy pond. Wild's lover, Margaret Payne, was given two years' probation. Their relationship had begun in April 1981 and they were living together in Somerset in what Charles Whitby QC, prosecuting, said was 'affluent domesticity' and employing a woman as a private tutor for the children.

In October 1981 Wild escaped capture in Somerset, and later Mrs Payne took him clothing and drove him to a hotel. She was arrested two days later and when Wild realised the police were holding her he threatened to go on a rampage. As a matter of expediency they released her, believing that she would lead them to Wild. They met on the Sussex Downs but Wild, who was having something of a charmed existence, escaped again and he was not recaptured for another five weeks.

Wild must have had powerful influences working for him, since he was paroled after serving a little over three years.

After the appeals were rejected, the families of both Dudley and Maynard launched a campaign to prove their innocence. This did not take the extreme course adopted by the friends of George Davis, but tee-shirts were sold and there was a march through Camden Town to Hyde Park Corner. Bobby Maynard junior stood as a candidate in the European Parliament elections in June 1984. Inevitably, however, the campaign suffered with Davis' conviction for the Bank of Cyprus raid.[41] Dudley appeared on television in the 1984 BBC programme *Lifers*. Nor was the North London Underworld convinced of their guilt; whilst it was accepted that Dudley was capable of great violence, few could believe that Maynard had the same capacity. Over the years various names have been put up as the potential killers, but no real inquiry has been undertaken by the authorities.

In 1991 Liberty, formerly the National Council for Civil Liberties, adopted the Maynard–Dudley case as one for special consideration in a campaign against wrongful convictions. With the passing of the Police and Criminal Evidence Act

41 The George Davis case was something of a cause célèbre. In 1974 a robbery took place at the London Electricity Board in Ley Street, Ilford, in which a PC Groves – who was in the vicinity quite by chance – ran to tackle the robbers and was shot in the leg for his pains. Whilst he was on the ground, another of the team stood over him threatening to shoot him again.

A name in the frame was George Davis. He was first seen by the police twenty days after the robbery, when he was arrested and gave an alibi that he had been driving a mini-cab. The books of the firm were gone through and one of his passengers was interviewed. Eight days later the same thing happened, but this time the log-books were taken away by the police.

Davis was identified by three officers. Three months after the robbery a second set of identification parades was held at Brixton prison. Davis was picked out by two other police officers, but another 34 people failed to pick him out and three made wrong identifications – two after he had changed his purple shirt with another man on the parade.

The jury did not accept his alibi and Davis was convicted in March 1975. He was sentenced to a total of twenty years' imprisonment, reduced on appeal to seventeen. So began an enormous campaign on Davis' behalf. There were allegations that he had been fitted up and on his conviction his supporters mounted protest marches, demonstrations, and the chalking and papering of most of East London with the slogan 'George Davis is innocent – OK'. In one incident the cricket pitch at Headingley was dug up during a Test Match.

The 'George Davis is innocent – OK' campaign was successful. He was released in a blaze of publicity on Tuesday 11 May 1976 by the Home Secretary, after the publication of the Devlin report on the dangers of convicting on identification evidence alone. It appears that an additional alibi witness had also come forward.

Unfortunately the rejoicing was short-lived. He seriously blotted his copybook as folk hero when, on 23 September 1977, he was captured *in flagrante* during a raid on the Bank of Cyprus in the Seven Sisters Road, Holloway. Davis' sentence in the Bank of Cyprus case was reduced to one of eleven years on appeal. But that was not his last brush with the law. On 21 January 1987 he received another sentence, this time of eighteen months (with nine of them suspended), following a raid on the London-to-Brighton mail train in March 1986. Police guarding postbags on the train tried to force their way into the mail van, but found Davis blocking the door. He pleaded guilty to attempted theft.

1984 it is doubtful if there would have been convictions in the Legal and General case. It is difficult to know just what, if any, effect the evidence of Wild had on the jury.[42]

Of course what England can do America can, at least in the courts, do a thousand times as well. On 25 April 1989 James Richardson, convicted of murdering his seven children, had his life sentence quashed. He had been convicted in 1967 exclusively on the evidence of three cell informers. On the other hand, the prosecution had declined to take action when another person apparently confessed to the crime.

Richardson's troubles began on 25 October 1967 at his home in, for him, the unhappily named Arcadia, Fla. He and his wife went fruit-picking and left the children in the care of Betsy Reese, a neighbour who fed them beans and rice for their lunch. Six died that afternoon, the seventh survived for twenty-four hours. Richardson's behaviour at the hospital where he went with his wife counted against him. Apparently he remained unmoved; she collapsed. There was also evidence that he had taken out modest insurance for the children of $500 each, as well as policies totalling $3,000 for himself and his wife. The local Sheriff Frank Cline, who was up for re-election, was convinced of Richardson's guilt. The Arcadia Police Chief Richard Barnard fixed his attention on Mrs Reese, who denied that she had either cooked the dinner for the children or even been to the Richardson house. Barnard knew she was lying about this part at least, for he had seen her there. He also discovered that her past was less than desirable: she had served four years in 1956 for shooting her second husband, and her first husband had died after eating her beef stew.

The Richardsons' house was searched for poison and none found, but the next day the police were called to find Reese and a local alcoholic fighting over a bag of parathion. Both said it had come from a shed in Richardson's yard.

The evidence which did for Richardson came from jailhouse

42 For a more detailed account of the case see B. Woffinden, *Miscarriages of Justice.*

informers. James Dean Cunningham was the first to come forward to say that Richardson had confessed to him. In return for his truthful testimony, he would have some time knocked off his sentence. However, he had problems with the facts. When first asked who poisoned the food he replied, 'the mother-in-law' and then when it was apparent that this was an incorrect answer, 'No – the babysitter. The lady who takes care of his kids.' The third time he got it right.

The second informer, gambler James 'Spot' Weaver, said that Richardson had confessed to him that he had poisoned the children while his wife was spending the night with Reese. The motive was jealousy over their uncorroborated lesbian affair. At the trial he said Richardson had never offered a motive. He was not pressed by the prosecution, and the defence were not shown his prior inconsistent statements. The third sneak was shot dead before the trial, but his evidence was read to the jury.

In 1988 Weaver, the only survivor of the trio of informers and then aged sixty-seven, recanted. He told the authorities that he had been beaten until he agreed to make a statement against Richardson. Cunningham had been shot to death in 1969. Meanwhile Betsy Reese, who appears to have been sliding into insanity, had allegedly confessed on numerous occasions to poisoning the children. Moreover, the confessions had been made to nurses well before she became incompetent.

At his re-hearing twenty-one years after he was convicted, it was ruled that Richardson had not received a fair trial because the prosecution had withheld evidence and knowingly used false testimony. There were no plans to re-try him.[43]

At the same time a furore arose in California when inmate Leslie White, who had amassed thirty arrests since the age of nine, decided to tell all and explain how he could garner sufficient evidence to make it seem as though he had been the recipient of a confession from the accused. In the past

43 Mark Curriden, 'No Honor among Thieves' in the *American Bar Association Journal*, June 1989.

he had used these confessions and his willingness to give evidence about them to bargain himself a lighter sentence. Now he changed sides, claiming that defence and prosecution lawyers and even judges knew he was lying. He appeared on CBS' *Sixty Minutes*, saying:

> I've had judges sit up on the bench and look at me like, you know, you lying piece of you-know-what. But what can they do. They can do nothing. If I say one thing, it's believed unless they can prove differently. The defense can't do anything. The defense lawyer will say, 'You're lying, aren't you?' I say, 'No, sir.'
>
> They have no other avenue to disprove my veracity other than the fact they're just trying to verbally attack me on the witness stand.

He went on to recount how he could get information from the telephone in the county jail. Having called the deputy district attorney and identified himself as a detective with the LAPD homicide unit, he then asked for and was given information which could only be known to the actual perpetrator and the police. Because of his disclosure the Los Angeles District Attorney's Office began a review into two hundred cases, including sixteen where the convicted person was on death row.

Eventually, just as they had in England, juries began to express their disapproval of the use of the informer and undercover sting. One of the most significant cases was that of John DeLorean whose trial began on 5 March 1984 in Los Angeles. The one-time millionaire car manufacturer was on a charge of plotting to import $24 million worth of cocaine into the United States. It had been done, said the prosecution, to try to raise money to save his ailing Belfast sports car factory. Time and again the television viewers in the United States had seen him reach into a suitcase of cocaine, lift a package and say, 'It's better than gold. Gold weighs more, for God's sake.'

276

His defence was that an FBI sting had been up and running to try to force DeLorean into buying the cocaine, something he had made every effort to avoid. A principal government witness was convicted cocaine smuggler James Hoffman who, DeLorean claimed, had threatened him and the life of his six-year-old daughter when he tried to back out of the deal. When it came to it Hoffman, who was cross-examined for twelve days, was never asked about the threats. Indeed the tapes showed the utmost friendliness between the men.

Commenting on the way the case was going, Michael Gillard wrote in the *Observer* (July 1 1984):

The defence has been helped by a steady stream of prosecution own goals. Missing tapes, erased tapes, destroyed notes, back-dated documents, breached guide-lines, contradictory testimony. These have been prised out of Government witnesses and have eaten into the prosecution case, if only around the edges. Only by testifying himself is DeLorean likely to be able to erase the impression on the tapes.

He was only partly right. DeLorean did not give evidence. However, on 16 August 1984 DeLorean was acquitted by the unanimous verdict of the jury who had deliberated for twenty-eight and three-quarter hours. DeLorean, who was by now a born-again Christian, called out 'Praise the Lord'.

Howard Weitzman, the chief defence lawyer, said:

The jurors are 12 citizens who have sent a message to the nation and the world that the type of conduct that was involved in the investigation, arrest, prosecution and ultimate vindication of John DeLorean will not be tolerated again.

Eight jurors spoke at a press conference after the hearing. They did not wish to be identified as they said they feared themselves being entrapped by government agents.

The veteran lawyer Melvin Belli is reported to have said:

It was one of the great jury verdicts of all time. They stood up and said they were not going to cotton on to cops acting like a bunch of bums.

Harvard Professor Allan Dershowitz, one of the leading American trial lawyers of today,[44] said:

His guilt or innocence played no role in this. All the attention was focused on the Government and he was presented as a victim.[45]

44 Amongst his more famous clients have been Claus von Bulow and O. J. Simpson.
45 *Daily Express*, 18 August 1984.

11

The Police – Undercover Work and Informants

In the manual of best practice provided in 1994 by the Association of Chief Police Officers and designed to overcome problems with informers, officers are enjoined not to use terms such as 'grass', 'snout' and 'snitch'. Nor should officers, however much they despise their informants, allow this to filter through into their dealings with them. As can be seen from the following examples, it will be hard to eradicate these words or thoughts from an officer's (or indeed anyone else's) vocabulary.

I'll tell you right now – it's a tricky game, being an informer. I'll tell you something else: in my seventeen years as a policeman up to 1945 I'd used scores of snouts, but out of them all I could name only ten who were absolutely top class: the men on whose unsupported word I could go in with my head down. It isn't really surprising when you know the circumstances. The snout is a game fellow. He's at one and the same time a crook, engaged in illicit operations, and a detective. He cops it both ways.[1]

1 John Gosling, *The Ghost Squad*, p. 39.

A rather younger officer recalls:

As an aide I was soon to learn the constant dangers that were always to be found with informants. My buck [colleague] and I had 'developed' an active villain – again the name is gone but I recall he lived in the Winchmore Hill area – and everything was going very smoothly. We were getting a job a month on average, receivers, the odd stolen car – all very much run-of-the-mill but very nice for all that. Then, after an association of about six months, trouble loomed. The informant had put us on to a young thief in Southgate who rejoiced in the soubriquet of 'Dig-'em-up Dave': the nick-name derived from the fact that for some years he had worked as a gravedigger and was able to effect no small amount of spare cash by the appalling practice of grave-robbing. It seemed that when Dave was required to dig into an existing family grave prior to the interment of a recently deceased husband or wife, he would return to the cemetery at night prior to the funeral, force open the coffin of the first occupant of the grave and rob the corpse of such rings and other effects as he could find.

In any event, as a result of information from our man we managed to catch 'Dig-'em-up Dave' with a stolen car. Unbeknown to us, Dave's father (Dave was adopted) was a lawyer of some esteem and, it turned out, not altogether unconnected in the 'right' circles. Scarcely before we knew what had happened, allegations of all sorts of malpractice on our part were flying about and a Chief Superintendent and Sergeant from C1 were deputed to investigate. It was suggested that the stolen car had been 'planted' on Dave by the informant and that the whole thing was a conspiracy between ourselves and the informant to implicate the wholly innocent Dave! As I recall, our houses were searched and we were interviewed at great length about the whole thing. Nothing came of it, though, and as both my buck and I continued as aides and were not reverted to uniform duty, I imagine that the powers that be had taken the lawyer's allegations with a pinch of salt.

The sensible use of a snout is essential in promoting career prospects. Even if an officer does not have one himself, from time to time an informer can be borrowed from another officer. A Flying Squad officer recalls his early days:

Towards the end of my aiding career I was to have my first experience of the 'professional snout'. I was due to go on a selection board for secondment to the permanent CID and in those days it was essential for such an interview to be able to present a comprehensive record of arrests. The one thing, it was reckoned, which would always impress was an 'off-duty job' and it was with this in mind that I was taken to King's Cross by an old and very experienced Detective Sergeant Brian Kelly to meet 'Spotty' Larwood.[2]

'Spotty', apparently, could invariably be found in an all-night snack bar in the Euston Road named 'Jon-Jaks' and sure enough this is where we found him. He was a small man, painfully thin and ultra-scruffy. In later years, when watching the TV programme *Callan*, I felt convinced that admirable actor Russell Hunter had known 'Spotty' Larwood well and upon him had based his portrayal of Callan's informant 'Lonely'.

'Spotty,' said Brian Kelly, with an air of authority, 'this is Mr R. He's going on a board in a couple of weeks and he needs a nice little job.'

'Hooo,' said 'Spotty' with a sharp sucking noise and in the manner adopted by car salesman when viewing one's prized Escort which is being presented for part-exchange.

2 A pseudonym.

'I don't know about that, Mr Kelly.' He produced a filthy diary or note-book and the conversation which followed took this form, and I give my word there is no exaggeration: *Spotty*: 'No, can't do nuffink for at least a munf, Mr Kelly (loud and very fluid sniff); 's'always the same, in't it, this time of the year – bloody aides boards[3] everywhere and they all want 'elpin', don't they?' Another quick look at the book followed by frenzied hacking at awful teeth with the pencil, and then: 'See, I got me own aides at Clerkenwell to look after, Mr Kelly, ain't I? Then I got to put one in for a skipper from the Cally (Caledonian Road) who's going on the DI's board, I got a DC at Narrowbone Lane (Marylebone Lane) in the shit and 'e needs a bit of 'elp (pause for disgusting throat clearance and relocation of nasal mucous), an' on top of all that, I got the 'Eavy Mob (Flying Squad) an' if I don't look after them Gawd knows what'll 'appen.' *Kelly*: 'And Gawd knows what'll happen if you don't help Mr R, you scruffy little bastard.'

What followed was pure theatre: for a quarter of an hour Brian Kelly alternated between threatening and pleading and Spotty, well, the man was a star! He moaned about the pressures of his profession and at the low rates being paid by the Informants Fund. He ridiculed the sentences being handed down by the stipendiaries at Clerkenwell Court and Messrs Seaton and Elam over at the London Sessions. Between sinus-clearing exercises and the insertion of various instruments into what I imagined must have been a whole cavern of dental cavities, he protested time, weather conditions, risk and likely reward. He (rightly) accused Kelly and I as being 'orf yer own manor' and suggested that before long there would be officers 'from bleedin' Brighton comin' up 'ere after me',

3 If an Aide to CID wished to be confirmed in the job he had to go before a promotion board, at the same time producing evidence (in the form of arrests) of his ability. The Aide to CID has been discontinued.

282

but eventually he came round. Ten minutes he'd give me,
he said grudgingly: 'Free o'clock Saturday afternoon –
outside the pictures in Clerkenwell Road.'

And so there I was, as directed; I recall it was
freezing cold and raining and a wind-swept corner in
the Clerkenwell Road is not the best place to be when one
is off-duty. After about a quarter of an hour I saw Spotty
walking towards me from the direction of the station on
the other side of the road. Beside him, and clutching an
enormous canvas sack, was a younger but equally scruffy
man. As they came adjacent with me Spotty looked across
and nodding towards his companion dodged up an alley
and disappeared. I ran across the road and producing my
warrant card stopped his friend, who was still striding
confidently along seemingly oblivious of Spotty's sudden
absence.

The sack contained about 60 towels and various other
linen articles, all marked as coming from one of the large
hotels round the Russell Square area. Spotty's chum was
charged with alternatively stealing them or receiving them
and he pleaded guilty the next morning, as they say 'like
a good 'un', and got three months without a word of
complaint.

As I gave the brief facts to the magistrate, I spied
Spotty in the public gallery watching the results of his
handiwork. I never knew whether his chum was some
sort of volunteer. I never knew how Spotty got paid and
I never saw him again.

Some years later, though, I heard that he was involved
in something of a scandal: it seemed that throughout
his professional career he had kept some sort of diary
(and probably accounts) relative to his activities, and
suddenly he decided to put this to good use. The story
– although it may be apocryphal – was to this effect:
late one winter's night Spotty was taking coffee at the
all-night coffee stall at The Cross [King's Cross] when

he encountered a down-and-out vagrant of even more straitened circumstances than himself. On learning that this poor man had neither lodgings nor the wherewithal to acquire them, Spotty immediately offered the spare bed in his room. He then treated the unsuspecting dosser to several cups of coffee and a bacon sandwich or two and then suggested they make their way to Spotty's drum. On the way, Spotty suddenly remembered a meeting that he had with a friend, and suggested that his new-found friend might like to continue on to the house and let himself in. For this purpose Spotty handed him an enormous bunch of keys and selecting one of these as being the key to the door of his lodgings, suggested that his friend may like to keep hold of it to save trying the lot in the lock. At the time he also happened to be carrying a large holdall which he handed over with instructions that his room was 'first on the left inside the front door' and that as he did not wish to take the bag with him on his 'meet' it should just be put on the bed.

He then disappeared into the night leaving the unsuspecting vagrant to make his way to some address off Argyll Square or that area. When he arrived, the key which Spotty had selected did not fit the lock of the front door and as he was trying key after key off the bunch in the lock he was collared by the local Q car crew – a plain-clothes mobile patrolling unit. The keys turned out to be a bunch of twirls (skeleton keys) and the holdall contained an assortment of housebreaking implements including, it was said, a rope ladder!

In those days possessing housebreaking implements by night was a matter for the Quarter Sessions (Crown Court) and it was there that things started to go wrong. It developed that the defendant was the errant son of very wealthy people from the North and, incensed by what had befallen their offspring, they instructed solicitors to brief the late Victor Durand QC to defend him. Private enquiry

284

agents were told to find Spotty Larwood but before he was located – and being well aware of what was going on – he turned up at New Scotland Yard one night complete with diary *et al* and put a lifetime of wickedness on paper. The defendant was quite rightly acquitted and in the months that followed countless CID officers from all over London were seen and interviewed.

As I say, this story may be apocryphal, but I recall speaking to several of the officers who were mentioned in his statement and from what they said I think it is true in substance.

More seriously, one of the problems with informants has been the danger that, to improve their standing with the officer running them, to get a licence, albeit a limited one, to steal or to deal in drugs or reward money, they will turn themselves into *agents provocateurs*. A very early example of this may have occurred in the running by the Special Branch of an informer, Auguste Coulon.

In 1892 a number of Fenians were arrested in connection with a bomb factory in Walsall. Almost certainly they had been acting under the aegis of Auguste Coulon. Indeed one of the conspirators Frederick Charles – who had the highest reputation in the area, 'would never,' – according to Patrick McIntyre, who on the eve of his promotion to inspector was suddenly demoted to constable – 'have gone of his own accord into any diabolical plot'. It may be that McIntyre, who made his denunciation of his superiors in *Reynolds Weekly*, had a grudge to argue, but Coulon was regarded as the property of a senior officer. Papers show that an order for the arrest of Coulon was countermanded by the Chief of Walsall police, Taylor.

Until the 1970s an informant to a Flying Squad officer could effectively remain anonymous. All the officer had to do was to put in a report to the information fund saying that an informant wished to be known as John Smith and had been instrumental (a favourite police word) in the arrest of Tom Brown, as a result of which a considerable amount of property had been recovered. The senior officer who authorised the ensuing payment did not have to know Smith's real name. It was a system which led to innumerable instances of abuse, one of which was the sharing of the reward money between the informer and the police officer.

It is also possible that the officers who run them, both for reasons financial and for advancement in the force, will turn their informers into *agents provocateurs*. Almost certainly in the bad days of Scotland Yard in the 1960s and 1970s, there were examples of officers who would arrange with an informer to set up a robbery and then after the arrest of his colleagues claim the reward from the bank which was never in real danger of an attack.

One of the more disturbing uses of the reward system came in 1968 in the case of David Cooper,[4] Michael McMahon and Patrick Murphy who were convicted of the murder of sub-postmaster Reginald Stevens who on 10 September 1969 was shot dead, probably accidentally, in his car in a Luton car-park. Four robbers had intended to persuade him to hand over the keys to the post office. The driver of one of the cars involved was thought to be in his forties or early fifties, with greying hair. A reward of £5,000 was offered by the Post-Master General.

A Vauxhall car, wiped clean of fingerprints and belonging to an Alfred Matthews, was identified as being in the area at the time of the murder. He had a number of convictions for violence and dishonesty, was known as a good getaway driver and had previously robbed a post office. The car had been transferred to a non-existent person at a non-existent address on the day before the murder. When the police went round, Matthews was said by his wife to be away. Eventually, his brother Albert Elliott told the police he was with him. Matthews was arrested, and by way of explanation

4 David Cooper was known also as John Disher. He died in 1993.

said that the man to whom he had sold his car must have been involved. He was never placed on an identification parade. He was, however, according to Detective Chief Superintendent Kenneth Drury, 'leaned on a bit' to turn Queen's Evidence against Cooper, McMahon and Murphy. This he did. Although charged with the others, no evidence was offered against him and he appeared as the major prosecution witness.

His story at the Crown Court was the traditional one of the informer – one which, in these less disingenuous times, might not have had the same degree of acceptance. He said that he had been asked to collect some parcels in his Vauxhall from the railway station at Luton, for which service he was to receive £10. By the time he realised that he was the dupe of the robbers, he was well on his way up the M1. Once in Luton the others went on ahead of him; he was asked to keep look-out on a shop which he suddenly realised was a post office. The three others, one of whom was covered in blood, collected him in a van. He wanted to drive away on his own but the man, wiping off the blood, got into the Vauxhall. After a mile or so he managed to persuade the man with him to get out.

Some of the other evidence against the men was provided by Thomas Weyers and Derek Jackson to whom McMahon, on remand in Leicester prison, supposedly confessed his guilt. He, Cooper and Murphy were convicted.

The reward money was duly paid with Alfred Matthews receiving £2,000, and his brother Albert Elliott, Thomas Weyers and Derek Jackson each receiving £500. There were suggestions that Drury had received up to half Matthews' share of the reward; his bank statement showed that when the £2,000 was deposited there was a withdrawal of £700.

Matthews was quite unable to accept that he had received a reward. He regarded the money as compensation for loss of work and inconvenience resulting from his decision to turn Queen's Evidence and the resulting police protection.

The struggles of Murphy, McMahon and Cooper to obtain their freedom, denied repeatedly by the Court of Appeal, occupied the next eleven years. On 13 November 1973, with a new alibi witness whom the court believed, Murphy was freed, the court having decided that the identification of Murphy by Matthews was too weak to be allowed to stand. Cooper and McMahon were not so fortunate. With the court protecting Matthews over the next decade, it was not until the Home Secretary, William Whitelaw, asked the Queen to remit the sentences that they were released on 18 July 1980.

In the meantime the officer in the case, Detective Chief Superintendent Kenneth Drury, had been promoted to Commander and then relegated to the status of prisoner. His downfall is an interesting insight into what happens when thieves, or grasses, fall out with their employing officers.

On 27 February 1972 the *Sunday People* announced that Commander Drury and his wife had recently returned from Cyprus, where they had been guests of porn dealers James and Rusty Humphreys.

For a time Drury tried to bluff his way out. Yes, he had been to Cyprus. No, he had not been a guest, he had paid his share. No, it had not been a holiday; in reality he was looking for the escaped train robber Ronnie Biggs. At the time, and for what it was worth, Humphreys supported him. But it wasn't worth much. On 6 March Drury was suspended from duty and served with disciplinary papers; he resigned on 1 May. Then foolishly he turned on his former friend. He sold his story to the *News of the World* for £10,000 and as part of his confessions amazingly he publicly named Humphreys as a grass. It is not surprising that Humphreys took umbrage and gave his alternative version, saying that far from being a grass or getting money from Drury it had all been the other way around. The money, the wine, the good life had all flowed from the Humphreys' cornucopia.[5]

On 7 July 1977 Drury was convicted of corruption for his part in the activities of some members of the Porn Squad.

5 Just to complete the somewhat tortuous story, in 1994 Humphreys returned to prison following his conviction at the Inner London Crown Court for dealing in pornography.

He received eight years' imprisonment, reduced on appeal to five. With the gift of hindsight it is possible to speculate that Matthews had been an informant for Drury all along, not simply on this one instance at Luton, and as such was protected by him. Even if that were not the case, the higher echelons of the police took a dim view of the shenanigans of Drury and Matthews. Commenting on the situation, Assistant Commissioner Gilbert Kelland later wrote:

> An immediate policy decision was made that no reward money would ever be recommended or paid by us to anyone who had turned Queen's Evidence.
>
> In 1980 I wrote a confidential letter to all the major banks, insurance companies and loss assessors pointing out the dangers of offering rewards so large that they might in themselves generate crime.[6]

It may be the case that subsequent to that no payments were made or recommended to those who turned Queen's Evidence, but certainly massive sums were paid out to actively involved criminals. In fact the rule was broken in spirit more than it was observed in practice.

However well-intentioned their plans, the police did not always achieve the desired ends when using informers. In St Paul, Minnesota, the Police Chief introduced the eponymous O'Connor system, the aim of which was to stem the flow of, and control, major crime within the system. The scheme was to allow hoodlums to use St Paul as a safe city to which they could go for rest, recreation and freedom from arrest provided they 'committed no depredations against the citizens of St Paul'. Gambling and prostitution were allowed to flourish on the basis that prostitutes and gamblers were the eyes and the ears of a police department.

The scheme appears to have worked well enough for a time

6 Gilbert Kelland, *Crime in London*, pp. 217–18.

in St Paul. Unfortunately, however, the effects were long-term. First, the local police force became lazy; it was now too easy for them to make arrests. More widely, criminals transferred their operations to other nearby towns and cities whose crime rates soared. The original *status quo* was restored.[7]

In more recent times members of the police have been used to infiltrate their own. In all instances this has been in an effort to eradicate corruption. In some cases the officers may have been reluctant but have been uncoerced; in others, it has been the price of their own freedom. As is almost invariably the case, the bulk of examples come from America. In 1970 the mayor of New York, John Lindsay, empanelled the Knapp Commission and over the next two years dozens of police officers were implicated in taking bribes and participating in gambling, prostitution and drug operations. Much of the evidence came from honest officers such as Sergeant David Durk and Detective Frank Serpico, who had infiltrated the operations of these corrupt officers. Sometimes officers were, like common criminals, given the option of turning informer or being prosecuted. One such was Officer William Phillips, accused of taking bribes and fixing court cases. Supplied with a tape recorder, he was used by the Knapp Commission to show that officers were obtaining up to $4 million a year in bribes. His evidence did not appeal to the Police Commissioner Patrick V. Murphy, who denounced the operation in general and Phillips in particular as a rogue cop caught in the act and 'squirming to get off the hook'. The Commission was disbanded with inconclusive results, but at the beginning at least it did have a dramatic effect. Two days after it first sat, 113 plain-clothes officers were transferred.

Another officer who gave evidence at the time of the Knapp Commission was the thirty-one-year-old Bob Leuci. He was

7 M. L. Harney and J. C. Cross, *The Informer in Law Enforcement*. In criminal circles St Paul was known as Home because of these facilities. It was not the only city which operated such a scheme. For a time at least Toledo, Ohio, had similar rules but was never given the accolade of a nickname.

called before the Commission in mid-February 1971 and left in an ante-room waiting to be interviewed by Nicholas Scoppetta. Leuci, one of the Princes of the City, so-called because the Special Investigating Unit for which he worked had a citywide jurisdiction, was not a happy man. Although he was unaware of it, the Crime Commission had nothing on him; he was not, however, clean and it did not take Scoppetta too long to suspect that Leuci was hiding something. According to Leuci's biography,[8] Scoppetta asked him to dinner and the two men struck an almost immediate rapport. Leuci admitted three occasions on which he had taken part in a scam – he had taken money from a drug-dealer on the premise that he and his colleagues could influence a prosecution which was in any event going to be dropped – but said he was otherwise clean. What he really wanted to do was not to inform on his colleagues but to go after the lawyers for both prosecution and defence who, depending upon which side of the fence they sat, were either taking bribes to drop cases or paying them to police officers. Leuci began to talk to Scoppetta, with everything being recorded. Unfortunately for posterity, the arrangement was that after the lawyer had finished with them the tapes should be returned to Leuci. He burned them.

At one time it was suggested by a superior of Scoppetta that there should be a scam practised on the criminals. Not only would Leuci find corruption, but it would be manufactured in the sense that active criminals would be told they were being prosecuted for tax evasion. Opportunities would then be created for active criminals to bribe Leuci – who was connected to the Mafia through family ties – to get their IRS files. They would then be arrested for attempting to bribe an officer. Leuci refused to play along, saying that this was a total frame.

Instead it was decided that an attack should be made on the Baxter Street gang, a group of lawyers and bail bondsmen who were suspected of fixing cases and who worked near the

8 R. Daley, *Prince of the City*, p. 13.

criminal courts on Center Street. Leuci went undercover, and the story of his investigation of lawyer Edmund Rosner and bondsman Nick DeStefano is an almost classic account of what can go wrong with undercover work and the subsequent court case. Both men were having considerable legal difficulties over an indictment alleging they had suborned perjury in a case involving Pedro Hernandez. Unfortunately for the Government, Hernandez had disappeared in July 1971 and without him there would be no case. It was thought that he might have been murdered. It seems that if they could not prevent the collapse of the Hernandez case, with the help of Leuci they could still put together another against Rosner. On 30 September 1971, Leuci, wearing a wire, had lunch with DeStefano and Nick Lamattina, a New York City police detective, in a Chinese restaurant. Leuci offered to find out whatever Rosner and DeStefano wished to know about the case. DeStefano seems to have relayed this most useful piece of information to Rosner, who said he did not wish to get involved. The next day DeStefano said that the lawyer was convinced he could win the case without help.

This did not actually suit DeStefano or Lamattina who wanted the information. The next step was to try to get Rosner to pay for the information for them even if he did not use it himself. DeStefano now told Rosner that Hernandez had been killed and that the government was putting a case together in which they would claim that Rosner was the contractor. Surely he now wanted information? It is easy to see how Rosner was in a bind. He had not arranged the killing. Was he being framed? Was Hernandez really dead? Could he explain his position to a judge? He agreed to see Leuci with DeStefano.

On the day of the meeting Leuci did not wear a wire. It was probably fortunate for him because this was the time when he was rubbed down by DeStefano and Lamattina. Immediately there were evidential problems. He maintained that Rosner had given DeStefano $400 to give to Leuci to give to his contact. Rosner's version was that he had resolutely refused to pay over any money. At the next meeting, however, Leuci was wired up but the results were inconclusive. The meeting had been in an Italian restaurant where the other customers, unaware of the importance of clarity on the tape, had inconsiderately laughed and talked, so ruining it. Thoughtlessly the management had had music playing as well.

It was arranged by Leuci's handlers that another meeting should take place, but this did not go too well either. It became apparent to DeStefano and Lamattina that Leuci was an undercover agent. Fearing for his life and after a series of misunderstood signals to his back-ups, he had them arrested. Within a few hours they had themselves become undercover agents. In terms Rosner didn't have a prayer.

What was more serious, however, was that Leuci's crimes were not limited to the three shake-downs of the drug-dealers. They amounted to a whole career of misbehaviour including destroying evidence and, when he finally confessed, enough crimes to fill an eighty-plus-page booklet. It did not do Rosner any good, however. At his trial Leuci stuck to the three crimes he had committed and the jurors tended to believe the good-looking police officer. Eventually Rosner served eight months of a three years' sentence. Leuci was never prosecuted and went on to become a successful crime novelist. One of the reasons for not prosecuting him was because it was thought that such an action would deter future informers.[9]

Despite the criticisms of the use of corrupt police to infiltrate and inform on other corrupt officers, this has become widespread in America. One major instance came in May 1986 when Henry Winter and his partner Tony Magno, from the notorious Precinct 77 in Brooklyn, were offered the choice of being indicted or turning informer/undercover officers on their own people. They had both been dealing in drugs and ripping off drug-dealers. The choice was clear: freedom or nine years.

9 For the record, Hernandez turned up alive and well in Mexico City.

—I want to go home tonight, Henry. Do you want to go home tonight?

—Yeah, I want to go home too.

—Then I guess we have no choice, Henry. I guess we'll cooperate.

And co-operate they did, to such great effect that at the end of their compulsory tour of duty one other officer had agreed to testify against his colleagues and one had committed suicide.[10]

There is, however, one entertaining instance from the fighting corruption days of the Met. It occurred in the Albion public house in Ludgate Circus, near the Old Bailey and used as a drinking hole for police and criminals alike (the Prince of Wales in Lant Street and the Premier Club in Soho were others) and as a place where business such as the arrangement of bail and negotiation of a reduction in charges could safely be undertaken.

Early one evening in March 1980 a scuffle broke out between two well-dressed men in the bar there, one of whom was trying to remove a tape-recorder from the other younger man. The story goes that the publican's wife leaned over the bar and said, 'Right. If you two don't stop now, I'll call the police. I'll call the police.'

The fighting stopped and the younger man hissed back at her, 'We are the police.' In fact they were Detective Superintendent John Keane and the younger Detective Inspector Bernard Gent. The fight had been in an endeavour to switch off a tape-recorder which had recorded an 'arrangement' that for £10,000 Gent, who had gone equipped with the device, would do his best to assist in the release of a man charged with robbery. At the Old Bailey, following a majority decision of the jury, Keane received a sentence of three years' imprisonment.

There has been little in the way of academic research into

10 M. McAlary, *Buddy Boys*, pp. 26–7.

the use of the informer in England and Wales, but recently studies have been undertaken at various universities, including the University of Hull, where Dr Clive Norris and Colin Dunnighan have carried out a survey of two forces, involving a sample of over 200 officers, both uniform and detective. Their findings, which seem to be matched by a second survey into another force, to a certain extent run counter to anecdotal evidence from officers who, it must be said, have been in the main from the Met, many dealing with serious organised crime.

Norris and Dunnighan issued a questionnaire to officers who were beginning their shifts. Generally these were completed in the canteen before starting work, although a number returned them at a later stage. They also had access to the records and people, based on the official payments made to informers. They then interviewed every detective (but not every officer) and a dozen informers. The first of their findings was that most officers said that the most important thing in the life of an informer was money. It was a response which Dr Norris doubted as being wholly accurate.

> Money is a way of negotiating trust. It is a way of cementing a relationship. Informers ask for money as a sign that what they are saying is valuable, but things cut across money particularly when you think that with a registered informer the average payment is £115.

Now, informers fall into two categories – registered and unregistered – with the difference being that as a rule (but not a completely inflexible one) only registered informers are paid. Since the cases of Macro and Birtles, this has become – in theory at least – standard police practice throughout the country. Indeed, the Association of Chief Police Officers has spent some time trying to arrange the adoption of a national policy, including providing an informer manual which includes 'best practice' for dealing with informers. In its unadopted form it has had a strong influence, but it has never been officially launched.

What Dr Norris and Colin Dunnighan found was that Home Office guidelines were regularly and routinely broken: 'For example – they ban the setting-up of jobs without authorisation from a senior officer. In practice, however, such authorisation was rarely sought.'

The statistics of the sample make for interesting reading.

Of registered informers, 80 per cent are male with half in their twenties, a third in their thirties and a fifth over 40. Two-thirds are unemployed. Half are either married or in a settled relationship. Only one in eight has no previous convictions; one-third have between one and five, and half have six or more.

A strong difference was found between registered and unregistered informers. The latter were more likely to be older, female, married, employed, and with significantly fewer convictions.

They also found that recruitment of registered informers almost invariably took place in the police station at the instigation of the police, with only one in ten of the informers beginning negotiations themselves. Half of the initial discussions occurred while the potential informer was under arrest, a third after an arrest but when they were no longer in custody, and one in ten came from those who were involved in an investigation into a crime but were not formal suspects. Sixty per cent of the negotiations began in a police station, with a further 25 per cent starting at either the recruit's home or place of work. Only one in seven conversations with people who became registered informers began in a club or pub. There was no single instance of a solicitor or his clerk acting as an initiator. As for unregistered informers, one-third volunteered themselves.

Once an informer is registered, it seems that officers spend a good deal of time keeping them sweet in what sometimes develops into a long-lasting relationship – although many informers give only one bit of information and are not heard of again. The longest-serving informer in the survey had been providing information for over twenty-two years. Nearly half of the officers had given their principal informer their home telephone number. The reason behind this is twofold. First, to maintain a successful informer twenty-four-hour-a-day access is little short of essential. Second are the childish names under which informers operate. It is hardly surprising that when 'Bugs Bunny' rings up Detective Sergeant White at the police station he has a hard time getting through or even leaving a message.

The research found that officers are extremely reluctant to ask for advice from their controlling officers, usually a Detective Chief Inspector and sometimes a Detective Inspector. Over half the officers running registered informers said that they had never asked for advice at all. Even then they would not, they said, ask the controller. Two-thirds would approach another constable or sergeant whom they would consider to be more sympathetic. Officers, in theory, should make applications to their controlling officer for authorisation of participating informers. It would seem that if the DCI is 'into' informers, the officer is likely to be given a free hand, and if the controller is not in favour of the informer scheme he will be subverted by the detective.

How does one handle an informer? Only slightly over a third of the officers said that they had received training, and half of those who had thought it to be of little use. Other training came from informal talks with other officers or was self-acquired. This presents a worrying feature, because it is clear that a number of younger officers are working without either training, instruction or support and consequently are likely to get themselves into problematical situations – for example, deals with their informers which they cannot possibly carry through. The use of the informer presents a dilemma. In theory, plea, charge and bail bargaining are frowned upon but, given there is no law requiring the police to charge anybody, there is no breach of the law if they do not. The use of the reduced charge and the grant of bail is essential to a successful relationship with an informer. Norris and Dunnighan found that was why so many officers said that money was the most essential part of a relationship with an informer. 'It doesn't raise moral questions.'

Much more worrying appears to be the disclosure, or rather non-disclosure, of the use of participating informers. In theory a decision to use a participating informer must be taken at either Head of CID or Assistant Chief Constable level. In fact the requests are granted rarely, particularly because, says Dr Norris, they are rarely made. And, when they are, his research suggests that they are not disclosed to the Crown Prosecution Service.

Whether they are granted will depend much on the person to whom they are made. A regional co-ordinator of the Regional Crime Squad is much more likely to sanction requests, since he will receive them on a regular basis. At force level, the authoriser is likely to be much more wary and will be bypassed.

From a detective's point of view informers are a continuous risk, one of the problems being the uncertainty of the information provided. There is the risk that the informer will provide the wrong information; he may provide the wrong time, date or place, or the job will simply not go down. This leads to a waste of time if, for example, the police have provided a stake-out, and it also leads to a loss of face for the detective running the informer. There is also the risk that the informer has watered down his actual role, and hence the problems that will arise when it is discovered he is in it up to his eyeballs rather than his ankles. Thirdly, there is the risk of physical harm being done to the informer.

On the other hand, 94 per cent of detectives were quite or very confident of the usefulness of the information supplied by their principal informer. Six out of ten thought that over three-quarters of the information he provided was useful. A substantial majority of the detectives (as opposed to the uniformed police who took part in the survey) believed that three-quarters of people turned in by their principal registered informer were actively involved in crime. Provided the informer was himself actively involved in the criminal sub-culture, they believed that some three-quarters of his information was useful. The less deeply involved, the less useful the information.

Anecdotal evidence that officers have paid informers out of their own pockets is substantiated. The last time an informer had been paid, slightly under half of the officers had paid from their own pockets sums up to £50, with half paying between £10 and £20. The highest sum ever paid from an officer's own pocket was £200, with only a handful paying more than £50.

Officers were found to be both protective and demanding of their informers. In one instance a detective had allowed his informer to escape, and to divert suspicion had taken him to hospital to have his arm put in plaster. In another, where good information was being received, an officer had protected a man whom he knew to be an escapee from prison. On the other hand, officers kept their informers in line by retaining papers which could lead to a prosecution and by threatening to blow their cover.

Only one in three had managed to recoup the money officially. There were, however, found to be a number of ways in which a sort of slush fund could be developed. For example, if an officer was over six miles from his station he could claim a luncheon allowance of £3.15, and supervisors encouraged officers to take advantage of this so that a fund of around £60 could be put together.

12

A Threatened Species?

Where does it all lead? Or is it just a circle with temporary breaks as the courts for a while turn against the testimony of the informer and undercover agent? Should a species seen to be endangered be protected? Apart from anything else a grass is cheap at the price. For example, the No.4 (Midlands) Regional Crime Squad had a £47,000 budget for the year 1993–94. On the other hand, in America there is a considerable reaction to the enormous sums being paid out to informants.

Critics of the supergrass system and of undercover police work argue that there are very considerable dangers not merely for officers but for the judicial system. One of the pre-eminent figures in American criminal law, Professor Alan Dershowitz, is clear:

Informers are very important. They give you leads and tips. They tell you where the guns are buried. That's all fine. It's when the informant's word, his credibility, is used in court – that's the problem.[1]

Stephen Trott, a judge on the US 9th Circuit Court of Appeals

1 Quoted in Mark Curriden, 'No Honor among Thieves' in the *American Bar Association Journal*, June 1989.

and former assistant attorney general for the Criminal Division, was quoted in the same article: 'I tell prosecutors, "Don't use these kinds of witnesses unless you absolutely have to."' He accepts, however, that the criminal justice system would collapse without the use of informants. The system tolerates informants – often the only witnesses – as essential:

> The FBI will tell you that if you don't have informants, you're out of luck when it comes to investigating heavy-duty crime. Out of luck! So you've got to balance this thing. It's not a question of not using them, it's a question of when and where.

Now in 1995, Professor Al Alschuler, of the University of Chicago, has firmed his opinion on the use of the supergrass:

> The informant system is a dark corner of law enforcement all but immune from judicial supervision. As the war on drugs escalates, so does the extent of the intrusion on privacy, the use of brutal methods to 'turn' snitches, and the unreliability of the informant-provided information upon which the police act.[2]

Unsurprisingly, there have also been problems with informants and supergrasses. Jack Slipper, who in principle likes the scheme, also recognises the dangers:

> I found the average informant was a man who had been dealt with by an officer who'd treated him fairly and not bullied him and the man had been fortunate enough to have got a light sentence. Then if the officer was any good he'd meet him soon after the case, if he hadn't gone away, or when he came out, buy him a drink and say, 'Look, it's up to you but if . . .'

2 Letter to the author.

Looking back, I think it is one of the most dangerous ways of retaining your credibility because no matter how clean, how straight you want to keep it the officers who run with professional informers find themselves bound in a web into which the layman would read corruption. But it could well have been nothing of the kind. I've known good officers, who've done excellent work and who've finished up their career with a cloud over their heads because of informers.

Over the years efforts have been made to provide a code for officers. In 1992 the Association of Chief Police Officers put together a document which was due to be put to the crime committee for ratification, but none was forthcoming. Some police forces used it as a blueprint, but for some reason it was never official policy. In September 1994 a document was prepared and accepted which sets out the rules to be followed by police using informers. To what extent it can or will be followed is another matter, and Clive Norris of Hull University has doubts:

In many respects the new guidelines merely codify the existing rules and regulations. Our research suggests that many of these rules were routinely broken. Unless there is a profound change in the manner in which detective/informer dealings are supervised, it is unlikely that they will have much impact on the day-to-day use of informers. In short, so-called 'noble cause' corruption will remain.

In the guide officers are urged to keep their distance from the informants. Whether it is actually possible to do this and maintain the necessary bond is another matter. Officers may be reminded that the informer belongs not to them but to the police, but the practice is a different matter entirely.

Here is a police officer who joined in the 1970s, speaking of

303

his younger days when the grass was loyal to the officer, and fine concepts of belonging to the police as a body did not occur to him:

In the 1970s the cultivation of informers was an active part of the CID. What are you doing? Are you getting to know them? These were questions asked by senior officers of young men in the CID. How you did it was left up to you. If it resulted in turning a blind eye and operating an unofficial licensing system, then that was not necessarily frowned upon. A set of double standards existed. The people you were sending to prison, as long as you treated them in a way they felt was their due, had no resentment. If you dealt with their family by their lights they'd be willing to become informers on their release.

I knew officers who looked after wives, making sure they didn't behave too widely; who looked after post office and building society books, bringing money each week for the wife.

The relationship between the police and villainy was wholly different from today. We were encouraged to be much closer.

Informers were a wholly personal thing. You didn't allow anyone else to know who your informant was. If you went to your DI or DCI and said, 'My informant tells me . . .,' if you were accepted as a working DC, then your superior officer would never dream of asking the informant's name, or if he did he wouldn't expect you to name him.

Informants expected to be paid out of the rewards, but in many cases the reward money paid out bore no resemblance to the amount the informant received. If they got a good drink they were lucky.

I was on late turn at the CID at Peckham one night. I was the only one in the office when the phone rang about 9.30 p.m. A voice said he wanted to speak to such and such an officer. I said he wasn't here and I'd leave a message for him. No, it was urgent. Would I meet the caller, who said he had information. I went and met him in a pub. He'd just come out of a three-year sentence. He'd been the driver in a robbery fifteen years earlier and had been grassed by a supergrass. He said whilst he was in prison he'd been visited by officers from Countryman who wanted him to tell them about Officer X. 'Tell us and you can walk out within the next few weeks.' He named the officer and I said I knew him well. 'If you know him, tell him I've nothing against him and I didn't tell on him. I did my full time but tell him they're looking into him.'

A new problem for the police and the courts has been the protection of their informers and ordinary witnesses from identification in court. In the past the witness appeared and then either took his chance or disappeared into a witness protection programme.

The Metropolitan Police have had a witness protection system for the last twenty years; it is one which has grown out of the use of the supergrass in the trials of the seventies. The police work on informality, and to make formal rules often presents problems. 'We wanted to make sure that people coming into the supergrass system survived giving evidence,' says Commander Roy Ramm, who ran the scheme.

The Metropolitan Police Criminal Justice Protection Unit (CJPU) has three categories into which witnesses in the context of organised criminal groups will fall. The witness is defined as being frequently a co-conspirator or associate mixing with members of the particular criminal group. They vary slightly from the ACPO definitions.

Resident Informant – An active participant in a succession of serious crimes who, after arrest, elects to identify, give evidence against and provide intelligence about fellow criminals involved in those or other offences.

305

Protected Informant – A person informing on associates participating in crime whose identity and activity is exposed.

Protected Witness – A person who can provide essential evidence, generally about the most serious offences, and a substantial threat exists to their well-being.

The scheme has dealt with several hundred witnesses over the years with, in 1994, about thirty cases outstanding. The figures provided by the Association of Chief Police Officers, Police Superintendents' Association and the Police Federation, in answer to a written question by the House of Commons Home Affairs Committee on Organised Crime, are:

In the period	No. of cases dealt with by the Witness Protection Unit	Breakdown by status
1977–82	48	96% Resident Informants 2%Protected Witness
1983–87	24	25% Resident Informants 50% Protected Witness 25% Protected Informants
1988–93	61	31% Resident Informants 58% Protected Witness 8% Protected Informants 3% Other

In cases where protection had been sought between 1 February and 20 June 1994, there had been fifty-seven applications for protection of which forty-one were witnesses seeking protection and forty dependants, making a total of eighty-one. Eight people were seeking resident informant status, forty-four protected witness status and five protected informant status.[3]

Curiously, Ramm believes that as more importance is placed on scientific evidence, so witness intimidation will increase:

> The more we are able to provide incontrovertible proof through DNA, fingerprints and forensic evidence in general, the more the witness provides the only vulnerable area in the prosecution.[4]

Nowadays, with (it appears) a much more active programme by professional criminals to discourage evidence being given against them, more steps have been taken to repair the situation. Quite apart from cases involving children, in what the authorities deem to be appropriate circumstances screens have gone up between the witness and the dock and the public gallery. There are now instances where pseudonyms and voice distorters are being used.

Nor is it clear what, if any, signal of guilt this sends out to the jury. The judge can say until he is blue in the face that the erection of such a screen should not be held against any of the defendants, but whether the jury puts two and two together and makes four or an even greater number, who can tell?

Given the self-interest of informers and the fact that they and ordinary witnesses have had very close links with the police for months, defence lawyers fear that there is likely to be a bond between them and the witnesses will be unlikely to say a word against their helpers. If the witness appears under a pseudonym, behind screens and with a voice distorter, it

3 House of Commons, Home Affairs Committee, *Organised Crime*, 1994, HMSO.
4 Michael Clarke, 'Witnesses in Fear' in *Police Review*, 6 May 1994.

is difficult to see how the defendant can mount any sort of cross-examination, let alone an effective one. It may be, for example, that he has had an abortive affair with the witness who holds a grudge against him. It may be the woman's husband. He may have sacked the witness, or fought him in a pub on a previous occasion. Who can tell?

The Court of Appeal was convinced that the defendant should have the right to know his accused even if he did not see him. In the case of Vincent Agar, heard at Teesside Crown Court, the judge had refused to allow the defence to put questions to police officers which might lead to the identification of the informer. Agar received eighteen months for possessing amphetamines with intent to supply. In February 1989 the Court of Appeal said that although there was a well-established rule of public policy inhibiting the disclosure of the identity of informants, there was an even stronger public interest in allowing a defendant to put forward a tenable defence in the best light.[5] The appeal was allowed.

One detective in a large metropolitan force is probably speaking for a great number of his colleagues when he says that:

> . . . it is a right of the defendant in British law to be faced by their accusers and this really flies in the face of that: but when you look at undercover officers or the security forces, they're allowed to do it, and this is just an extension of that.[6]

It is small wonder that the defence, where the money is available – and that of course is only in serious crime cases – have resorted to employing private detectives to try to identify the witnesses.

5 (1989) 90 Cr. App. R. 318.
6 Michael Clarke, *op. cit.*

Part of the problem has come about because of the reluctance of the prosecution over the years to disclose to the defence what material it has which it is not using. There have, unfortunately, been a number of highly publicised cases at appeal level which have shown that the prosecution has, before trial, had in its possession evidence which would either tend to show the innocence of the defendant or actually exculpate him completely.[7] In theory, for many years the prosecution has had a duty to pass over unused material but has not been doing so. Now the defending lawyers have adopted a more aggressive stance, and to a great extent they have been supported by the courts.

In 1993 David Shattock, Chief Constable of Avon and Somerset, spoke up against the practice of disclosure, saying that since the previous September at least ten cases had been withdrawn because the disclosure rulings would have put witnesses or informants at risk:

> Certain solicitors and barristers are exploiting the rules of disclosure, knowing we will withdraw the prosecution rather than face the fear of reprisals when information becomes known to their clients.
>
> One never wants to stop information being passed on to solicitors and barristers who have a duty to look after the best interests of their clients. After what has happened in the past, we don't want to be the sole keepers of information.
>
> But there are occasions where we think that the information that they are asking for is not necessary.

Examples given by the Avon constabulary – not one would

---

7 A particularly sad example is that of Stefan Kisko, convicted of the rape and murder of Lesley Molseed. The prosecution, which relied heavily on a confession, had evidence to show that physically he could not have been her attacker. Kisko was released from a mental hospital after many years and died before he could be awarded compensation for his ordeal. Later, after Kisko's release, another man was arrested but was never charged.

immediately think of as being the centre for major organised crime – included the kidnapping of two men who were taken to a flat, tied up and handcuffed. Their money was stolen from them and their kidnappers threatened to pour boiling water over them. The offenders were caught in the act, but the witnesses failed to appear at court, telling the police they were in fear of their lives. A second case involved a man who was hacked with a meat cleaver, and others were attacked with baseball bats. Several days later one of the victims was threatened by men who stole and burned his car; he later withdrew the complaint. The third of Avon's instances involved a man who was beaten unconscious and when he awoke found himself naked in a bath; he then had boiling water poured over him. The case was dropped after witnesses were too scared to help the police.

On average it appears that the police (really the Crown Prosecution Service) are dropping a case a week to protect informants. Assuming it is a multi-handed defence case, this means that over the last two years 200–300 serious criminals are on the streets who would, and should, have been in prison. This is the opinion of Detective Chief Superintendent Brian Ridley of the Metropolitan Police.

The police also complain that the disclosure rulings are physically restrictive and financially ruinous. Lawyers defending Robert Black, the paedophile convicted of killing three girls in April 1994, asked for and received twenty-three tons of documents obtained in the ten-year investigation. In the Asil Nadir – Polly Peck fraud case, over one million documents were produced.

The police have also complained about the tactics used by defence lawyers when they have obtained the information. In one rape case in the South of England, it is claimed that the police had routinely interviewed a man who had had a rape conviction many years earlier. The defence obtained this information under the rules of disclosure and called the man as a defence witness. He was asked whether he had ever been convicted and whether he had been questioned over the present incident. Their defendant was acquitted.

In the case of an allegation of a robbery at a supermarket in the Midlands, details were obtained of all other supermarket robberies in the area – on which there was no evidence against the defendant – and for which he was able to supply alibis. He was acquitted.

This, say the police, is unfair play, maintaining that in the first case the jury had the impression that the witness was the guilty man, and in the second that they had never made any allegations against the accused in relation to the other robberies.[8]

It may be that there can be restrictions on the amount of documents to be produced, but that still does not solve the problem of protecting the identity of witnesses.

As for the use of the informer, now big business for drug-enforcement agencies, there are allegations that there is little control exercised by the agencies that use and pay them, and that many informants continue their illegal activity while being paid by the agencies. Further it is claimed, particularly in America, that deals are concealed from the defence.

There is clear evidence that informants have lied on oath, so sending innocent people to jail, and that the informers frequently entrap people to build cases for the agents for whom they work and with whom they bond.

In Great Britain there is a suggestion that informers should be put on a weekly wage, and this is almost the practice at present in the case of a principal registered informer. It certainly appears to have been the case in Northern Ireland. As always, America is ahead of the game. Back in 1991 FBI agent Bensch, who at the time supervised over 250 confidential informants, acknowledged that:

Many informants working on a long-term case will get

8 *Independent on Sunday*, 18 December 1994.

a weekly allowance of $1,000 and a large reward at the
end, as much as $100,000 . . . actually, some of the bigger
informants are a downright bargain.[9]

'We will pay an informant anything from £50 to £100 at the
bottom to several thousand pounds of public money for the
recovery of large quantities of drugs,' says Detective Chief
Superintendent Roy Ramm, thereby showing that Scotland
Yard is in a different league from the forces researched by
Dr Norris. He adds:

And I wouldn't want to put a ceiling on it, because, so
far as we're concerned, there is no ceiling. We don't say
we pay up to a maximum, it depends on the work.[10]

Apart from paying from their own resources, informants are
funded by Scotland Yard which sends out begging letters to
banks, building societies, and insurance companies asking for
a contribution for informers. 'Informing has become, if not an
honorable trade, a mass occupation,' says Dershowitz. 'They
manufacture crime to sell their product. They lie to give their
employers – the authorities – what the informant thinks they
want to hear.'

Says Professor Al Alschuler:

With money and leniency, there are tremendous pressures
on informants just to make things up. Any honest law
enforcement officer will tell you informants put spins on
their stories all the time. You cannot trust these people.
What is more disturbing is that the government is giving
informers a licence to conduct their criminal conduct. The
government is basically subsidizing the drug trade.

9 *American Bar Association Journal*, June 1991.
10 R. Fleming with H. Miller, *Scotland Yard*, pp. 126–7.

There is plenty of anecdotal evidence that this is being mirrored here, with drug shipments being allowed through to wait for 'the big one'. If concrete evidence is needed, then a case which was eventually heard at Newcastle Crown Court gives ground for considerable concern.

At the beginning of 1994 there was a major disaster in the case of Joseph Kassar, a Manchester businessman convicted of a plot to smuggle £67 million of cocaine imported amongst lead ingots from Venezuela. The shipment had gone through and had been distributed through sources in Liverpool, but the planners tried a second time. On this occasion Customs and Excise found nearly £150 million, in street terms, of 95 per cent pure cocaine at a warehouse in Stoke-on-Trent. They removed the drugs from the crates of thirty-two lead ingots which, this time, had come in through Felixstowe and were on their way to Liverpool. Customs tried to prove that the £67 million had gone through Kassar's hands, but in the end they were able to show that only £300,000 had passed that way.

That was bad enough, but the full story of the investigation and its repercussions was yet to come out. When it did, it showed a complete lack of co-operation between the Customs and the police. The success story which turned to ashes had begun on 26 June 1992 when the Customs were waiting as Brian Charrington landed in his private aircraft at Teesside airport. Six months previously Customs officers had drilled into the lead ingots stored in the Stoke warehouse, and they believed Charrington was the organiser of the shipment.

It appears that members of the drug wing of the No. 2 (North East) Regional Crime Squad had been working with Customs to prepare a case against him. Unfortunately, what appears not to have been mentioned is that quite apart from him being Target One, Charrington was just about the *Numero Uno* police informant. The moment he was arrested, the police went to his rescue. If need be, they would give evidence in his defence.

In fact this is not uncommon practice. For example in January 1989 Detective Superintendent Tony Lundy was allowed to give evidence *in camera* on behalf of his protégé, supergrass Roy Garner, and towards the end of 1994 a major furore broke out when it was discovered that Commander John Allinson, former head of operations at Scotland Yard, had privately intervened at the trial of a man linked to a contract killing. Allinson later resigned.

During the search for the killer of Donald Urquhart, shot in a professional hit, a suspect's home in Sussex was raided. There detectives found a huge cache of arms and ammunition. Allinson gave evidence in the judge's private room, saying that the man had helped to solve a major robbery ten years previously. It was a move which did not please either London or Sussex detectives. In the end the weapons were confiscated and the man fined.

The Customs officers in the Charrington case complained that, far from producing major drug-related arrests, Charrington had only implicated small-time if professional criminals. Gilbert Gray QC, the barrister for Charrington, asked for and was granted a meeting with Sir Nicholas Lyell, the Attorney General. Five weeks later, on 28 January 1993, all charges against Charrington were withdrawn by the Crown Prosecution Service; he and ten others were due to be committed for trial to the Crown Court. In their turn the police complained that the bust of Charrington had pre-empted a major strike against a Colombian cartel.

In January 1994 the only person to be convicted for his part in the whole affair was Kassar, described by the trial judge, Mr Justice May, as 'not one of the principal organisers, but very much a middleman'. It is interesting to speculate on the sentences which would have been passed on the leaders. His solicitor complained that the case had been surrounded by secrecy and that the press had been deliberately gagged to prevent the truth being known. John Merry, who runs a news agency in Darlington, claims that a prominent politician telephoned him urging him not to publicise the case. At the time of Kassar's trial, Charrington was believed to be in Hong

Kong. According to the *Observer*, one of the police officers involved in thwarting the Customs inquiry left the force in January 1993 and that September drove to Spain with his wife, a serving police constable, in an £87,000 BMW registered to Charrington.[11]

It is only when a situation or an informer begins to unravel that the damage he or she has caused can begin to be seen, and by then it is often too late to do anything about it except to begin a damage limitation exercise.

One such American informer was the former nude dancer, Darlene McKinney, who became so addicted to cocaine that the only person she could find to employ her was not a topless-bar-owner but the Georgia law authorities. She laid the first information because a supplier refused her credit, and from then an officer in the drug squad in Rome, Georgia, took her up with some enthusiasm. She was told there was more money in addition to her first reward if she continued to help bust drug-dealers and she co-operated enthusiastically. Later she turned on the agent who ran her when the head of the town's narcotics unit was himself charged with trafficking.

During spring 1988 her activities, which included luring men into using or selling drugs after sex with her, led to eighteen arrests. McKinney also maintained that her supervisor not only had sex with her but let her walk off with part of the drugs. She also received 10 per cent of cash or assets seized.

> The reason I was doing all these things [offering sex if friends would buy her cocaine specifically from the undercover agent] was because I would do anything for drugs.

She went on to testify that after each arrest agents would spread the bags of cocaine they seized on the table.

11 The *Observer* was about the only newspaper to carry what would appear to be a major story. See David Rose and John Merry, 'Drugs bust victory turned to dust' in the *Observer*, 16 January 1994.

I'd just get a little out and he'd kind of turn his back. He never actually handed me the bags and said, 'Here, take some cocaine out of it,' but he knew what I was doing. He'd have to be pretty dumb not to.[12]

Apart from those who suffered at Darlene McKinney's hands, all this may seem mildly amusing and remote from the real world. After all, where exactly is Rome, Georgia? Of course, the denizens of that town may ask, who is John Banks? The sort of question a judge asks on a slack afternoon, or late morning, with an eye on a place on page one of the tabloids: 'Who are the Beatles?' He might also have asked, 'What on earth were the authorities doing using him?'

The Beatles may have written and performed 'Lucy in the Sky with Diamonds', said to be a homage to LSD, but John Banks was another proposition altogether. In April 1993 the thief, mercenary, blackmailer and would-be contract killer, as journalist David Rose described him, was in hiding, protected by police and Customs squads who, Rose said, had paid him as an agent for many years. The wheels had finally come off.

In the first week of April a jury at Southwark Crown Court had unanimously found an alleged heroin dealer, Raymond Okudzeto, not guilty. Okudzeto was, he claimed, the victim of a classic reverse sting. He thought he was acting with and on behalf of the authorities, but he was not. The jury found that he had been entrapped by Banks acting as an *agent provocateur*, and threw out the case.

Banks' career is both lengthy and noteworthy, and it is

12 *American Bar Association Journal*, June 1991. Another story in the same article tells of how a sixty-year-old electronics expert was prevailed upon to make a briefcase bomb. He was told that the explosive was necessary to destroy a Mafia shipment of drugs. He wanted to back out but he was then told the Mob would harm his family. In a third story, marijuana dealer Woody Moore seems to have gone completely off the rails. First he testified that leading Georgians, including a judge and his law partner, had helped him launder drugs. The partner was indicted but along with all other defendants was acquitted. During this period Moore had continued importing drugs. He then turned on the authorities, alleging they had known all the time he was still importing.

interesting that anyone should have used him as a trustworthy informer for any period of time at all. A self-styled major, he served in the British Army from which he was dishonourably discharged in 1969 for theft. The commission was, he said, awarded him by the government of South Vietnam shortly before its collapse.

His career as a mercenary began some six years after his compulsory retirement from the British Army. Operating from an office above a laundrette in Sandhurst, he endeavoured to recruit mercenaries for the African cause in what was then Rhodesia with an advertisement in the *Daily Telegraph*. The initial group of dogs of war did not last long; some were discharged for getting drunk in a London hotel, and within six months Banks was back recruiting once more – now for the anti-Marxists in Angola.

This time some of the dogs did not return to home kennels. Of the 180 who went, fourteen were murdered by a Greek fighting on their side. Two were executed by the victorious MPLA, and others were killed in action.

Banks' first appearance as a government witness was in the spring of 1977, when he appeared at the Old Bailey in a case where three men were said to have negotiated a deal to buy what now seems to be a modest £25,000 of arms. They received long sentences. At the trial Rock Tansey, appearing for the defence, alleged that Banks had incited the men into dealing in arms, probably against their will and certainly against their better judgement. Gerald Smiley, Joseph Higgins and James Davidson were found guilty on 10–2 majorities of being involved in soliciting Banks and two other men to supply 1,000 American-made M1 carbines. Smiley called to the judge, 'You gave Banks a chance to perjure himself and these fools [the jury] believed him.'

Three years later Banks was back in the Old Bailey, this time in the dock accused of blackmail and uttering threats to kill. So far as the blackmail went, he claimed he had information about a Cuban plot to assassinate the Nicaraguan president, Antonio

317

Somozo. Banks had sent two men to collect $250,000 from the Nicaraguan embassy in London. His defence was interesting, including not only claims that he was a past agent for the British Secret Service but also details of plots to kill 'Carlos the Jackal' and of assassinations in Yemen. He received two years' imprisonment.

Six months later in April 1981, he was in Coldingley open prison and absconded, staying out for eight months. On his return, he lost twenty-eight days' remission and suffered fourteen days' loss of privileges, a punishment which hardened prison discipline observers would describe as little more than a slap on the wrist.

Throughout the remainder of the 1980s Banks seems to have flourished. He became a security consultant, a military adviser and a wheeler-dealer. He had a substantial property in Lincolnshire. Nevertheless, he found time to become involved in situations which led to his appearances as a prosecution witness or a behind-the-scenes manipulator in cases where others gave evidence. In 1991 he was giving evidence in the contract killing of a former-loved-one case; the woman was acquitted. That same year, allegations of dishonest handling and theft against a man said to be a member of the Ulster Defence Association were dropped at Isleworth Crown Court. They related to some £20 million worth of paintings, part of the theft of the Alfred Beit Collection stolen in Ireland. He had posed as a potential buyer at the Penta Hotel at Heathrow.

Next year, he did not give evidence when Martin Poole and James Collis were prosecuted at Winchester Crown Court for trying to buy 75 kilos of cannabis from the Customs in the form of officer Michael Stephenson in an undercover scam. Their defence was that Banks had bullied them into purchasing the cannabis, telling them that it was compensation for the failure of a deal he had made with one of their associates.

The defence, although severely hampered, managed to provide at least marginal evidence that Banks existed and was involved. They found his computer telephone records, but Stephenson gave evidence that he did not know the whereabouts of Banks. Later, it would appear that he was in regular contact with Banks, who was 'an informant whose identity we were trying to protect'. This would seem to be not the only time that Banks was being protected.

The Okudzeto trial related to £40,000 of heroin found at the defendant's flat shortly after he had offered a sample to an undercover Customs officer, who went to the flat, posing as a buyer for £15,000 of heroin. Okudzeto had been approached in Kenya by a man called Evans Anyona, and had immediately told Banks, his former business associate, in the belief that he would pass the information on to the authorities. Instead, Banks persauded him to take an active part in the sting.

The Customs sheltered Banks for eight months, refusing to admit that he had played any part in the sting; it was only at a pre-trial review that his existence was admitted. When he did give evidence, Banks denied he had ever spoken to Anyona. Later during the trial a logged record was produced showing that Michael Stephenson, the undercover officer in charge of the case, had spoken with Banks about putting in a buyer, and that Banks had been in touch with Anyona in Kenya.

Banks gave evidence and under cross-examination denied setting people up. He also denied he owed Okudzeto money and claimed he had been paid £750 by customs officials. His only motivation, he said, was his hatred of drugs. Asked about his involvement in Africa, he cannot have charmed the jury when he replied, 'I didn't mind which side [I was working for] as long as it was paid for.' He was asked how much he charged for a contract assassination and replied, 'There is no fixed price. I'm sorry, we're not Tesco's.'

Summing up, Judge Eugene Cotran said:

The log reveals the discrepancy between Banks and Stephenson. The credibility of one or both of them is suspect. There was some misdemeanour by the Customs team . . . There were certain disturbing features. You

319

must ask yourself why were these things done. You may say the rot starts from the top downwards or you may question the credibility of this case.

The jury failed to agree, and now Okudzeto, who had been in custody for eleven months, was released on bail. The re-trial took place the following April. At the second trial Banks did not give evidence and Okudzeto was acquitted.

In July 1994 Banks resurfaced in South Africa organising bodyguards for Winnie Mandela. He was now, it appears, her main security adviser, and had been in the country since October 1993 when he came to the notice of the police over a Mercedes Benz hired car. He was held in prison until payment of £21,000 was made anonymously.

As for the use of undercover police, there is an argument that this itself leads to the licensing of criminals to commit crime. Jean-Paul Brodeur argues that whilst all guidelines on handling informers proclaim that the law is not to be broken in the course of their assignment with the police, the application of the guidelines is progressively suspended as handlers get more deeply involved with their informers in risky operations. He cites the case of a Royal Canadian Mounted Police officer who appealed against his conviction for drug trafficking on the grounds that he accepted only a part of the benefits that his informer was making in selling drugs. The informer apparently had found it unfair that his handler should not get his slice of the cake.[13] He also sees the subversion of the law as inevitably following, and the informer as a shield for misconduct:

> I was struck by how often police officers whose behaviour was under review tried to justify the the fact that they were at the wrong place (e.g. a strip joint), at a wrong time (being on duty) and doing the wrong thing (getting drunk) by alleging that they were 'meeting with an informer'.

13 J.P. Brodeur, 'Undercover policing in Canada: Wanting what is wrong' in *Crime, Law and Social Change* 18.

A senior Scotland Yard officer believes that undercover officers have to be committed.

> Totally. And they have to keep remembering where they come from. They have a need to be conscious of what their parent organisation is trying to achieve.

There is also the danger, more prevalent in America than here, that the undercover officer will become a casualty. Gary Marx cites a number of cases when undercover black officers have been killed in mistake for offenders.

The benefits are, however, attractive. Police morale can be strengthened by the knowledge that officers are actively taking steps to prevent and detect crime. The results of an undercover operation can serve as a warning to the semi-professional as opposed to career criminal. For the latter, undercover work may not break up an organisation but its presence, perceived or real, may serve to disorganise their businesses.

On a lighter side, surveillance and undercover investigators are used by insurance companies investigating fraudulent claims. Willy McNicholas was injured carrying mats at the Moss Side Leisure Centre in 1987. He was still claiming to be suffering from the effects of his injuries when he went to Fuertaventura where he carried the luggage for his family, swam and carried his son's buggy. Posing as a tourist, the investigator filmed him in these operations. McNicholas was later invited to see edited highlights of the film of his holiday. Within half an hour he abandoned his claim, though he thought the behaviour of the council was unsporting: 'It's normal business practice to check out compensation claims but to video my wife and kids as well as me is a bit much. No privacy laws were broken because we were filmed in public places, not in our room or anything like that.'[14]

Many would like to see the range of undercover work extended. A senior Scotland Yard officer believes that the

14 *Observer*, 25 September 1994.

road down which the police should think of travelling is that of the undercover officer, and says:

> Courts seem to be much more comfortable with under-cover officers than with informers. Society is better off with undercover officers, but the historical context says that society is uncomfortable with secretive let alone secret police.

More positively, he notes that there is an increasing number of appearances of undercover officers because of the difficulties with informers.

> We can protect undercover officers better. For decades we have been seeking to limit the role of the informant, looking to get an undercover officer in or to get corroboration.

Rowan Bosworth-Davies, formerly a police officer and now with a major City firm of solicitors, comments:

> I'm a fan of undercover policing. The future of investigating real City crime is the use of undercover policing with target surveillance and target hardening. If you accept City crime is organised crime then why not investigate it as such? If the authorities want to combat City fraud effectively then the way they go about it at present is farcical.

In America, where perhaps the technique of the use of the informer has been most highly developed, it would seem that in 1993 the Justice Department spent some $97 million on informers of one kind or another annually. It has raised the hackles of many, including one lawyer who commented:

> Many of these individuals, because of their special relationships with law enforcement or prosecutors, are

able to continue committing crimes and doing drugs. I consider this to be an absolute disgrace. As a lawyer I understand that the government may need informants at times, but this level of cash payments (let alone other benefits conferred on informants) is outrageous.

As with all forms of policing, there is a price to be paid. There is little doubt that, if asked to vote on the subject, the vast majority of the public would shut their collective minds to the dangers of the informant, the informer, the entrapper and the cell fink. They would think only of the resulting convictions and say, 'Yes, siree, that is indeed what we want.'

Appendix

STATEMENT OF WITNESS

(M.C. Act, 1980, S101; C.J. Act, 1967, s.9; M.C. Rules, 1981, r. 70)

Statement of ....

Age of Witness (if over 21 enter 'over 21') ....

Occupation of Witness ....

Address and Telephone Number ....

....

....

This statement, consisting of   pages each signed by me, is true to the best of my knowledgevidence, I shall be liable to prosecution if I have wilfully stated in it anything which I know to be false or do not believe to be true.

Dated the   day of   , 19   .

Signed ....

Signature witnessed by ....

On Saturday 22nd June 1985 with a man called Roger I and a man known as Tom MORRIS went to the roundabout on the North Circular Road at the junction of the M1 motorway where we met a man known as Tony, I now know this man to be Michael BAILEY, and another man named Garry, I now know this man to be Harry Brand. I had £10,000 in cash in my constructive possession with the authority of my Detective Inspector. BAILEY and BRAND arrived in a Ford Granada colour blue index no: CEV 185R. I was introduced to them and we then followed to the Woodman Public House, in Highgate, N.6 where we entered the car park at the rear. BAILEY and I discussed the fact that he said that he had a quantity of forged £50 notes for sale. He said that he had £50,000 worth and wanted £10,000 sterling for them. I agreed to this and I said I would show him my money (i.e. £10,000) BAILEY also said,

325

that he had one sample on him but it was down his trousers and he would show it to me at a later stage. Then Roger, BAILEY and I went in Roger's car to the Archway Public House, Archway Road, N.19 where I showed BAILEY my £10,000. He said that there was no need as he trusted me fully. He also said that everything was sweet and that he would take us to a public house in the East End where we could exchange the £50,000 worth of forged £50 notes for my £10,000 cash. Meanwhile we had left Harry and MORRIS drinking in the Woodman Public House. With BAILEY Roger and I went to the Swan Public House, Kingsland Road, Dalston, E.8. where I met a number of men and was introduced by BAILEY to a man named Frank. I now know this man to be Jack TAYLOR. TAYLOR stated that they had £50,000 worth of forged £50 notes in a car nearby and he wanted to do the swap i.e. £10,000 sterling for the forged £50,000 rather quickly. I said to TAYLOR, 'As they had seen my money, I wanted to see theirs before the transaction was completed.' TAYLOR was reluctant to show his forged £50 notes at this stage. TAYLOR said that he wanted my £10,000 first before he passed me his forged £50,000 currency. I would not agree to this and insisted that I had to see their money first. TAYLOR said that as we all trusted each other there were no problems and that he had definitely got the forged money in a car nearby. I said that if that is so, show it to me. TAYLOR was still reluctant to do this. BAILEY who was present all the time during this conversation then said that he [had] a forged £50 note in his possession and that I could have a look at it in the toilet if I wished. He gave me a £50 note and I went into the Gents toilet with BAILEY, and carefully examined this particular £50 note. The note appeared to me to be a genuine £50 note. BAILEY and I returned to the bar, again to the company of TAYLOR. BAILEY said to TAYLOR, that he had shown me a forged sample and TAYLOR asked me what I thought of the quality of the forged £50 note. I said to BAILEY and TAYLOR that if the rest of their merchandise was as good as that one then they would be just about perfect. I said to TAYLOR, 'Would you show me the £50's.' TAYLOR said, 'There are too many people about, I can't show it to you in the car.' I said to TAYLOR and BAILEY, 'In that case, I'm going to return to Nottingham.' Roger and I returned to the Woodman Public House where we met BRAND and MORRIS. I said to BRAND that TAYLOR and BAILEY would not show their £50's and that I was going to return to Nottingham. BRAND used the telephone and he told me that TAYLOR would contact me in due course at Nottingham.

On Tuesday 2nd July 1985 I went to Nottingham where at 7.30 pm BAILEY telephoned me from London to say that the deal was on and that business could definitely be done this time. He also said he could double up. I asked him to explain this and he said that he had £100,000 in forged £50 notes and wanted me to produce £20,000 for this amount. I said that this was okay. He then said he would ring me the following evening and confirm when and where we should meet in London. BAILEY did in actual fact telephone again the following evening, 3rd July 1985, but stated that he would definitely confirm a meeting in London for Saturday morning, but before he was able to do this he would ring again at 7.30pm on the following Friday night. I stated I may be unable to take his telephone due to business I had to do in Manchester. As a result of further information received on Saturday 6th July 1985, Roger and I met BAILEY and TAYLOR in the Woodman Public House, TAYLOR stated that they had the forged £50 notes nearby and they had £100,000 worth. BAILEY said that it is all good stuff and that it was as good as the sample he had shown me previously. We had a few drinks and then TAYLOR suggested we leave the Woodman Public House and follow him. TAYLOR left alone in his Vauxhall motor car and BAILEY came with Roger and I in Roger's car. We followed TAYLOR down the Archway Road and eventually stopped outside Marlers Wine Bar, Archway Road, N.6. where TAYLOR, BAILEY and I had a drink at the table outside the Wine Bar. Roger stayed in his car. BAILEY then introduced me to a young man who had in his possession a plastic shopping bag with some shopping in it. BAILEY then took the bag from the young man and showed me a large quantity of forged £50 Bank of England notes, which were at the bottom of the bag underneath the shopping. I checked them, they looked good and all the numbers appeared to be the same. Due to the length of time I spent checking them, BAILEY said, 'You're not going to count them all one by one.' I said, 'No, I trust you.' Whilst checking the forged money it did not appear to me that there was £100,000 notes present, and it was in my opinion their idea to 'have me over'. (By pretending there was £100,000 but in actual fact there was approximately £50,000) I then arranged to go and get my money: (i.e. £20,000). I returned a short time later to Marlers Wine Bar and again spoke to TAYLOR and

BAILEY. I was carrying a flight bag and said I had the £20,000 in there. TAYLOR and BAILEY then signalled to the young man who was in the vicinity. The young man approached and then BAILEY handed me the plastic bag. I looked inside and checked to see that the forged money was still there. It was. I then gave a pre-arranged signal to my colleagues and I ran away up Highgate Hill.

Bibliography

Agnew, D., *Undercover Agent – Narcotics* (1959), London, Souvenir Press.

Albanese, J., *Organised Crime in America* (1989), Cincinnati, Anderson Publishing Co.

Allen, M., *Pioneer Policewoman* (1925), London, Chatto & Windus.

————*Lady in Blue* (1936), London, Stanley Paul.

Archer, J.E., *By a Flash and a Scare* (1990), Oxford, Clarendon Press.

Ayling J., with Barnao, T. and Lipson, N., *Nothing But the Truth* (1993), Chippendale, Pan Macmillan.

Babington, A., *A House in Bow Street* (1969), London, Macdonald.

Bamford, S., *Passages in the Life of a Radical* (1984), Oxford, Oxford University Press.

Bean, J.P., *Over the Wall* (1994), London, Headline.

Bergreen, L., *Capone* (1994), London, Macmillan.

Bland, J., *Crime, Strange but True* (1991), London, Futura.

Bleakley, H., *The Hangmen of England* (1929), London, Chapman & Hall.

Block, A., *East Side – West Side* (1980), Cardiff, University College Cardiff Press.

Bogen, J.I., *The Anthracite Railroads* (1927), New York, Roland Press.

Bonanno, J., *A Man of Honor* (1983), New York, Simon & Schuster.

Borrell, C. and Cashinella, B., *Crime in Britain Today* (1975), London, Routledge & Kegan Paul.

Boyd, A., *The Informers* (1984), Dublin, The Mercier Press Ltd.

Brown, M. (ed), *Australian Crime* (1993), Sydney, Lansdowne.

Burke, S., *Peterman* (1966), London, Arthur Barker.

Campbell, D., *That was Business, This is Personal* (1990), London, Secker & Warburg.

————*The Underworld* (1994), London, BBC Books.

Campbell, P., *A Molly Maguire Story* (1992), New Jersey, Templecrome.

Capstick, J., *Given in Evidence* (1960), London, John Long.

Coleman, J.W., *The Molly Maguire Riots* (1936), Richmond, Va., Garrett & Massie.

Colquhoun, P., *A Treatise on the Functions and Duties of a Constable etc.* (1803), London.

Colquhoun, R., *Life Begins at Midnight* (1962), London, John Long.

Cox, J., *A Faithful Narrative of the Most Wicked and Inhuman Transactions of that Bloody-Minded Gang of Thief-Takers alias Thief Makers,* in *Villainy Detected, Being a Collection of the Most Sensational True Crimes and the Most Notorious Real Criminals that Blotted the Name of Britain in the Years 1660–1800* (1947), New York, D. Appleton-Century.

Cyriax, O., *Crime* (1993), London, André Deutsch.

Daley, R., *Prince of the City* (1978), New York, Houghton Mifflin.

Darbyshire, N. and Hilliard, B., *The Flying Squad* (1993), London, Headline.

Demaris, O., *The Last Mafioso: The Treacherous World of Jimmy Fratianno* (1981), New York, Times Books.

Dershowitz, A.M., *The Best Defense* (1983), New York, Vintage Books.

Detroit, M., *Chain of Evidence* (1994), London, Headline.

Donaghue, A., and Short, M., *The Krays' Lieutenant* (1995), London, Smith Gryphon.

Dunne, D., *Fatal Charms* (1988), New York, Bantam.

Dvornik, F., *Origins of Intelligence Services* (1974), New Brunswick, N.J.

Enright, S. and Morton J., *Taking Liberties* (1990), London, Weidenfeld & Nicolson.

Fitzpatrick, W.J., *Secret Service Under Pitt* (1892), London, Longman.

Fleming, R. with Miller, H., *Scotland Yard* (1994), London, Michael Joseph.

Follain, J., *Dishonoured Society* (1995), London, Little, Brown.

Fordham, P., *Inside the Underworld* (1972), London, George Allen & Unwin.

Fox, S., *Blood and Power* (1990), London, Penguin.

Frankos, D., *Contract Killer* (1993), London, Warner.

Fraser, F., *Mad Frank* (1994), London, Little, Brown.

Friedman, M., *The Pinkerton Labor Spy* (1907), New York, Wilshire Book Co.

Fry, C. with Kray, C., *Doing the Business* (1993), London, Smith Gryphon.

Gardner, P., *The Drug Smugglers* (1989), London, Robert Hale.

Giradin, G.R. and Helmer, W.J., *Dillinger: The Untold Story* (1994), Bloomingdale, University of Indiana Press.

Goddard, D., *The Insider* (1992), New York, Arrow Books.

Gosling, J., *The Ghost Squad* (1959), London, W.H. Allen.

Graeff, R., *Talking Blues* (1989), London, Collins Harvill.

Greenham, G.H., *Scotland Yard Experiences from the Diary of G H Greenham* (1904), London, George Routledge.

Greere, S., 'The Rise and Fall of the Northern Ireland Supergrass System' in *Criminal Law Review*, October 1987.

————*Supergrasses* (1995), Oxford, Clarendon Press.

Grover, D.H., *Debators and Dynamiters: The Story of the Haywood Trial* (1964), Corvallis, Oregon State University Press.

Hammer, R., *Playboy's Illustrated History of Organised Crime* (1975), Chicago, Playboy Press.

Halper, A. (ed), *The Chicago Crime Book* (1968), London, Souvenir Press.

Hammond, J.H., *The Autobiography of John Hays Hammond* (1935) (2 volumes), New York, Farrar and Rinehart.

Harney, M.L. and Cross, J.C., *The Informer in Law Enforcement* (1960), Springfield, Ill, Charles C. Thomas Publishers.

Hay, D. et al, *Albion's Fatal Tree* (1977), London, Peregrine Books.

Horn, T., *Life of Tom Horn: Government Scout and Interpreter, written by Himself* (1964), Norman, University of Oklahoma Press.

Irey, E.L. and Slocum, W., *The Tax Dodgers: The Inside Story of the T-Men's War with America's Political and Underworld Hoodlums* (1948), New York, Greenberg.

Irwin, W.R., *The Making of Jonathan Wild: A Study of the Literary Method of Henry Fielding* (1966), Hamden, Conn., Archon Books.

Jennings, A., Lashmar, P. and Simson, V., *Scotland Yard's Cocaine Connection* (1990), London, Jonathan Cape.

Kelland, G., *Crime in London* (1981), London, Bodley Head.

Knightley, P., *Second Oldest Profession* (1986), London, André Deutsch.

Korson, G., *Minstrels of the Mine Patch* (1938), Philadelphia.

Kray, R., *Villains We Have Known* (1993), Leeds, N.K. Publications.

Lacey, R., *Little Man* (1991), London, Constable.

Lansdowne, A. A., *Life's Reminiscences of Scotland Yard* (1890), London, Leadenhall Press.

le Caron, H., *Twenty-five years in the Secret Service: The Recollections of a Spy* (1892), London.

Lee, R. and Pratt, C., *Operation Julie* (1978), London, W.H. Allen.

Lee, W.M., *A History of the Police in England* (1901), London, Methuen.

Lewis, A.H., *Lament for the Molly Maguires* (1964), New York, Harcourt, Brace & World Inc.

Littlechild, J.G., *Reminiscences of Chief Inspector Littlechild* (1894), London, Leadenhall Press.

Lock, J., *Scotland Yard Casebook* (1993), London, Robert Hale.

Maas, P., *The Valachi Papers* (1970), St Albans, Panther.

Marx, G. T., *Under Cover: Police Surveillance in America* (1988), Los Angeles, University of California Press.

Maxwell, W.H., *History of the Irish Rebellion of 1778* (1845–1903), London.

McAlary, M., *Buddy Boys* (1988), New York, G. P. Putnam's Sons.

Mills, L., *Crimewatch* (1994), London, Penguin.

Morn, F., *The Eye that Never Sleeps* (1982), Bloomington, Indiana University Press.

Morton, J., *Gangland* (1992), London, Little, Brown.

———*Bent Coppers* (1993), London, Little, Brown.

———*Gangland* 2 (1994), London, Little, Brown.

Murphy, R., *Smash and Grab* (1991), London, Faber & Faber.

Nash, J.R., *World Encyclopedia of Organised Crime* (1993), London, Headline.

Nash, J.R. and Offen, R., *Dillinger: Dead or Alive?* (1970) Chicago, Henry Regnery.

Nelli, H.S., *The Business of Crime: Italians and Syndicate Crime* (1981), Chicago, University of Chicago Press.

Niederhoffer, A., *Behind the Shield* (1969), New York, Anchor.

Noble, T., *Neddy* (1993), Balmain, Kerr Publishing Pty Ltd.

Norman, F., *Bang to Rights* (1958), London, Secker & Warburg.

O'Brien, J. and Kurins, A., *Boss of Bosses*, (1991), London, Simon & Schuster.

O'Mahoney, M., *King Squealer* (1978), London, W.H. Allen.

Petrow, S., *Policing Morals* (1994), Oxford, Clarendon Press.

Pistone, J.D. with Woodley, R., *Donnie Brasco* (1988), London, Sidgwick & Jackson.

Porter, B., *The Refugee Question in Mid-Victorian Politics* (1979), Cambridge, Cambridge University Press.

————*The Origins of the Vigilant State* (1987), London, Weidenfeld & Nicolson.

————*Plots and Paranoia* (1989), London, Unwin Hyman.

Poulter, J., *The Discoveries of John Poulter, alias Baxter* (1778), Worcester, Michael Russell.

Powis, D., *The Signs of Crime* (1977), Maidenhead, McGraw-Hill.

Pringle, P., *The Thief Takers* (1958), London, Museum Press.

Pritchard, M. and Laxton, E., *Busted!* (1978), London, Mirror Books.

Radzinowicz, L., *A History of the English Criminal Law, volume ii* (1956), London, Stevens.

Read, L. and Morton, J., *Nipper* (1991), London, Macdonald.

Renner, T.C. and Kirby, C., *Mafia Enforcer* (1988), London, Corgi.

Rozenberg, J., *The Case for the Crown* (1987), Wellingborough, Equation.

Rowan, R. W., *The Pinkertons* (1931), London, Hurst & Blackett.

Scott, H., *Scotland Yard* (1954), London, André Deutsch.

————(ed), *Crime and Criminals* (1961), London, Bookplan.

Short, M., *Crime Inc.* (1991), London, Mandarin.

————*Lundy* (1991), London, Grafton.

Sifakis, C., *An Encyclopedia of American Crime* (1982), New York, Facts on File.

Siringo, C.A., *Two Evil Isms: Pinkertonism and Anarchism* (1915), Chicago, Charles A. Siringo.

Slipper, J., *Slipper of the Yard* (1981), London, Sidgwick & Jackson.

Smith, D.C., *The Mafia Mystique* (1975), New York, Basic Books.

Spiering, F., *The Man Who Got Capone* (1976), Indianapolis, Bobbs-Merrill.

Starr, C.G., *Civilisation and the Caesars* (1954), Ithaca, NY.

Stone, I., *Clarence Darrow for the Defense* (1941), New York, Doubleday.

Summers, A., *Official and Confidential: The Secret Life of J. Edgar Hoover* (1993), London, Gollancz.

Sunday Times Insight Team, *Ulster* (1972), Harmondsworth, Penguin.

Taylor, L., *In the Underworld* (1983), London, Guild Publishing.

Teresa, V. with Renner, T.C., *My Life in the Mafia* (1973), London, Hart-Davis, MacGibbon.

Thompson, E.P., *The Making of the English Working Class* (1963), London, Victor Gollancz.

Thompson, J., *My Life in the Klan* (1988), Nashville, Tenn., Rutledge Hill Press.

Thurston, G., *The Clerkenwell Riot* (1967), London, George Allen & Unwin.

Tremlett, G., *Little Legs* (1989), London, Unwin Hyman.

Unger, S.J., *FBI* (1976), Boston, Little, Brown.

Whittington-Egan, R. and M., *The Bedside Book of Murder* (1988), Newton Abott, David & Charles.

Wilkinson, L., *Behind the Face of Crime* (1957), London, Frederick Muller.

Williams, W. W., *The Life of General Sir Charles Warren* (1941), Oxford, Oxford University Press.

Wilson, F.S. and Day, B., *Special Agent: A Quarter Century with the Treasury Department and the Secret Service* (1965), New York, Holt, Rinehart and Winston.

Woffinden, B., *Miscarriages of Justice* (1987), London, Hodder & Stoughton.

Index

Bergreen, Laurence 186
Berkley, Alf 93
Berman, Otto 'Abbadabba' 128
Berry, John 43–4
Bessell, Peter 92
Beutler, Seymour 16
Biggs, Ronnie 57
Bindon, John 261, 264–5
Birnie, Sir Robert 192
Birtles, Frank Alexander x, xii, 243
Black, Christopher 149–50
Black, Robert 310
Black, Sonny 190
Blake, Ann & Ian 224
Blake, Joseph (aka Blueskin) 41
Bleackley, Horace 42n., 43
Bliss, John 222
Bloefeld, John 77
Boal, Desmond 153, 154–5
Bonanno, Joseph 134
Bonanno, Salvatore 136
Bosson-Williams, Tony 209n.
Bosworth-Davies, Rowan 322
Bott, Dr Christine 225–7, 229
Botting, James 193
Bow Street Runners 33n.
Boyd, Andrew, *The Informers* 156
Boyle, James 174
Brady, Dave 20, 105
Brady, Joseph 145
Brand, Harry 232–6
Brazil, Freddie 117
Brett, George 106, 107
Brett, Terence 106, 107
Bridges, Keith 4–5
Brindle, David 127n.
Brindle family 100
Brindle, 'Whippo' 100
Brinks-Mat robbery 71, 104
Brinn, Det. Sgt. Matthew 205
Britton, Paul 251
Brodeur, Jean-Paul 320
Brothers, Leo V. 187

Brown, John (aka Dawson) 35–6
Brown, Mary 35–6
Brown, Robert ('White Angel') 106n., 107
Brown, Tommy ('The Bear') 21
Buckley, Father Pat 156
Burden, Richard 226
Burke, Thomas 145
Burke, William 45–6
Burton, Det. Sgt. George 205

Cain, Lawrence ('The Snake') 123–4
Campbell, Alec 175–6
Campbell, Duncan 78, 248, 268n., 271
Campbell, Sgt. P.J. 152–3
Cameron, Prof. James 108, 271
Cannon, Joe 26, 81
Canter, Ben 210–11
Capone, Al 29, 121–2, 127, 183–7
Capone, Louis 127
Cappelletti, Pete 11
Capstick, ex-Det. Supt. John 205–6, 208
Carey, James 145–6
Carroll, James 174
Caruana, George 112
Cassells, Timothy QC 111
Castellammerese War 133
Cato Street Conspiracy 191
Cavendish, Lord Frederick 145
Chan, Jackie 126
Charles, Frederick 285
Charrington, Brian 313, 314–15
Cheung, George Wai Hen 125–6
Child, Det. Chief Insp. 224
Childs, John Henry ('Bruce') 105–6, 108–9
Chinese tongs 16n.
Chrastny, Mrs 110–11, 113
Chrastny, Nikolaus (aka

338

343